SIXTH EDITION

CONTEMPORARY ISSUES IN LEADERSHIP

SIXTH EDITION

CONTEMPORARY ISSUES IN LEADERSHIP

Edited by

William E. Rosenbach

and

Robert L. Taylor

Westview Press

A Member of the Perseus Books Group

Find us on the world wide web at www.westviewpress.com

Westview Press books are available at special discounts for bulk purchases in the United
States by corporations, institutions, and other organizations. For more information, please
contact the Special Markets Department at the Perseus Books Group, 11 Cambridge
Center, Cambridge, MA 02142, or special.markets@perseusbooks.com.

Designed by Brent Wilcox

Library of Congress Cataloging-in-Publication Data
   Contemporary issues in leadership / edited by William E. Rosenbach and
Robert L. Taylor.—6th ed.
      p.   cm.
   ISBN-13: 978-0-8133-4331-0 (pbk.)
   ISBN-10: 0-8133-4331-3 (pbk.)
   1. Leadership. I. Rosenbach, William E. II. Taylor, Robert L. (Robert Lewis), 1939-
HM1261.C69 2006
303.3'4—dc22

                                                                    2005023651

06 07 08 / 10 9 8 7 6 5 4 3 2

*Dedicated to our students who made teaching
the highlight of our careers*

Contents

– I –
THE HEART OF LEADERSHIP

– II –
LEADERSHIP LEGACIES

– III –
THE FOLLOWER FACTOR

– IV –
LEARNING TO LEAD

– V –
LEADERSHIP AS A PARADOX

Exhibits, Tables, and Figures

Figures

Preface

In preparing for this sixth edition we found the leadership literature to be broader, and crossing more disciplinary boundaries. This is consistent with our experience for previous editions of the book. In the sixth edition, we reprised ten chapters from the fifth edition, two chapters have been revised, and we selected nine new chapters. You will find that the twenty-one chapters come from a variety of academic, professional, and practitioner-oriented publications from the United States and abroad. We believe that the broader perspective of leadership provides a deeper appreciation and understanding of the topic. But it also results in ambiguity, dilemmas, and paradox. The differences in leadership research methodology and conclusions, as well as the absence of consensus on what leadership really is and how one behaves as a leader, are a reflection of the diversity of people, organizations, and cultures. The search for easy and simple answers to the leadership question is futile in our opinion, because something as ambiguous and complex as leadership defies an easy answer.

Confusion on the relationship between management and leadership continues to exist. However, we find that confusion to be not as great as it once was. The assumptions that management and leadership are the same thing or, if not, that one is better than the other, or that if you are good at one you will be good at the other, or that if you are the boss then you are the leader, have all been successfully challenged. Most of us agree that good management *and* good leadership are necessary for groups and organizations to effectively accomplish their goals and objectives and translate their vision into reality. There is now general agreement that management and leadership are both sources of influence but that one is based on positional power and the other on personal influence. Therefore, in this edition you will not find the leadership-versus-management argument.

We continue to be disappointed that the literature identifies countless articles and books that described leadership as a set of tools and techniques that really relate to management rather than leadership. Through electronic and manual searches, we identified more than fifteen hundred possible articles written since the last edition in 2000. After eliminating those that dealt with management concepts, those in which statistical methods overshadowed the substance of conclusions, and those that were overly narrow in focus, we were left with a little more than a hundred articles to seriously consider for this edition.

Transformational and transactional leadership remain the theories of choice and elaboration. Scholars continue to explore the nuances and pursue empirical outcomes in meaningful ways. Finding the right balance between transactional and transformational leadership sets expectations for effective leadership outcomes.

The concept of followership continues to gain recognition as a legitimate area of leadership study as scholars explore the reciprocal relationships between those who lead and those who are led. The literature describes varying follower styles just as it does leadership styles. Models of follower behavior are emerging in the literature and are described in this edition. Through observation, empirical studies, and anecdotal evidence, the role of the follower is becoming more appreciated and recognized. We believe the *follower factor* has become more important than ever and have therefore organized the three chapters on followers and followership into a separate section, Part 3.

We have organized the book into five sections. Part 1 focuses on the individual as a transactional and transformational leader and what is required of a person to motivate and enable others to follow her or him and what is necessary to build an enduring culture of success in the leadership endeavor. The historic legacies and lessons of great leaders make up the theme of Part 2. In Part 3, we examine the follower factor and how leaders develop followers as partners in a way that makes leaders and followers comfortable switching roles. We examine leadership development from a variety of perspectives that range from the emotional intelligence of individual leaders, mentoring of people who find themselves in the dual roles of follower and leader, formal leadership development programs, and global leadership education in Part 4. Finally, in Part 5 we explore some of the paradoxes of leadership.

In this edition we recognize the critical need for effective leadership in government, not-for-profit organizations, business, military, education, and social movements. We drew upon a wide variety of journals and authors from the United States and abroad for ideas, opinions, and perspectives so that a diverse body of readers can study leadership without the constraints of a specific frame of reference.

We are indebted to the authors and publishers of the readings included in this edition as well as to our students and colleagues, who continue to ask questions about leadership that have no easy answers. Our special thanks to Heather Ruby, who discovered a myriad of articles in expected and unlikely places and also assisted us with many of the mundane chores associated with a project such as this. We thank our colleagues from around the world who provided suggestions, meaningful feedback, and thoughtful criticism, which resulted in a much better book. Continuing support from our editor, Steve Catalano of Westview Press, inspired us to be thoughtful and thorough. Without the caring and professional support of Rosalyn Sterner and Marda Numann, the manuscript would not have been completed—they really are the best. Finally, we treasure the support of Colleen and Linda, particularly their understanding of our crazy way of working together.

William E. Rosenbach
Robert L. Taylor

— I —

THE HEART OF
LEADERSHIP

Leadership is widely discussed and studied but continues to remain an elusive and hazy concept. Although the study of leadership has emerged as a legitimate discipline, one still finds little agreement about what leadership really is. There are almost as many definitions of leadership as there are people attempting to define it. Yet we know good leadership when we experience it! Today, as in the past, the definitions are very often bounded by the academic discipline or the experience of those attempting definition. In 1978, Pulitzer Prize winner James McGregor Burns wrote that we know a lot about leaders but very little about leadership. However, Walter F. Ulmer, Jr., former president and CEO of the Center for Creative Leadership, believes that we know more than we used to about leaders, but that much of our knowledge is superficial and fails to examine the deeper realms of character and motivation that drive leaders, particularly in difficult times. If one is to begin to understand what leadership is, it is worthwhile to examine what leadership is not. Leadership is not hierarchical, top-down, or based on positional power and authority. Although effective managers must practice good leadership and effective leaders must possess managerial skills, leadership is not management or some part or principle of it. To understand leadership, one must understand its essential nature, that is, the process of the leader and followers engaging in reciprocal influence to achieve a shared purpose. Leadership is all about getting people to work together to make things happen that might not otherwise occur or to prevent things from happening that would ordinarily take place.

Looking through the history of the study of leadership, we find that the earliest coherent thrust centered on an approach now referred to as the Great Man or Great Person theory. For a full generation, leadership scholars concentrated on identifying the traits associated with great leadership. At first it seemed obvious: Are not great leaders exceptionally intelligent, unusually energetic, far above the norm in their ability to speak to followers, and so on? However, when these "obvious" propositions were subjected to test, they all proved false. Yes, leaders were found to be a bit more intelligent than the average, but not much more. And yes, they were more energetic and dynamic—but not significantly so. True, they were better-than-average public speakers with some charm, but again their overall advantage was not very great. And so it went: Each of these and other leadership myths evaporated under the glare of scientific scrutiny.

What followed was a focus on the behavior of leaders. If the key was not *who* they were, perhaps the crux of leadership could be found in *what* they did. In fact, researchers were able to identify two crucial types of leader behavior: behavior centered on task accomplishments and behavior directed toward interpersonal relations. Their peers typically reported individuals who consistently exhibited high levels of both of these types of behavior as leaders. Those who engaged in a high level of task-related activity but only an average level of relationship-centered behavior were sometimes still designated leaders. Those who engaged only in a high level of relationship behavior were rarely designated leaders by their peers. Finally, those who did little in the way of either task- or relationship-centered activity were never seen as leaders.

Perhaps, then, the essence of effective leadership is engaging in high levels of both task-oriented and relationship-centered activity. To test this possibility, researchers trained factory foremen in the two types of behavior and put them back on the job. For a while things did seem to improve, but the effects were short lived. After only a few weeks the foremen went back to their old behaviors; performance and productivity also returned to their prior levels. Although further research showed that even sustained high levels of the new behaviors had limited long-term effects on employees' performance, productivity, or satisfaction, the leadership-training programs developed in the early 1960s are still popular. Serious students of leadership, however, soon recognized the need to look further for answers to the riddle of effective leadership.

Some took a new path, suggesting that leadership effectiveness might require different combinations of task and relationship behavior in different situations. Theoretically, the most effective combination would depend upon certain situational factors, such as the nature of the task or the ability level of employees reporting to a certain supervisor. Another somewhat different path was to combine the situational hypothesis with some variations of the personal characteristics approach. Like earlier attempts, however, these efforts to explain effective leadership met with limited results.

Interestingly, the theme of focusing on relationship and task behaviors is common to the many theories developed over the past decades. The attempts to develop predictive and prescriptive models led to serious research and popular fads as scholars worked to solve the leadership puzzle. As popular literature focused on leadership tools and techniques, we note that most people remain skeptical about leaders and leadership. Thus, we must ask, what have we really learned?

In this book we distinguish between two basic types of leadership. *Transactional* leadership clarifies the role followers must play both to attain the organization's desired outcomes and to receive valued personal rewards for satisfactory performance, giving them the confidence necessary to achieve those outcomes and rewards. Transactional leadership is the equitable transaction or exchange between the leader and followers whereby the leader influences the followers by focusing on the self-interests of both. The self-interest of the leader is satisfactory performance, and the self-interests of the followers are the valued rewards gained in return for good performance. Used well, and in appropriate situations, transactional leadership will result in good performance. Transactional leadership is simply good management and might be considered managerial leadership.

Transformational or *transforming* leadership involves strong personal identification of followers with the leader. The transformational leader motivates followers to perform beyond expectations by creating an awareness of the importance of mission and the vision in such a way that followers share beliefs and values and are able to transcend self-interests and tie the vision to the higher-order needs of self-esteem and self-actualization. Transformational leaders create a mental picture of the shared vision in the minds of the followers through the use of language that has deep meaning from shared experiences. In addition, they are role models: In their daily actions they set an example and give meaning to shared assumptions, beliefs, and values. Transformational leaders empower or, better yet, enable the followers to perform beyond expectations by sharing power and authority and ensuring that followers understand how to use them. These leaders are committed to developing the followers into partners. In the end, what transformational leaders do is to enable followers to transform purpose into action.

LEADERSHIP PERSPECTIVES

In "Leadership That Matters: A New Vision of Leadership" (Chapter 1), Marshall Sashkin proposes that there has been a paradigm shift in leadership theory and practice. He reviews the evolution of the concepts of transactional and transformational leadership and describes transformational leadership behaviors and characteristics as well as the social context of leadership. Sashkin also explains how The Leadership Profile (TLP) measures leadership effectiveness. Leadership matters, he writes, because it makes a difference.

In Chapter 2, "Challenge Is the Opportunity for Greatness," James M. Kouzes and Barry Z. Posner posit that when times are stable and secure, leaders and potential leaders are not severely tested. It is challenge that produces the opportunity for greatness, and given the extraordinary challenges the world faces today, the potential for greatness is monumental.

Vision is presented as an essential element of leadership in Neal Thornberry's "A View About 'Vision'" (Chapter 3). There are many interpretations of vision, and the concept is not well understood by those who are setting the stage for future action in organizations. Thornberry describes the key components of vision and argues that much of the ability to be visionary can be taught. Vision is not a passing fad; it is an increasingly important part of an organization's struggle to be fast, flexible, and competitive. He draws several conclusions that will help leaders manage the visionary process.

In an outstanding piece, "Moral Person and Moral Manager: How Executives Develop a Reputation for Ethical Leadership" (Chapter 4), Linda Klebe Trevino, Laura Pincus Hartman, and Michael Brown outline the perceptual differences between you as a moral person and you as a moral leader. You are defined as a person by how others perceive who you are, what you do, and what you decide. They note that you must clearly communicate these elements to those you lead. The second aspect is that of moral manager. Here the authors cite the importance of being a role model, communicating regularly about ethics and values, while using rewards to ensure that everyone in the organization accepts and adheres to those standards. The result is a shared pride, commitment, and loyalty that are the key elements in attracting and retaining the best people.

Mathew Valle, in "Crisis, Culture, and Charisma: The New Leader's Work in Public Organizations" (Chapter 5), suggests that the changing nature of public service requires a "new" leadership. This is an important addition to the text because Valle specifically addresses the public sector organization, where accountability for performance is based on perceptions of service rather than profit. There are external and internal environmental forces impacting public organizations, especially as responsibilities for social needs are shifted from one venue to another. Valle describes the interactions of the environment, the followers, and the leader, characterizing this interplay as a combination of culture, crisis, and charisma. Leadership is now the development of an adaptive organizational culture in response to environmental changes.

1

~

Leadership That Matters:
A New Vision of Leadership

Marshall Sashkin

THE PUZZLE OF LEADERSHIP

There have been almost as many leadership theories and models as authors who have written on the subject. Our approach has been aimed at integrating as much as possible that is of value into an overall leadership approach. We originally called this *visionary leadership theory* but, in the most recent treatment, refer primarily to *leadership that matters*. In part, this is because we use the term *vision* in a way quite different from most of those who write about leadership. Why we prefer the term *leadership that matters* will also become evident in the following presentation.

The history of leadership thought and research is generally recognized as having followed a sequence of three primary areas of study. The first was the study of leadership traits. When this seemed to have been relatively unprofitable, as summarized in Ralph Stogdill's (1948) classic research review, the second area, the study of leader behavior, dominated research and theory for about twenty years. However, when this area, too, proved to provide a less comprehensive explanation to the puzzle of leadership than had been hoped, the third area of study came to the fore. This was, and is, the examination of leadership in the context of its setting. Even this approach failed to offer as powerful an answer to the question "What is leadership?" as had been hoped.

This chapter is based on and incorporates materials originally prepared by Marshall Sashkin and William E. Rosenbach.

One way to resolve the puzzle of leadership is to simply insist that the way one has defined and measured leadership is the correct and only way to do so. Many writers on leadership have taken this approach and many continue to use simple, unsubstantiated assertion as their answer to the question of the nature of leadership. Some take a different approach and suggest that all three of the leadership aspects we have mentioned—personality, behavior, and the situational context—must be taken into consideration if we are to fully understand leadership. Although this makes sense, it still fails to provide a coherent answer.

We propose a somewhat different approach. Although accepting the premise that personality, behavior, and situation are all important, we take a step back. We start with a reexamination of the personal nature of leadership, not in terms of simple traits but in the sense of the basic element of human nature. This provides us with a central organizing framework for our concept of leadership.

LEADERSHIP CHARACTER

What is the nature of the leader's character? Is it simply a new set of traits? Though some had long dismissed traits as an adequate explanation for leadership, it is quite common for leadership scholars and practitioners to use traitlike models to assess individuals' "leadership competencies." Yet the approach we present here is as old as Stogdill and as current as the most recent "five-factor" personality theory (Costa and McCrae, 1992; Digman, 1990; McCrae and Costa, 1997; Wiggins, 1996).

Stogdill observed that although no single trait or set of independent traits seemed to be strongly associated with leadership, there were five *clusters* of traits that when taken together seemed to be linked to leadership. He identified the clusters listed in the middle column of Exhibit 1.1.

The five personality factors of the five-factor model are shown in the left-hand column of Exhibit 1.1. As can be seen, this approach is in many ways quite similar to Stogdill's five clusters.

Taken together, Stogdill's cluster list and the five factors fit rather well with what we see as three elementary aspects of leader character, as shown in the right-hand column of Exhibit 1.1.

Although these three basic aspects of leadership all concern the leader personally, it would be overly simplistic to call them *personality characteristics*. The three aspects we refer to are, nonetheless, the fundamental building

EXHIBIT 1.1   Personality Factors in Leadership
Parallels across the five-factor model, Stogdill's five clusters, and the three leadership characteristics basic to leadership that matters

Five Personality Factors	Stogdill's Clusters	Leadership Character Elements
1. Openness to Experience	A. Capacity Intelligence Judgment	Visionary Leadership Cognitive capability
1. Openness to Experience	B. Achievement Scholarship Knowledge	Visionary Leadership Cognitive capability
2. Dependability/ Conscientiousness	C. Responsibility Dependability Aggressiveness Self-confidence Desire to excel	Confident Leadership Self-confidence
3. Agreeableness	D. Participation Activity Sociability Cooperation Adaptability	Follower-Centered Empowerment orientation
3. Agreeableness 4. Extroversion	E. Status Position Popularity	Follower-Centered Empowerment orientation
5. Emotional Stability/ Neuroticism		Follower-Centered Empowerment orientation

blocks of personality. None are newly discovered; in fact, all have been recognized for several thousand years as aspects of human nature. Plato, for example, considered human nature as having three aspects. The first (and "highest" in his view) was reason. The second was courage—the potential for action consistent with what is "good" or "right." The third element Plato defined as "appetite," that is, emotional desire. A few thousand years later the psychologist Ernest Hilgard (1980) spoke of *cognition* (thought), *emotion* (feeling), and *conation* (action) as the three basic elements of the human psyche—thinking, feeling, and behaving.

Thus, ancient philosophy and modern psychology seem to agree on certain fundamental facts of human nature. However, unlike Plato or Hilgard, we see emotion as the centerpiece element, the lynchpin that ties thought to action. We believe that Freud, too, saw things this way. That is, it is the *feelings* of the infant that are at the core of early human awareness. Thought and action come to be enlisted in the service of satisfying emotional needs or what Plato dismissively called "appetites." What makes the difference in terms of what one might consider a "higher order" of functioning is, first, the way the relationships among the three elements actually play out. That is, the term *courage* links emotion to action in a positive sense and facilitates one's use of reason—thought—to act effectively. Second, the purpose or meaning of this process of emotion as guiding positive action through reason is, in the context of leadership, the achievement of common aims and mutual moral development. It is difficult not to see this as a "higher order" of things.

We will briefly give our interpretation of the three basic elements of leadership character. We use the term *will* to introduce each, because we want to emphasize that these are not necessarily inborn or genetic traits. Rather, each can be—at least to some degree—developed and increased by almost anyone.

The Will to Act: Confident Leadership

One central element of human nature is the orientation toward action. Psychologist Julian Rotter (1966) observed that some people act as though what happens to them is a matter of chance or, at least, beyond their control. Such individuals are, he said, "externally controlled." Others appear to act in ways that show they personally feel in control of their lives—their actions and the consequences. These individuals are, Rotter says, "internally controlled." Stanford social psychologist Albert Bandura (1982) referred to the same dimension as "efficacy." He went beyond Rotter by pointing out that efficacy is learned through actions and outcomes in social contexts. Former president of the American Psychological Association Martin Seligman built his long research career around what he now calls "learned optimism." We prefer a label more simple than any of these: *self-confidence,* that is, the confidence to act.

This characteristic is also similar to the "big five" factor of conscientiousness. But however labeled or measured, this personal characteristic comes into operation by the will of the individual leader, who elects to act and to engage in goal-directed behavior, rather than to sit back and observe.

The Will to Use Power: Follower-Centered Leadership

This second element centers on feeling or affect. In our view it is power or control that is at the core of human affect. Harvard social psychologist David McClelland (1987) detailed how this central emotion and need develops over time, from birth and infancy through adulthood. Although the issue of using power to gain control over one's life is, then, a primary concern for all of us, it is also the foundation of leaders' *development* of the power need. That is, our instinctual need for power centers on personal survival, but for leaders a higher stage of development of this power need involves the ability to use power in positive, or what McClelland called "prosocial," ways. This benefits groups of others, not just oneself. Thus, what might otherwise be simple narcissism, or what former CIA personality analyst Jerald Post (1986) has, in referring to Saddam Hussein and some other leaders, called "malignant narcissism," can be turned into a more healthy orientation to the need for power.

The Will to Think Critically About Cause and Effect over Time: Visionary Leadership

The third and final element concerns cognition. Plato called it "reason," and learning theorist Hilgard labeled it "conation," but they were referring to the same thing. Reason is not simply intelligence. Our way of looking at reason is based on the work of Elliott Jaques (1986). In this view, reason, or what Jaques called (at different times) "cognitive complexity" and "cognitive capability," has three important aspects beyond generalized intelligence. First is the ability to think in terms of cause and effect, that is, to understand the "levers" that, by one's actions, determine whether or not one's goals are attained. Second is the ability to extend such thinking over time, into the relatively distant and not just the immediate future. Third is the ability to think critically, to make meaningful judgments about actions that involve use of power and influence in ways that produce positive outcomes.

CHARACTER DRIVES BEHAVIOR

Our earliest efforts to develop our approach to understanding leadership centered on the behaviors of leaders. The actions of effective leaders, who as

Burns said transform followers into more self-directed leaders and transform social organizations into more productive and meaningful institutions, do seem to involve certain sorts of behaviors. These behaviors are more subtle than those that are at the center of older leadership behavior theories. Although there is no definitive list of the specific behaviors, it is still possible to identify some that are especially useful. Among the most important of the behaviors that transformational leaders rely on in order that their leadership might matter are the following four.

Communication Leadership

This first category of transformational leadership behavior involves focusing the attention of others on key ideas, the most important aspects of the leader's vision. In practice, this means using metaphors and analogies that make clear and vivid what might otherwise be abstract ideas. Of course, communication leadership does not neglect the basics of effective communication practices, skills such as active listening and giving and receiving feedback effectively. These actions contribute to effective communication between leaders and followers.

Consistent Leadership

Leaders establish trust by taking actions that are consistent both over time and with what the leader has said. Leaders must also be sure to follow through on commitments, to do what they say they will do. Trust, of course, exists in the minds and hearts of followers and is not a directly observable leader behavior. But it is *consistency* over time and between words and actions and *credibility* in terms of fulfilling commitments that *produce* feelings of trust in followers.

Caring Leadership

This behavior involves showing respect and concern for people. Psychologist Carl Rogers called this behavior "unconditional positive regard." By this he meant caring about and respecting another person despite one's feelings or judgments about that person's actions. As religious leaders have said, one may hate the sin yet still love the sinner. Visionary leaders show that they care not just by "big" actions, such as ensuring employees' job security. They show it through everyday actions, such as remembering people's birthdays or even something as basic as learning and using their names.

Creating Empowering Opportunities

Transformational leaders empower followers by allowing them to accept challenges, such as taking on and "owning" a new project. But transformational leaders also are careful to plan for success. This means that leaders don't ask more of followers than they know the followers can accomplish. Followers might still feel a sense of risk in accepting what they see as a challenge. However, a transformational leader does what is necessary to ensure that real risk is low. The leader makes certain that empowered followers have the resources, skills, and knowledge they need to succeed.

Note that, unlike older behavioral theories of leadership, effective transformational leadership does not simply mean doing a lot of each of these four behaviors. It may be that one or another of them is most needed at a particular time or with regard to particular followers or groups of followers. Neither can the transformational leader simply follow some standard rule or prescription that calls for certain actions under certain conditions. Transformational leaders aim to define and construct those conditions by their actions. We can briefly consider just what organizational conditions— the *organizational culture*—transformational leaders want to create.

THE LEADER'S ROLE IN SHAPING THE ORGANIZATION'S CULTURE

Edgar H. Schein (1993) has said that the *only* important thing leaders do may well be constructing culture. They somehow help define and inculcate certain shared values and beliefs among organizational members. Values define what is right or wrong, good or bad; beliefs define what people expect to happen as a consequence of their actions. The values and beliefs shared by people in an organization are the essence of that organization's culture.

The elements of organizational culture are not a matter of random chance. They concern the most important and fundamental issues faced by people in organizations. These issues are *adaptation,* how people deal with external forces and the need to change; *goal achievement,* the nature of organizational goals, how they are defined, and their importance; *coordination,* how people work together to get the job done; and *the strength of shared values and beliefs,* that is, the degree to which people in the organization generally agree that these values and beliefs are important and should guide their actions. We will briefly consider each issue and the values and beliefs relevant to it.

Adaptation

Consider two specific beliefs about change and adaptation. The first goes like this: "We really just have to go along with outside forces; what we do can't make much of a difference." Such a belief has some clear implications for action—or inaction. After all, why bother? Contrast this outlook with the belief, "We can control our own destiny." The former belief may be more accurate in an objective sense. However, it also pretty much ensures that nothing will be done and that what is done will not make a difference. After all, no one expects it to. Even if the second belief is not as accurate, it makes it more likely that people will take actions to affect short-range outcomes as well as their long-range destiny. Perhaps their actions will have positive effects. What people expect becomes more likely. This is called a *self-fulfilling prophecy.*

Beliefs concerning change and adaptation are the organizational analog of self-confidence, the belief that one's destiny is a matter of internal control. It is especially important that leaders teach followers self-confidence, since only then is it likely that the organization will develop the sort of culture that results in successful adaptation to change.

Goal Achievement

"Every person, every department, has its own goals; the organization is best served by competition among them." Does that sound like a typical organizational value? Unfortunately it is; it's unfortunate because such values don't serve the organization well. Contrast it with this one: "We are all here to serve our customer by identifying and meeting the customer's needs, whatever they may be." That value says a lot about how goals are defined and what goal achievement is all about. And unlike the first value, this one does benefit the organization.

The issue of goals relates to the leader's need for power and what attempts are made to satisfy that need. The leader may benefit the organization by empowering others. Or the leader may benefit only himself or herself, through narcissistic self-aggrandizement. Leaders' empowerment of others is important because it places the value of goal achievement in a larger, organizational context. Achievement of goal becomes important not just in a personal, or even a group, sense, but as an organizational value.

Coordinated Teamwork

Many organizations seem to operate on the maxim "Every person for himself or herself; we all compete to be best." But this is not a very functional value when the very essence of organization is to perform tasks that require the coordinated work of several individuals and groups. In contrast, the value "We all must work together" is a much better expression of the reality of organization. Only when people work together effectively can an organization prosper.

We spoke of vision or cognitive power as the means by which leaders think through complicated chains of cause and effect and decide how to create desirable outcomes. This means looking at the organization as a system and thinking about how it fits together, which happens, of course, through the coordinated efforts of organization members. This is one reason leaders must help followers develop their cognitive power, their own vision. Then followers will be better able to coordinate their efforts effectively.

Shared Values and Beliefs

In some organizations one hears people say, "Everyone has the right to his or her own philosophy." Although that might seem to be a sound democratic ideal, it makes poor organizational sense. Such a value destroys the potentially positive effect of the three beliefs and values just identified. If everyone can buy into or reject them at will, how can these values and beliefs have a consistent impact on people's behavior?

Contrast this with a very different value: "Everyone here is expected to adhere to a common core of values and beliefs." This value supports and strengthens positive values related to adapting ("We can control our world"), achieving goals ("Results for our customers are what counts"), and coordinating efforts through teamwork ("Cooperative teamwork is what counts around here"). Of course, such a value would make values and beliefs that lead to *ineffective* adaptation, goal achievement, or teamwork even more dysfunctional. That's why cultural strength alone, the degree to which the members of the organization share a common set of values and beliefs, is a poor predictor of organizational effectiveness. Shared values and beliefs can support increased organizational effectiveness. They can also impair effectiveness. When all hold to the same flawed beliefs, their combined efforts may lead to total disaster! Thus, the results of a strong organizational culture depend on the specific values and beliefs that culture is built on.

HOW LEADERS CONSTRUCT CULTURE

It is relatively easy to see how the personal characteristics required for transformational leadership relate to the fundamental aspects of organizational culture. It is another thing, however, to ask how leaders actually construct cultures. How do they go about defining and inculcating values and beliefs? There are three general approaches that are especially important.

First, leaders develop a clear, value-based *philosophy*, a statement of organizational purpose or mission that everyone understands. This task is anything but simple. A philosophy does not spring fully formed from the brow of the leader. Leaders must use their cognitive power to assess the organization's context, its environment, and the key factors in that environment. Then, they must solicit and incorporate into the vision the thoughts, values, and beliefs of others: executives, managers, and front-line employees.

Second, leaders empower others to define organizational *policies* and develop *programs* based on the values and beliefs contained in the philosophy. It is programs and policies that put values and beliefs into organizational action. For example, hiring and promotion policies should take into account values consistent with those in the organization's philosophy, as well as applicants' knowledge and skill. Reward systems and bonus programs should be based on the values of cooperation and innovative action, not on competition over a limited pool of resources.

Finally, leaders inculcate values and beliefs through their own individual behaviors, their *personal practices*. Leaders model organizational values and beliefs by living them constantly and consistently. This is why the leadership behaviors we described earlier are so important. Many people think of these behaviors as tools with which leaders explain their vision to followers and convince them to carry out that vision. There is some truth to this. However, these behaviors are most important because leaders use them to demonstrate and illustrate the values and beliefs on which organizational visions are founded. That's why transformational leadership takes so much time and effort—and why transformational leaders must be good managers with strong management skills.

Leaders use everyday managerial activities—a committee meeting, for example—as opportunities to inculcate values. In such a meeting the leader may guide a decisionmaking process while making it clear that final authority and responsibility rest with the group. By doing this a leader takes what might otherwise be a bureaucratic process and instills the value of empowerment into that process. Whenever possible, leaders overlay value-inculcating actions on ordinary bureaucratic management activities. It's now clear why, without a sound base of management skills on the part of leaders, transformational leadership is not possible.

We have also, now, come full circle in that we can see how culture is constructed by the behavioral actions of transformational leaders. We see how the leader's character drives those behaviors. Character also enables transformational leaders to see what actions are needed to establish within an organization's culture the values and beliefs that transform followers into self-directed leaders and create high-performing transformational cultures.

SOUNDS GOOD: DOES IT REALLY WORK?

The test of any theory is, of course, the degree to which it helps one predict future results on the basis of current information and the extent to which it proves useful for designing actions that produce desired results. A great social scientist said, "There is nothing as practical as a good theory!" From the initial development of "visionary leadership theory," the precursor to leadership that matters, there was a strong emphasis on measuring the concepts being defined and linking those measures to practical outcomes.

The most current version of these measures is called The Leadership Profile (TLP). It is a fifty-item assessment questionnaire completed by a leader and by several of the leader's associates, to give a comprehensive measure of the leader's behavior, character, and culture-building actions. The TLP consists of ten "scales," each one measuring a specific aspect of leadership behavior or character. The scales are briefly defined in Table 1.1. Note that the first two scales measure the essence of good management. That's because good management is an important foundation for effective leadership. Repeated refinement of the TLP has produced an assessment tool that has been demonstrated to yield a reliable and valid measure of leadership that matters.

Dozens of research studies have been conducted since the early 1980s to test the theory described in this chapter. Details of some of these studies can be found in the book *Leadership That Matters* (2003), by Marshall and Molly Sashkin. Overall, it has been demonstrated that leadership that matters is strongly and consistently associated with sound measures of effective organizational culture. Most important of all, it has been repeatedly shown that in banks, schools, manufacturing facilities, and a wide range of other organizations there is a strong and significant relationship between leaders' Leadership

TABLE 1.1   The Leadership Profile

Scale	What the Scale Measures
I: Capable Management	Measures how well a leader accomplishes day-to-day basic administrative or managerial tasks. Capable managers make sure that people have the knowledge, skills, and resources they need to get the job done right and know what is expected of them.
II: Reward Equity	Effective leaders promise followers what followers value in exchange for good performance, and they deliver on their promises.
III: Communication Leadership	Assesses the ability to manage and direct the attention of others through especially clear and focused interpersonal communication, by using metaphors and analogies that make abstract ideas clear and vivid.
IV: Credible Leadership	Measures whether a leader "walks the talk" by engaging in behavior that is consistent both over time and with what the leader has said.
V: Caring Leadership	Measures the degree to which a leader demonstrates respect and concern for others.
VI: Creative Leadership	Effective leaders create opportunities for followers to be empowered, to "own" the actions that yield successful results.
VII: Confident Leadership	Effective leaders believe they control their own fate. This scale measures the extent to which the leader possesses and displays this sort of self-confidence.
VIII: Follower-Centered Leadership	Measures the degree to which a leader sees followers as empowered partners rather than as subordinates to be manipulated.
IX: Visionary Leadership	Assesses the extent to which a leader sees and takes actions that will produce successful outcomes over the long term.
X: Principled Leadership	Measures the extent to which a leader builds a culture based on shared values and beliefs that facilitate effective performance.

Profile assessments, which measure the degree to which a leader exhibits leadership that matters, and measures of organizational performance.

IN SUM

Leadership involves the will to act, to use power in a positive or prosocial manner, and to think through the consequences of actions, over time. Leaders who possess these characteristics are able to determine and to carry out the specific actions needed to transform followers into more capable self-leaders and to construct the sort of transformational organizational culture we have described.

Simple as this prescription may sound, it is far from simple in action. Understanding of the real, underlying nature of leadership, as described here, is sorely lacking both in organizations and among leadership experts. And the development of leaders who are capable of leadership that will truly make a difference and matter to people and organizations remains an abiding challenge.

But it is crucial to remember that it is character that is at the heart of transformational leadership, that drives transformational leadership behavior, and that enables such leaders to construct transformational organizational cultures. This is why we close by returning, briefly, to the essential nature of leadership. The three personal characteristics, based in the underlying aspects of human nature, seem to be at the heart of everything we do to develop and improve leadership. They are so important that they deserve a final emphasis, by means of a true anecdote.

Some years ago dancer Ray Bolger, the scarecrow in *The Wizard of Oz* movie, was asked what he thought was the underlying lesson or theme of the story. He replied that a person who saw *The Wizard of Oz* should leave with the understanding that *every* person has a heart, a mind, and the potential for courageous action. These are, of course, the three personal characteristics at the core of this presentation and of our understanding of the nature of leadership. They are, Bolger also observed, the essential gifts that make us human.

Leadership that matters does so because it makes a difference. This difference occurs in the lives of followers, in a group or organization. There's also a difference in group or organizational performance. And there is an important difference in the organization itself as a result of leadership that matters. Thus, our approach to leadership differs from others most basically in our view of the *purpose* of leadership. The English author and essayist Samuel Johnson said, "The only aim of writing is to enable the readers better to enjoy life or better to endure it." This happens, we think, because great authors lead readers to find or make meaning in their own lives. The same can be said of good leaders in general.

This chapter is intended as an introduction to leadership that matters and does not include a comprehensive research bibliography. For a more extensive review of formal research, see Sashkin and Sashkin (2003).

REFERENCES

Axelrod, R. H., & Sashkin, M. (2000). Outcome measurement in a leadership development program. Paper presented at the annual meeting of the Academy of Management, Toronto, August.

Bandura, A. (1982). Self-efficacy mechanism in human agency. *American Psychologist, 37,* 122–147.

Burns, J. M. (1978). *Leadership.* New York: Free Press.

Costa, P. T., Jr., & McCrae, R. R. (1992). Normal personality assessment in clinical practice: The NEO Personality Inventory. *Psychological Assessment, 4,* 5–13.

Digman, J. M. (1990). Higher-order factors of the Big Five. *Journal of Personality and Social Psychology, 73,* 1246–1256.

Hilgard, E. R. (1980). The trilogy of mind: Cognition, affection, and conation. *Journal of the History of the Behavioral Sciences, 16,* 107–117.

Jaques, E. (1986). The development of intellectual capability. *Journal of Applied Behavioral Science, 22,* 361–383.

McClelland, D.C. (1987). *Human motivation.* Cambridge, UK: Cambridge University Press.

McCrae, R. R., & Costa, P. T., Jr. (1996). Toward a new generation of personality theories: Theoretical contexts for the five-factor model. In J. S. Wiggins (Ed.), *The five-factor model of personality: Theoretical perspectives* (pp. 51–87). New York: Guilford.

McCrae, R. R., & Costa, P. T., Jr. (1997). Personality trait structure as a human universal. *American Psychologist, 52,* 509–516.

Post, J. M. (1986). Narcissism and the charismatic leader-follower relationship. *Political Psychology, 7*(4), 675–687.

Rotter, J. (1966). Generalized expectancies for internal versus external control of reinforcement. *Psychological Monographs, 80* (Whole No. 609).

Sashkin, M., & Sashkin, M. G. (2003). *Leadership that matters.* San Francisco: Berrett-Koehler.

Schein, E. H. (1993). *Organizational culture and leadership.* San Francisco: Jossey-Bass (2nd ed., 1993).

Stogdill, R. M. (1948). Personal factors associated with leadership. *Journal of Psychology, 25,* 37–71.

Wiggins, J. S. (Ed.) (1996). *The five-factor model of personality: Theoretical perspectives.* New York: Guilford.

2

~

Challenge Is the
Opportunity for Greatness

James M. Kouzes
Barry Z. Posner

Are we on the verge of a leadership explosion? Caught in today's hurricane of discouraging news, some may see little reason to be optimistic. We, on the other hand, are full of hope. We expect the emergence of a whole new breed of energetic leaders who will work to restore people's faith in one another and revitalize society's capacity to excel.

This is neither Pollyanna-ish cheerfulness nor wishful thinking. Our belief is completely consistent with history. To test this for yourself, try this exercise. Take out a piece of paper and draw a line down the middle. Think of a few well-known historical figures you consider exemplary leaders. Think about the men and women who've led organizations, communities, states, nations, or the world to greatness. Write their names in the left-hand column. In the right-hand column opposite each name, record the events, circumstances, or historical contexts with which you identify each of these individuals.

Now cover the names in the left-hand column and look only at the right-hand column listing the events, circumstances, or contexts. What pattern do you notice among the leadership *situations*?

We predict that your list will be made up of leaders you identify with the creation of new institutions, the resolution of serious crises, the winning

---

Reprinted with permission from *Leader to Leader* (Spring 2003), pp. 16–23.

TABLE 2.1   Historical Leaders and Their Contexts

Historical Leaders	Situation or Context
Queen Elizabeth I	Revival of order in 16th-century England
Winston Churchill	World War II
Mahatma Gandhi	National independence for India
Abraham Lincoln	U.S. Civil War
Florence Kelley	Struggle for child labor laws
Martin Luther King, Jr.	U.S. Civil Rights movement
Nelson Mandela	National liberation movement in South Africa
Rosa Parks	U.S. Civil Rights movement
Eleanor Roosevelt	Women's participation in U.S. public life

of wars, the organization of revolutionary movements, protests for improving social conditions, political change, innovation, or some other social transformation.

The table shows a few representative examples of historical leaders people have mentioned when we've asked this question.

Consistently over time, we've found that when we ask people to think of exemplary leaders, they recall individuals who served during times of turbulence, conflict, innovation, and change. Skeptics might say that this is true only for those few great leaders who've made their mark on history, and it can't be true for those less famous. Absolutely not so. When we analyzed the personal-best cases in our leadership research from "ordinary" people, we discovered *exactly the same thing*. Virtually all the personal-best leadership cases were associated with a challenge. The challenges faced by the leaders we studied may have been less grand and global, but even so they involved *major changes* that had a significant impact on their organizations.

The fact is that when times are stable and secure, no one is severely tested. People may perform well, may get promoted, and may even achieve fame and fortune. But certainty and routine breed complacency. In times of calm, no one takes the opportunity to burrow inside and discover the true gifts buried down deep. In contrast, personal, business, and social hardships have a way of making us come face-to-face with who we really are and what we're capable of becoming. *Only challenge produces the opportunity for greatness.* Given the extraordinary challenges the world faces today, the potential for greatness is monumental.

Although we're confident that exemplary leaders will emerge from the chaos and uncertainty of the present, we're not comfortable with the notion of just waiting around for them to arise from the ashes. Society can't afford to leave it to chance. Moreover, we need all the leaders we can get in all sectors of society and at all organizational levels, from the front line to the boardroom and beyond. It's essential to create a climate in which a new breed of leaders is supported, nurtured, and encouraged. Based on our research into the practices of exemplary leadership, we can highlight the essential leadership actions for establishing a culture that's conducive to the growth of leaders.

SET THE EXAMPLE

People become the leaders they observe. If we want to become good leaders, we have to see good leaders. "Modeling is the first step in developing competencies," said Albert Bandura, Stanford University professor of psychology and the world's leading authority on the topic. We had this idea reinforced for us when we did some research on the leader-as-coach. In that study we found that of all the items used to measure coaching behavior, the one most linked to success is "this person embodies character qualities and values that I admire."

To increase the quality and supply of exemplary leaders in the world, it's essential to give aspiring talent the chance to observe models of exemplary leadership. To develop ethical leaders, allow aspiring talent to observe leaders behaving ethically. To build leaders who think long term, allow aspiring talent to observe leaders taking a long-term view. To have leaders who treat people with dignity and respect, make sure aspiring talent can observe leaders treating people with dignity and respect.

When we asked Taylor Bodman, general partner at Brown Brothers Harriman in Boston, about his personal leadership role models, he was able to name six. For each one he was able to tell us in great detail why he selected each person, what each did, how he felt about each, and what he had learned from them. Here's an abbreviated description of one of his role models, Peter J. Gomes, the minister of Harvard's Memorial Church:

> I learned from Gomes that people burn out less from a lack of energy than
> from a lack of a sense of purpose. That insight changed the way I lead at work.
> I started to engage others in some large, obvious, and therefore long-absent

questions, such as "Why are we here?" and "What are we trying to do?" Observing Gomes also taught me that it is possible to honor the past and at the same time to learn from our failures so that we succeed in the future.

I have found for myself that stories can offer the perspective and meaning that generate energy in others. I try to do this at work. I try to determine the cause that is greater than ourselves and to convey it.

Taylor Bodman considers himself very fortunate to have had many exceptional role models in his career. He found from each rich lessons that enable him to be a better leader. It's absolutely essential to the growth and development of leaders—or of anyone, for that matter—that they're exposed to the behaviors they're expected to produce. You can't do what you say if you don't know how, and you can't know how until you can see how it's done. Without exemplary role models, all the training in the world won't stick.

MAKE CHALLENGE MEANINGFUL

There's an oft-repeated management maxim that says, "What gets rewarded gets done." If this were actually true, then we'd be hard-pressed to find an explanation for why people embrace challenges that don't offer a lot of money, options, perks, power, or prestige. There is absolutely no correlation between courage of convictions and pay for performance.

Just ask Arlene Blum. Arlene earned a doctorate in biophysical chemistry but has spent most of her adult life climbing mountains—literally and figuratively. She's had more than three hundred successful ascents. Her most significant challenge—and the one for which she is most well known—was not the highest mountain she's ever climbed. It was the challenge of leading the first all-woman team up Annapurna I, the tenth-highest mountain in the world. We've learned many leadership lessons both from her book, *Annapurna: A Woman's Place*, and from talking with her.

"The question everyone asks mountain climbers is 'Why?' And when they learn about the lengthy and difficult preparation involved, they ask it even more insistently," said Arlene. "For us, the answer was much more than 'because it is there.' . . . As women, we faced a challenge even greater than the mountain. We had to believe in ourselves enough to make the attempt in spite of social convention and 200 years of climbing history in which women were usually relegated to the sidelines."

In talking about what separates those who make a successful ascent from those who don't, she said, "The real dividing line is passion. As long as you believe what you're doing is meaningful, you can cut through fear and exhaustion and take the next step." It wasn't because Annapurna was there. It was because the climb was *meaningful.*

Experience, we've learned, is the best leadership teacher, and challenging experiences offer the most opportunities. But it's not about challenge for challenge's sake. It's not about shaking things up or tearing things down just to keep people on their toes or give them a chance to show what they're made of. It's about challenge with meaning and passion. It's about living life on purpose. To create a climate for developing the best leaders, we must make the challenge meaningful. As E. L. Deci pointed out, there has to be something significant in the challenge itself that makes the struggle worthwhile. When it comes to excellence, it's definitely *not* "What gets rewarded gets done" but "What *is* rewarding gets done."

PROMOTE PSYCHOLOGICAL HARDINESS

Challenge brings with it a much higher degree of risk and uncertainty. That's why it's rich in learning opportunities. It's also why it can be a breeding ground for stress.

Many of us associate stress with illness. We've been led to believe that if we experience serious stressful events, we'll become ill. Yet it isn't stress that makes us ill, it's how we respond to stressful events.

There is a clear attitudinal difference between high-stress–high-illness people and high-stress–low-illness people. Salvatore Maddi and Suzanne Kobasa have found in over thirty years of research that this latter group make three key assumptions about themselves in interaction with the world. First, they feel a strong sense of *control,* believing that they can beneficially influence the direction and outcome of whatever is going on around them through their own efforts. Lapsing into powerlessness, feeling like a victim of circumstances, and passivity seem like a waste of time to them. Second, they're strong in *commitment,* believing that they can find something in whatever they're doing that's interesting, important, or worthwhile. They're unlikely to engage in denial or feel disengaged, bored, and empty. Third, they feel strong in *challenge,* believing that personal improvement and fulfillment come through the continual process of learning from both negative and positive experiences. They feel that it's not only unrealistic but also stultifying to simply expect, or even wish for, easy comfort and security.

To create a climate that fosters the development of leaders, we not only need to set an example and make the challenge meaningful, but we also have to promote "psychological hardiness"—a condition in which stress does not promote sickness but instead promotes success.

People can't lead if they aren't psychologically hardy. No one will follow someone who avoids stressful events and won't take decisive action. However, even if leaders are personally very hardy, they can't enlist and retain others if they don't create an atmosphere that promotes psychological hardiness. People won't remain long with a cause that distresses them. To accept the challenge of change, they need to believe that they can overcome adversity. Leaders must create the conditions that make all that possible.

Take Dick Nettell, for example. As corporate services executive for Bank of America, Dick greets challenge as if it were his best friend. He's been doing it since he first began his career at the bank. Dick doesn't let circumstance overwhelm him, and he's never been intimidated by higher authority.

When Bank of America was acquired by NationsBank, creating the new Bank of America, there was a major restructuring, to put it mildly. Two huge organizations merged, and two very different cultures collided. There were sizable layoffs and wholesale changes at the top. Dick was asked to stick around and to help pick up the responsibilities of his former manager.

Early in the process of this painful transition, Dick's manager at the time came out from bank headquarters (in Charlotte, North Carolina) to San Francisco to address Dick's group and talk about the cuts and all the changes. It was a bit of a risk, but Dick asked her if he could say a few words to the group of about two hundred employees assembled in the room. In his familiar straightforward style, Dick said:

> Let's cut to the chase. David Lynch (the former head of the business unit that had been merged into Dick's part of the organization) built this organization. He was here for thirty-five years, and he did an outstanding job. We're at a crossroads right now. We can sit here and moan and feel sorry for ourselves because it's not the same old bank. Or we can do what he would want us to do, which is build on the legacy he left behind and really show people what this organization is made of—its pride, its personal responsibility in delivering excellence. That doesn't change.

You could feel the spirits lift and the attitudes shift the day that Dick made those comments. What Dick did in this situation promoted psychological hardiness in three simple ways. First, he was proactive and encouraged others to be proactive—to take charge of change. He showed them it was within their abilities to do it. Second, he infused the challenge with meaning by invoking the work of his predecessor and values that people shared. Third, he increased commitment by recognizing the ability of everyone in the group to do it. He appealed to their personal pride and their ability to deliver excellence.

This is the kind of fertile field that makes leadership everyone's business and enables people to grow and develop.

CREATE A CLIMATE OF TRUST

In the thousands of cases we've studied, we've yet to encounter a single example of extraordinary achievement that didn't involve the active participation and support of many people. We've yet to find a single instance in which one talented person—leader or individual contributor—accounted for most, let alone 100 percent, of the success. Throughout the years, leaders from all professions, from all economic sectors, and from around the globe continue to tell us, "You can't do it alone." Leadership is not a solo act; it's a team performance.

Turbulence in the marketplace, it turns out, requires more collaboration, not less. The increasing emphasis on networks, business-to-business and peer-to-peer e-commerce, strategic acquisitions, and knowledge work, along with the surging number of global alliances and local partnerships, is testimony to the fact that in a more complex, wired world, the winning strategies will be based on the "*we* not *I*" philosophy. Collaboration is a social imperative. Without it people can't get extraordinary things done in organizations.

At the heart of collaboration is trust. It's *the* central issue in human relationships both within and outside organizations. Without trust you cannot lead. Without trust you cannot get extraordinary things done. Exemplary leaders are devoted to creating a climate of trust based on mutual respect and caring. Individuals who are unable to trust others fail to become leaders, precisely because they can't bear to be dependent on the words and work of others. Their obvious lack of trust in others results in others' lack of trust in them.

Creating a climate of trust is exactly what Jeanne Rosenberger, dean of student life at Santa Clara University, did when she was faced with a very challenging situation on campus. Jeanne found herself the link between the administration and a student group protesting SCU's acceptance of a $50,000 gift from a major government defense contractor. Jeanne needed to find a way to keep the protest from escalating, to ensure everyone's safety, to safeguard the health of the students who were fasting as part of their protest, to use the event as a learning opportunity, and to formulate a win-win outcome.

Jeanne's aim was to create a calm, collaborative setting rather than a confrontational one. This she managed step by step, gaining agreements and trust from both groups along the way. She made sure that a neutral location was used for meetings. She emphasized the importance of face-to-face communication and careful listening. She began each conversation with the students by asking about their health and well-being—not with an ultimatum. She gained the students' trust by advocating that the university call the local police department or campus safety office only if needed, rather than having a constant police presence or threat of action.

As a result, the protest remained peaceful, the students fasted for four days—all with no health problems—and a dialogue began about the development of a gift policy. In addition, after the demonstration, Jeanne made use of the educational opportunities, involving students in reflecting on what they had learned—about the demonstration, about the university, about corporations, about leadership, and about themselves. For these youthful activists, learning the importance of trust in the resolution of differences is a powerful leadership lesson they will carry with them beyond the grounds of the campus.

DEVELOP RELATIONSHIP SKILLS

Leadership is a relationship between those who aspire to lead and those who choose to follow. Sometimes the relationship is one-to-one. Sometimes it's one-to-many. But regardless of the number—whether it's one or one thousand—leadership is a relationship. If leaders are going to emerge, grow, and thrive in these disquieting times, they must become socially competent. We can't have positive face-to-face interactions if we don't have competence, and competence is crucial to our personal and organizational success.

Daniel Goleman has generated widespread awareness of this set of abilities, which he and others refer to as "emotional intelligence" (EI). He described it this way: "Emotional Intelligence—the ability to manage ourselves and our relationships effectively—consists of four fundamental capabilities: self-awareness, self-management, social awareness, and social skill."

Emotional intelligence is no passing fad, and because of the vital importance of this competency to executive success, Egon Zehnder International has become a leader in applying emotional intelligence to the world of work. That effort has been spearheaded by Claudio Fernandez-Aråoz, EZI partner and a member of its executive committee. Claudio knows from personal experience the significance of this burgeoning field, having conducted hundreds of senior executive searches and supervised a number of studies on EI. He said:

> This experience has left me with no doubts about the relevance of emotional intelligence to senior management success. . . . The classic profile organizations look for in hiring a senior executive (relevant experience and outstanding IQ) is much more a predictor of failure than success, unless the relevant emotional intelligence competencies are also present. In fact, serious weaknesses in the domain of emotional intelligence predict failure at senior levels with amazing accuracy.

What Claudio said is serious stuff. Senior executives can graduate at the top of the best business schools in the world, reason circles around their brightest peers, solve technical problems with wizardlike powers, and have all the relevant situational, functional, and industry experience—and *still* be more likely to fail than succeed, unless they also possess the requisite personal and social skills.

Mastery of any vocation requires skill-building efforts. You can't paint without skills, you can't write software code without skills, you can't sell without skills, and you can't lead without skills. Mastery of leadership requires mastery of those skills central to developing and maintaining positive relationships with others. This is no time to cut training and coaching budgets. This is no time to skimp on teaching people the skills that will enable them to listen, to communicate, to resolve conflicts, to negotiate, to influence, to build teams, and otherwise to strengthen the capacity of others to excel. Organizations serious about leadership will make the appropriate resources available, and individuals who recognize the opportunities for greatness inherent in today's challenges will make the time available to improve their leadership skills.

LEADERSHIP MATTERS

Recently Vince Russo, executive director of the Aeronautical Systems Center at Wright-Patterson Air Force Base, related to us that in his forty-year career he'd been part of more than fifteen strategic initiatives—from zero defects to management-by-objectives to total quality management to lean thinking to reengineering. "You name it," he said, "and we've done it." They've come and gone, but "I've observed one constant theme across all of them," he continued. "The theme is that leaders have to step forward and get involved with change. Although each idea on how to do change is somewhat different—and they all have some good parts—without leadership, nothing works."

Leadership is not a fad. It's a fact. It's not here today, gone tomorrow. It's here today, here forever.

Leadership matters. And it matters more in times of uncertainty than in times of stability. And since leadership matters more in times of uncertainty, then leadership development should matter more now than ever. If today's leaders want tomorrow's organizations to thrive, they have an obligation to prepare a new generation of leaders.

Stuff happens in organizations and in our lives. Sometimes we choose it; sometimes it chooses us. People who become leaders don't always seek the challenges they face. Challenges also seek leaders. It's not so important whether you find the challenges or they find you. What is important are the choices you make when stuff happens. The question is: When opportunity knocks are you prepared to answer the door?

3

~

A View About "Vision"

Neal Thornberry

Any modern manager who has not heard the word *vision* used in relationship to his or her own or another organization must surely be undereducated regarding today's latest buzz words. The term *vision* may actually lead in frequency of usage in the mahogany halls of senior management, ahead of *total quality, reengineering, strategic intent,* and *competitive advantage.*

The concept of vision is not the problem, but the fact that most business leaders who use the term don't really understand it and worse still don't have the faintest idea how to create and deploy it. It's not entirely their fault since most of the literature and research on vision have accurately identified its importance and pointed out individuals who seem to be visionary but have done little to help leaders at all levels in the organization actually do it (Krug and Oakley, 1993; Capowski, 1994).

Some of the fault lies in the nature of the concept. A simple definition of vision is a picture or view of the future. Something not yet real but imagined. What the organization could and should look like. Part analytical and part emotional. This definition is actually no more concrete to managers than the concept of vision itself. Herein lies both the challenge and the difficulty of vision. It is very hard to define. In fact in some Spanish-speaking countries the translated words for vision are more closely defined as "nightmare" or "apparition," a definition some English-speaking managers may find closer to reality after trying to develop and implement a vision within their own companies.

Reprinted by permission from *European Management Journal*, 15: 1 (February 1997), pp. 28–34. Copyright 1997. Published by Elsevier Science Ltd. All rights reserved.

Unfortunately the concept is itself very "woolly" or "fuzzy," so it creates various individual interpretations with little consensus to be found. The author was recently asked to review and evaluate the vision statement of an international finance company. Senior management had spent over a year trying to evolve this vision. Many meetings had been held, and after much debate they had arrived at an acceptable "vision" statement of which they were quite proud. They had it engraved on a gold plaque, which was conspicuously displayed in the corporate boardroom. The plaque had the following elements:

- We aspire to be number one in our marketplace.
- We respect and value our customers and our employees.
- We will work diligently to build value for our shareholders and investors.

I will not bore you with further elements of this "vision statement," but as you can see, it really tells us nothing. I was not popular with this company when I suggested that they had actually purchased this "vision" from some "vision" warehouse that sells the same generic statements to hundreds of other companies in all kinds of industries. They were not amused. One would be hard-pressed to find a company that did not publicly agree with all of the above platitudes. Can you imagine a company that wants to be mediocre, is mean to its employees, and tries to screw its customers?

What they had done was mix generic concepts and ideas. In their vision statement they had mixed values with mission but had not really created a picture of the future, nor had they come to grips with their fundamental purpose or reason for being.

CONFUSING TERMINOLOGY

With one notable exception, the literature on vision has not been very helpful in sorting out and differentiating these concepts. Most vision statements that I have reviewed seem to be a mix of strategy, goals and objectives, values and beliefs, slogans, purposes, and so on. Vision statements should be designed to be vivid, memorable, inspiring, meaningful, and brief. Some of these statements, especially those found in annual reports, are boring at best and indecipherable to the general public; clearly they are not memorable. In addition, words alone rarely carry long-term meanings for people unless the message behind them can be visualized. We recently asked over two hundred managers from a large European IT company to tell us their company's vision. Some people had no idea what it was. For those who thought they knew, there was no consensus. A number of these managers volunteered to retrieve materials from offsite to clear up the confusion. This in itself was indicative of a less than effective visioning process. The company's vision was neither clear nor memorable.

KEY COMPONENTS OF VISION

Perhaps the most coherent differentiation of some of these concepts comes from the work of Collins and Porras (1991, 1994). They studied over seventy-five organizations and isolated twenty of those that seemed to have gotten this "vision thing" down. Among those were Procter and Gamble, 3M, Ford, Sony, and Compaq. They analyzed these organizations to determine what constituted the anatomy of vision. They found that the most obvious and memorable part of the vision was what they called the "vivid description." Bennis and others have called this the picture or painting of the future entity, what the company aspires to become (Bennis and Goldsmith, 1994).

From the my work at Babson College in the United States and at Ashridge Management College in the United Kingdom, this is the part of vision that people actually remember. It is the part that gives direction, helps focus effort, and stays etched in one's mind. This is also the component of vision that is the most difficult for business leaders to comprehend and develop. It involves both an artistic and an emotional component that many managers feel ill equipped to cope with.

PURPOSE OR REASON FOR BEING

Collins and Porras (1994) further argued that visions also have other components that are necessary to support this vivid description. The first is purpose. It is the fundamental reason that the organization exists. Many of today's managers will say the purpose of their organization is to make a profit and to increase shareholder value. My friends in financial circles will not like my view, but ROE (return on equity) is not the organization's purpose. It may be a goal or mission, but purpose refers to the fundamental need in the marketplace that a company's goods or services fulfill.

The new president of an international division of a financial services company, with whom I work, had an opportunity to communicate the purpose of his company to three hundred of his managers at a conference held in Canada. His speech was spent mostly in talking about his company's existing for the purpose of building value for the company's shareholders. Rubbish—the real purpose of the company was to help people who can't get conventional banks to loan them money to buy the things that so many of us take for granted. This company exists to help low-wage earners satisfy some of their physical and psychological needs through loans and revolving credit. It also gives their low-wage-earning customers respect and attention, something that typical banks do not do. The shareholders are the least important for this purpose. If a company can't satisfy some basic human need or want in the marketplace, then there won't be any equity for shareholders to share. Furthermore, very few of the managers in the room were shareholders, so from an inspirational perspective this purpose fell on deaf ears.

The best way to understand purpose is to ask the question that Collins and Porras ask: "What would the world lose if your company went out of business tomorrow?" Purpose tends to be long term and often helps to define the industry that a business is really in. Automobile manufacturers are not really in the car business; their purpose is to provide transportation. Purpose should be inspiring. Company employees should be able to see how what they do affects other people, especially the customer whose wants and needs the employee is trying to satisfy.

CULTURAL BELIEFS AND VALUES

The second element of the overall vision deals with values and beliefs. A Swedish-German combine in the paper industry is spending a great deal of time and energy on just this one component of vision. They realize that in order to fulfill their vision, they will have to have values that support it. For example, they envision their future organization as much flatter, leaner, and more decentralized. Yet many of their current values support hierarchy, power and authority, and the chain of command. Furthermore, the Germans have different values from the Swedes in terms of empowerment and delegation. This focus on values is seen as critical to the CEO because he knows that the company must create a new value system in order to meld the two cultures together. Clearly managers' values have to change if power and decisionmaking are to be pushed down to lower levels (*Business Week,* 1994a, b; *Canadian Manager,* 1993).

Values are extremely important if an organization is to realize its vision. Jack Welch of GE has always believed in promoting risk taking. Yet GE had traditionally "shot" risk takers who failed. Not exactly an action conducive to developing risk taking and entrepreneurship within the company. So Welch decided to reinforce this value by promoting even someone who had taken a risk that failed and lost the company money. Welch felt that the risk was a good one and that it had been well thought out. Risk taking wouldn't be risk taking if there weren't a significant chance of failure. Welch's action sent a real and symbolic message around GE that the company was serious about supporting a risk-taking culture. Welch's vision of a new GE that was fast, flexible, and opportunity focused could only be realized if people lived values that supported this vision.

MISSION, GOALS, AND OBJECTIVES

Mission, the third element of the visioning process, is not purpose, although it is often used as a synonym. Mission is bounded by time, and it usually involves some sort of target that can be either qualitative or quantitative. Welch wanted GE businesses to be first or second in all of their marketplaces or GE would sell them. This mission could be measured in terms of market share or volume or any number of indices. Operating plans can often be cascaded from a well-developed and thought-out mission statement.

The financial services company mentioned earlier has a mission of 15 percent growth annually. Missions usually allow for the derivation of specific goals, objectives, and measures so that the accomplishments of the mission can be determined. Collins and Porras (1994) described mission as a "bold, hairy, audacious goal." What they were really saying is that mission should stretch the organization but be possible to achieve given the company's aggressive pursuit of that goal—to be number one, to be world-class, and so on. Although these are both very broad statements, companies that are serious in reaching these lofty goals can actually develop measures that will allow them to determine their degree of success. Since missions are time-bound, they force the company to try to achieve their missions by a certain time. Some missions are never accomplished but always sought. Toyota has a mission of producing zero-defect automobiles. Unlikely to ever happen, but it has driven the company to be the best in accomplishing much of this mission. Missions are milestones on the way to realizing the vision.

A PAINTING OF THE FUTURE

The last part of the Collins and Porras (1994) model is what they described as the "vivid description." This is the crux of the vision concept. It embodies purpose, values, and mission in a picture of how the future organization will look and operate. This vivid description is a state to be aspired to. It is not yet real but what the organization would aspire to be in the future, given some realities of its current market position, financial health, competitors, and so on. It is not strategy. *Strategy* refers to plans and actions to be taken to meet strategic targets and objectives, to achieve the organization's mission. Strategy is hard; the picture of the future is soft. It is a dream. Individuals dream all the time about the future. Why shouldn't an organization dream as well? Organizations should have dreams that are built around a combination of reality and fantasy.

Isadore Sharp, founder and CEO of Four Seasons Resorts and Hotels, started his career as an architect and with his father built one small motel, but he *dreamed* of creating a luxury hotel where employees would want to bend over backward to serve their guests. So he built his first luxury hotel in a seedy area on the outskirts of Toronto, but with an inward-looking courtyard and garden so that guests would see beauty regardless of where the hotel was actually situated. The reality for Sharp was that he had the skills to design and build motels but dreamed of something greater, and the rest is history. In fact, Sharp's dream or vision is so instilled in its culture that a hotel employee flew to a nearby city at his own expense to return a bag that he had forgotten to load for a hotel guest. Thus Sharp's dream is not only a reality in stone and brick but also a reality in the hearts and minds of his employees *(Canadian Manager,* 1993).

If you are currently feeling a little unsettled by my use of language, you are in good company. Very few self-respecting CEOs, MDs, or division heads would admit to dreaming. Their world is the world of numbers, market share, ROI (return on investment), and so on. It is the world of management, not leadership or art. To lead means to take people somewhere. In today's extremely competitive and changing environment, that "somewhere" can be quite frightening. The somewhere part can be determined in part by careful analysis, planning, and strategy development. Taking people there requires the ability to paint that somewhere in an understandable and motivational picture and the courage to commit to this picture with one's heart and soul.

Visioning is not for the faint of heart. Many people in the organization will purposely take issue with the picture. The colors aren't right, the frame is the wrong size, the picture is fuzzy, the cost is too high, the picture is frightening, you're not a good artist, and so on. This is probably the clearest line of demarcation between management work and the work of leadership.

TEACHING MANAGERS TO BE VISIONARIES

One can argue whether the ability to be visionary can be taught at all. My experience at two business schools and in numerous training sessions suggests that much of it can be taught. There are, however, two elements that probably can't be taught. The first is conceptual ability and the second is courage. Conceptual ability is critical because it allows the individual to conceive of the future: to think in conceptual terms and to see the interrelationships between concepts, such as purpose, mission, and values. Most higher-level managers in today's businesses have a fair degree of conceptual abilities or they wouldn't be where they are. There are exceptions. In some old-line businesses like utilities, mining, and some elements of manufacturing, conceptual skills are not necessarily prized. With the recent upheavals in these industries, however, conceptual skills, like strategic planning, have become much more important, and we have seen a new brand of leader emerging.

Courage is about deciding where you want to go and then committing to it. We suspect that many managers are afraid to do this for fear that the direction might be wrong and therefore it is better to take no stand at all. Any leader who is unwilling to put his or her stake into the ground is not really a leader. This kind of courage is also not easily taught. If one does not have the courage of one's convictions, then it will be very hard indeed to get others to have courage about these convictions. Interestingly, vision workshops have demonstrated that some people have very strong convictions and the courage to stand behind them, once they discover that they have convictions. This is no small thing. A number of the managers who attend these vision workshops start out with very little understanding of what they really care about. During the day-and-a-half workshop, they actually find out that they care very deeply but were unaware of the depth of their caring or had not been able to communicate it.

In the vision workshop, we ask managers to practice communicating their vision to a small group of other people in the course, who then critique this communication process. This vision presentation is videotaped and reviewed. Participants often start out mouthing the platitudes about vision and mission that they have literally taken out of the company brochures or annual report. This is usually very boring and very predictable, an excellent antidote for insomnia. The real test comes when the platitudes are exhausted and there is nothing "out there" to rely on. This is the point where some participants are forced to look inward and get in touch with their own views and feelings about what is important. The workshop design also encourages listeners to challenge the presenter's vision. This often helps presenters to further refine and hone their views, and it helps them deal with the inevitable challenges that they will actually face when trying to implement their visions back in the organization.

An Asian manager from one of our sessions was surprised to find out how angry he was about the lack of individual ownership and responsibility shown by the employees and managers in his company. Everyone waited for orders and was quick to blame the person in charge. This anger helped him form a vision of his company as one that encouraged lateral communications, a profit-centered orientation, and individual accountability. His company manufactured farm equipment, mostly tractors and tractor components. To express his vision of the future, he used a tractor metaphor, showing a drawing of a tractor that represented the current state of his company and another tractor that represented the desired future state. The first tractor was slow and outdated. It had weak internal parts that constantly broke down, affecting the performance of every other part. The tractor was only effective on flat terrain, not rolling hills or unpredictable landscapes. It did not have much pulling power and was unattractive to customers. It did not do very well in pulling or pushing.

The new tractor, on the other hand, was just the opposite: fast, powerful, attractive, capable of carrying a heavy load, and good on all types of terrain. It was easy to see the connections between the tractor and the company, both in terms of how he saw the company today and what he wanted it to be tomorrow. The picture of the new tractor was simple and easily remembered, using a metaphor that all employees, including those on the shop floor, could understand. And it travels well.

This manager then made the connections for us. The terrain for his company was the competitive landscape. It used to be flat and predictable; now it was competitive and constantly changing. The tractor's weak parts were his internal departments, which didn't take the responsibility to develop themselves, and the parts were not well integrated. These parts referred to lack of communication and cooperation among the various internal company departments. Making the new tractor or the new company would require some major changes in the way the tractor was made, the way the company operated. It is easy to see the power of this image.

On his first attempt at developing a vision, this manager used typical managerial tools. He stood over an overhead filled with goals and objectives, market share, and so on. All important data to be sure, but not visionary. He started with mission, not vivid description, and used a lot of supporting financial data. Neither motivating nor inspirational. He made the mistake of thinking that mission is vision. Goals and objectives are data-driven, whereas the tractor is clearly image- or vivid-description-driven.

ART OR SCIENCE?

The videotape reviews are quite remarkable because we are able to define the distinct line of demarcation, from the mouthing of someone else's words to the "real" person emerging. There is a distinct change in body language, tone, enthusiasm, conviction, and emotion that is clearly evident. Program participants are often unaware of this transition until they see it on tape. Once we have identified what the participant really cares about, then the development process becomes much easier. The biggest challenge for us as educators is knowing when the participant makes this transition. Some of these individuals are very adept speakers—highly literate, loquacious, and extremely good presenters. But all of us, teachers and participants alike, are usually able to see when the words and the emotions don't connect, in spite of excellent presentation and communication skills.

We are currently examining how we might employ techniques used by actors to help some of our workshop participants. This is where we see a connection between business and art that might be worth exploring. Actors are taught how to interpret text and convey it directly to an audience so that the text becomes real. They breathe life into words. We are asking corporate leaders to do the same. The difference is that corporate leaders must write their own script or it becomes obvious that they are "acting" and therefore suspect. But the actor's skill allows the translation to carry some emotion that does tend to support and reinforce the conceptual message.

The director of a large hospital in the United Kingdom, part of the NHS (National Health Service), had a very difficult time with the vivid description part of our workshop. She was all business, numbers-oriented, and a very logical, detail-oriented thinker. The idea of painting a picture or showing emotion was too much for her. One of our theater consultants took her aside and worked with her on expressiveness. She asked her to imagine her mother as a patient in her hospital: "How would your mother be treated and how would you like her to be treated? How would you personally feel and act if she were mistreated?"

From this exercise came one of the best visions we have seen. The hospital director gave us two scenarios: The first involved a sickly old woman coming to a hospital. She described in painful imagery what this woman experienced. Insensitive treatment, being left on a trolley unattended to for two hours, cursory examinations, and uncaring health care people. The second scenario involved the same woman attending another hospital and having a completely different experience. The hospital director then described the first hospital as illness, a virus with all the typical attributes of a virus: spreading malaise, difficult to control, impersonal, and so on. The second hospital was described as healthy, self-diagnosing, and self-treating. She then made the links to her organization. Her hospital was the sick one, where the old woman was treated poorly. The other was the one she wanted her hospital to become, and she then laid out a plan for getting there. The picture was clear to all of us listening to her presentation, and it was indelibly etched on our memories.

Again, she had planned to give a statistical and data-laden presentation as her first attempt at communicating her vision. She was pleased that with time and the right coaching she was able to develop and internalize a clear vision for herself, one that could be communicated easily to others. And this was from an individual who did not believe that she had the ability to be a visionary leader.

IS THIS JUST A FAD?

But why should today's leaders worry about this vision thing at all? Is it just the latest fad, which will go the way of quality circles or job enrichment? We don't think so. The difference is that many of today's organizations have taken out or significantly "downsized" the middle management or "glue" that has traditionally held organizations together. Flatter, leaner, meaner, downsized, and right-sized all mean removal of layers of management that are supposed to provide order, integration, and direction. Many of today's companies have cross-functional team structures, self-directing groups, and large spans of control.

The "glue" has weakened. So how does the organization keep itself integrated and organized? There is still some structure to be sure, but flattening requires everyone in the organization to be less managed and more self-directed. If you no longer have a boss who tells you what to do, either you need to have a vision of where to go or you have to guess. Today's managers don't have time to hold their employees by the hand, so they need to get the right people. Give them the right information (desktop computers have allowed us to give just about any information to anyone), and let them make the right decisions. At the core of this information is what we want the organization to be. Thus the ability to paint, communicate, and anchor a vision (Bennis and Goldsmith, 1994) will become more, not less, important as organizations struggle to be fast, flexible, and competitive.

CONCLUSIONS

First, vision is neither rhetoric nor platitude. It provides organizational direction, it aligns people so that they move in roughly the same line, and it forces senior management to come to grips with their strategic obligation. Others, lower down in the organization, should not have to guess where it is going. Developing a vision requires strategic planning, industry analysis, risk taking and decisionmaking, imagination, and commitment. This doesn't mean that senior management should not get help from both inside and outside the organization to help them craft this vision, but in the end, it is *their* job to make sure that it gets done and it is *their* view not someone else's.

Second, a vision must give guidance. Thus wordy documents without a painting of what the company will be like when we arrive at our destination aren't very helpful. This painting must be understood and communicated throughout the organization. With rare exceptions, wordy documents do not travel well. Thus vision must be simple, easily communicated, and memorable. Paintings do this well; words do not. This means that senior management must communicate both the content and the intent of this painting in symbolic, artistic ways as opposed to mere numbers and text. Slogans can help. For instance we all know that at Ford, "Quality is job one," and that GE "makes good things for life." Slogans can be extremely powerful reflections of both vision and values, and they are memorable. Also, we know that visions tend to get blocked or retranslated by middle and upper middle management. Effective leaders make sure that they deliver their messages to the lowest level as well. Sam Walton used to visit his distribution warehouses at midnight, bringing coffee and doughnuts. He took this opportunity to communicate Wal-Mart's vision in a direct, informal manner.

Third, the visioning process requires that senior management get in touch with their leadership responsibilities, namely, the ability to help plot the future course of the organization so that it develops and sustains a competitive advantage in the marketplace. This means that senior management must get in touch with what they really care about and where they think the organization should be going. It is very typical for senior managers to be so obsessed with the short-term quarterly numbers game that this becomes their only field of "reference." One can look only at the quarterly numbers and go out of business in the process. The Japanese have taught us that there is real strength in planning for the long run, not just jumping for the "jelly bean" in the short run. This is a lesson that only some Western businesses have taken to heart. Japanese leaders are willing to accept short-term losses in pursuit of long-term success. U.S. managers are not. So the visioning process is a real test of an organization's leadership.

Fourth, visions are crafted. They need thought to develop, nurturing, and practice to deliver effectively. These are not skills taught in business school. Thus senior management may have to call upon creative help in developing their organization's vision. More than likely, this help will come from outside the organization unless it has some very talented and savvy communications people. This is that intersection between art and science. Don't be ashamed to get help from the non-business-oriented community. We have used some theater and broadcast consultants in our UK seminars to help participants with the visioning process. The theater people have been received with mixed reviews, but they are excellent at challenging the closed and self-limiting attitudes of many of the senior managers with whom we have worked. The media people are excellent at asking participants to communicate their vision in "sound bites" that force participants to distill their visions into easily communicated and remembered messages. The broadcast people are also skilled at getting our participants to say things that they don't really mean. Working with them helps participants identify the traps that others may want to spring on them in the organization, and gives them communication skills for dealing effectively with these traps.

Fifth, don't wait for perfection. Paintings are by nature imperfect. The colors may not be true to life, the brushstrokes may not be uniform, and the closer to the painting one gets, the more flaws one might see. The same is true of visions. They can be nitpicked to death. The real test is whether they convey a direction forward. There may be detours in the path and the road will be bumpy, but we know where we are heading. Get the vision out. Get feedback. Refine the vision, develop it, and recommunicate it. It is a process, not a destination. Things happen so that the painting of the future may change. The picture may be smaller, the colors may be brighter or less bright, or the painting may need reframing. Still, we have an idea of where we are headed.

Sixth, have fortitude. Courage can be brought out in people who have it and may not know it. It takes courage to paint a picture of the future that may be inaccurate. It takes even more courage to set sail to unknown lands when sharks and storms await the ship on its journey. But if the captain does not have the courage to head for the destination, then the passengers are unlikely to have faith in the captain. Visioning is taking a risk. It is what we think leaders are paid for.

Finally, the ability to develop a vision is not the sacred territory of senior management alone. Unit managers can create visions for their units. Divisional heads can do the same. It helps if there is a corporate vision to connect to, but in its absence, people in the middle have to make their best guess. A middle manager at Toomey-Delong, a food brokerage company in Boston, attended one of our visioning seminars. He came back to his company, developed a vision for his account management group, and then went to the senior manager and asked him to relate the company vision to his. Interestingly, this pressure and that of his colleagues caused the senior manager to go through the same process, so it doesn't always have to start at the top.

REFERENCES

Bennis, W., and Goldsmith, J. (1994) *Learning to Lead.* Addison-Wesley.
Business Week (1994a) "It's warm not fuzzy." July 18 (Editor's Page).
Business Week (1994b) "Managing by values." August 1.
Canadian Manager (1993) "Isadore Sharp, outstanding CEO of the Year." Spring.
Capowski, G. (1994) "Anatomy of a leader." *Management Review,* March.
Collins, J., and Porras, J. (1991) "Organizational vision and visionary organizations." *California Management Review,* 34, Fall.
Collins, J., and Porras, J. (1994) *Built to Last.* Harper Publishing.
Krug, D., and Oakley, E. (1993) *Enlightened Leadership.* Simon & Schuster.
Nice, R. C. (1994) "Empower the leaders." *Credit Union Management,* April.
Quigley, J. (1993) *Vision: How Leaders Develop It, Share It, Sustain It.* McGraw-Hill.
Smith, R. (1994) "Inspirational leadership." *Executive Speeches,* February-March.

4

~

Moral Person and Moral Manager: How Executives Develop a Reputation for Ethical Leadership

Linda Klebe Trevino
Laura Pincus Hartman
Michael Brown

Plato asked, "Which extreme would you rather be: an unethical person with a good reputation or an ethical person with a reputation for injustice?" Plato might have added, "Or would you rather be perceived as ethically neutral—someone who has no ethical reputation at all?" Plato knew that reputation was important. We now understand that reputation and others' perceptions of us are key to executive ethical leadership. Those others include employees at all levels as well as key external stakeholders.

A reputation for ethical leadership rests upon two essential pillars: perceptions of you as both a moral person *and* a moral manager. The executive as a moral person is characterized in terms of individual traits such as honesty and integrity. As moral manager, the CEO is thought of as the chief *ethics* officer of the organization, creating a strong ethics message that gets employees' attention and influences their thoughts and behaviors. Both are necessary. To be perceived as an ethical leader, it is not enough to just be an ethical person. An executive ethical leader must also find ways to focus the

Reprinted from the *California Management Review*, 42: 4, by permission of The Regents. Copyright 2000 by The Regents of the University of California.

organization's attention on ethics and values and to infuse the organization with principles that will guide the actions of all employees. An executive's reputation for ethical leadership may be more important now than ever in this new organizational era when more employees are working independently, off-site, and without direct supervision. In these organizations, values are the glue that can hold things together, and values must be conveyed from the top of the organization. Also, a single employee who operates outside the organizational value system can cost the organization dearly in legal fees and can have a tremendous, sometimes irreversible, impact on the organization's image and culture.

MORAL PERSON + MORAL MANAGER = A REPUTATION FOR ETHICAL LEADERSHIP

These ideas about a dual-pillar approach to ethical leadership are not brand-new. As the opening quotation suggests, the emphasis on reputation goes back to Plato. Chester Barnard addressed the ethical dimension of executive leadership sixty years ago. Barnard spoke about executive responsibility in terms of conforming to a "complex code of morals"[1] (moral person) as well as creating moral codes for others (moral manager).

If Plato and Barnard had this right, why bother revisiting the subject of ethical leadership now? We revisit the subject because, in our forty structured interviews (twenty with senior executives and twenty with corporate ethics officers), we found that many senior executives failed to recognize the importance of others' perceptions and of developing a reputation for ethical leadership. To them, being an ethical person and making good ethical decisions were enough. They spoke proudly about having principles, following the Golden Rule, taking into account the needs of society, and being fair and caring in their decisions. They assumed that if they were solid ethical beings, followers would automatically know that. They rejected the idea that successful ethical executives are often perceived as ethically neutral. Furthermore, they assumed that good leaders are by definition ethical leaders. One senior executive noted, "I don't think you can distinguish between ethical leadership and leadership. It's just a facet of leadership. The great leaders are ethical, and the lousy ones are not."

However, a *reputation* for ethical leadership cannot be taken for granted because most employees in large organizations do not interact with senior executives. They know them only from a distance. Any information they receive about executives gets filtered through multiple layers in the organization, with employees learning only about bare-bones decisions and outcomes, not the personal characteristics of the people behind them. In today's highly competitive business environment, messages about how financial goals are achieved frequently get lost in the intense focus on the bottom line. We found that just because executives know themselves as good people— honest, caring, and fair—they should not assume that others see them in the same way. It is so easy to forget that employees do not know you the way you know yourself. If employees do not think of an executive as a clearly ethical or unethical leader, they are likely to think of the leader as being somewhere in between—amoral or ethically neutral.

Interestingly, perceptions of *ethically neutral leadership* do not necessarily arise because the leader *is* ethically neutral. In fact, many of the senior executives we spoke with convinced us that it was impossible for them to be ethically neutral in their jobs, given the many value-laden decisions they make every day. Rather, the perception of ethically neutral leadership may exist because the leader has not faced major *public* ethical challenges that would provide the opportunity to convey his or her values to others. As one executive noted, "They haven't had to make any decisions on the margin. . . . Once you're faced with [a major public ethical dilemma], you bare your soul and you're one or the other [ethical or unethical]." On the other hand, a reputation for ethically neutral leadership may exist because the leader has not proactively made ethics and values an explicit and evident part of the leadership agenda. Executives must recognize that if they do not develop a reputation for ethical leadership, they are likely to be tagged as "ethically neutral." As a result, employees will believe that the bottom line is the only value that should guide their decisions and that the CEO cares more about himself or herself and the short-term financials than about the long-term interests of the organization and its multiple stakeholders.

Figure 4.1 provides a summary of our study's findings.

PILLAR ONE: MORAL PERSON

Being an ethical person is the substantive basis of ethical leadership. However, in order to develop a reputation for ethical leadership, the leader's challenge is conveying that substance to others. Being viewed as an ethical person means that people think of you as having certain traits, engaging in certain kinds of behaviors, and making decisions based upon ethical principles.

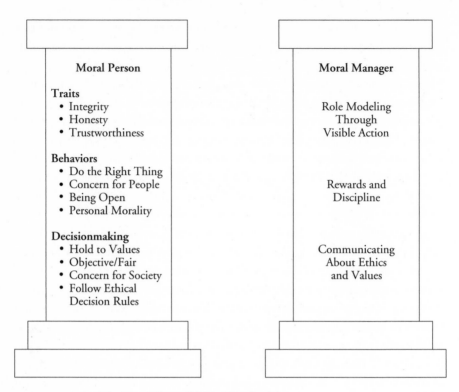

FIGURE 4.1   The Two Pillars of Ethical Leadership

Furthermore, this substantive ethical core must be authentic. As one executive put it, "If the person truly doesn't believe the ethical story and preaches it but doesn't feel it . . . that's going to show through. . . . But [a true ethical leader] walks in [and] it doesn't take very long, if you haven't met him, before [you think] there's a [person] with integrity and candor and honesty."

Traits

Traits are stable personal characteristics, meaning that individuals behave in fairly predictable ways across time and situations and observers come to describe the individual in those terms. The traits that executives most often associate with ethical leadership are honesty, trustworthiness, and integrity. A very broad personal characteristic, *integrity* was the trait cited most frequently by the executives. Integrity is a holistic attribute that encompasses the other traits of honesty and trustworthiness. One executive said that average employees would say that the ethical leader is "squeaky clean." They would think, "I know that if I bring an issue to him or her, I can count on the person's honesty and integrity on this because I've seen the standard of integrity is one that's very important to him or her."

Trustworthiness is also important to executives. Trust has to do with consistency, credibility, and predictability in relationships: "You can't build a long-term relationship with a customer who doesn't trust you." Finally, *honesty, sincerity,* and *forthrightness* are also important: "An ethical leader . . . tends to be rather candid, certain, [and is] very careful to be factual and accurate. . . . An ethical leader does not sugarcoat things. . . . He or she tells it like it is."

Behaviors

"Your actions speak so loudly, I can't hear what you're saying." That is the sentiment expressed by one executive. Although traits are clearly important to ethical leadership, behaviors are perhaps more so, and these include "the way you act even when people aren't looking"; "People are going to judge you not by what you say but by what you do"; "People look at you and understand over time who you are personally as a result of their observations." Important behaviors include "doing the right thing," showing concern for people and treating people right, being open and communicative, and demonstrating morality in one's personal life.

First and foremost, executives said that ethical leaders *do the right thing*. One retired CEO talked about the founder of his firm, a man who "was known for his strong belief that there is only one way to do business and that's the right way."

Second, executive ethical leaders *show concern for people* through their actions. They treat people well—with dignity and respect:

> I think [the ethical leader] treats everybody with dignity—meaning everybody—whether they're at the lowest level or higher levels. . . . Everyone gets treated with dignity and respect. I've also found that if you treat people with dignity and respect and trust, they almost invariably will respond in that fashion. It's like raising children. If you really don't trust them, they don't have much to lose by trying to get away with something. If they feel you trust them, they are going to think long and hard before they do something that will violate that trust.

Several of the executives used the military example: "In the military, the troops eat before the officers. . . . Leaders take care of their troops. . . . A leader is selfless, a leader shares credit, a leader sees that contributors are rewarded."

Being open means that the executive is approachable and a good listener. Employees feel comfortable sharing bad news with the ethical leader. One executive said, "An ethical leader would need to be approachable so that . . . people would feel comfortable raising the tough issues . . . and know that they would be listened to." Another put it this way: "In general, the better leaders that I've met and know are more than willing to share their experiences of rights and wrongs, successes and failures." These leaders do not kill the messenger who brings bad news. They encourage openness and treat bad news as a problem to be addressed rather than punished.

Finally, *personal morality* is associated with ethical leadership. We asked explicitly about personal morality because our interviews with executives took place during the Monica Lewinsky scandal in the Clinton presidency and the topic was prominent in everyone's mind. When we asked whether personal morality was linked to ethical leadership, most executives answered yes: "You cannot be an ethical leader if your personal morality is in question. . . . To be a leader . . . what you do privately reflects on that organization. Secondly, to be a leader you have a greater standard, a greater responsibility than the average person would have to live up to."

Decisionmaking

In their decisionmaking role, executive ethical leaders are thought to *hold to a solid set of ethical values and principles.* They aim to be *objective and fair.* They also have a perspective that goes beyond the bottom line to include *concerns about the broader society and community.* In addition, executives said that ethical leaders rely upon a number of ethical decision rules such as the Golden Rule and the *New York Times* Test. The *New York Times* Test says that, when making a decision, ethical leaders should ask themselves whether they would like to see the action they are contemplating on tomorrow morning's front page. This question reflects the ethical leader's sensitivity to community standards.

To summarize, the "Moral Person" pillar of ethical leadership represents the substance of ethical leadership, and it is an important prerequisite to developing a reputation for ethical leadership because leaders become associated with their traits, behaviors, and decisions as long as others know about them. With the moral person pillar in place, you should have a reputation for being an ethical person. You can think of this as the ethical part of the term *ethical leadership*. Having a reputation for being a moral person tells employees what *you* are likely to do—a good start, but it does not necessarily tell them what *they* should do. That requires moral managing—taking the ethics message to the rest of the organization.

Many of the executives we interviewed thought that being an ethical person who does the right thing, treats people well, and makes good decisions was necessary *and* sufficient for being an ethical leader. This is not surprising because executives know other executives personally. They have served under them, worked with them, and observed their behavior at close hand. Therefore, in their minds, an executive's ethical traits, behaviors, and decisions are automatically associated with a reputation for ethical leadership. However, some of the executives and even more of the ethics officers noted that being an ethical person was not enough. To develop a reputation for ethical leadership with employees, leaders must make ethics and values a salient aspect of their leadership agenda so that the message reaches more distant employees. To do this, they must be moral managers as well as moral persons. As one executive expressed it,

> Simply put, ethical leadership means doing the right thing, and it means communicating so that everyone understands that [the right thing] is going to happen at all times. . . . I think that most of the people I've been in business with adhere to the first but do less well with the second. And, in my experience, it is something that has to be reinforced constantly. . . . The second part is the hardest.

PILLAR TWO: MORAL MANAGER

In order to develop a reputation for *ethical leadership,* a heavy focus on the leadership part of that term is required. The executive's challenge is to make ethics and values stand out from a business landscape that is laden with messages about beating the competition and achieving quarterly goals and profits. Moral managers recognize the importance of proactively putting ethics at the forefront of their leadership agenda. Like parents who should explicitly share their values with their children, executives need to make the ethical dimension of their leadership explicit and salient to their employees. Executives who fail to do this risk being perceived as ethically neutral because other more pervasive messages about financial success take over. One CEO put it this way:

We do some good things [turn down unethical business opportunities, develop people, champion diversity], but compare the number of times that we recognize those [ethical] achievements versus how much we recognize financial achievements—it's not close. I mean, I cringe . . . saying that . . . I'm not saying we don't work at these other things, but . . . the recognition is still very much on financial performance and . . . it's true in almost all organizations. . . . And that's what's wrong. That's what's out of kilter.

Our study identified a number of ways moral managers can increase the salience of an ethics and values agenda and develop a reputation for ethical leadership. They serve as a role model for ethical conduct in a way that is visible to employees. They communicate regularly and persuasively with employees about ethical standards, principles, and values. Finally, they use the reward system consistently to hold all employees accountable to ethical standards.

Role Modeling Through Visible Action

Role modeling may seem similar to the "doing the right thing" category above. However, role modeling emphasizes *visible action* and the perceptual and reputational aspects of ethical leadership. Some ethical behaviors will go completely unnoticed whereas others will be noticed and will contribute to a reputation for ethical leadership. Effective moral managers recognize that they live in a fishbowl of sorts and employees are watching them for cues about what's important. One manager explained, "You are demonstrating by your example on and off the job, in other words, twenty-four hours a day, seven days a week, you're a model for what you believe in and the values." In addition, "if you're unethical . . . people pick up on that and assume because you're the leader that it's the correct thing to do, . . . that not only are you condoning it, but you're actually setting the example for it."

The effective moral manager understands which words and actions are noticed and how they will be interpreted by others. In some cases, visible executive action (without any words at all) is enough to send a powerful message. One executive offered the following as an example of the power of executive action:

Some years ago, I was running one of our plants. I had just taken over and they were having some financial troubles. . . . Most of our management was flying first class. . . . I did not want . . . my first act to be to tell everybody that they are not gonna fly first class anymore, so I just quit flying first class. And it wasn't long before people noticed it, and pretty soon everybody was flying coach. . . . I never put out a directive, never said a word to anybody . . . and people noticed it. They got the message. . . . People look to the leader. If the leader cuts corners, they say its okay to cut corners around here. If the leader doesn't cut corners, we must be expected not to do any of that around here.

Negative signals can also be sent by visible executive action, and moral managers must be particularly sensitive to these. For example, what kind of signal does it send when your organization's ethics policy prohibits employees from accepting any kind of gift from a prospective client and then employees see a group of senior executives sitting in a client's box enjoying a professional football or basketball game? Unless the CEO is wearing a large sign that says, "We paid for these tickets," the message is clear. Ethics policies do not apply equally to everyone. It becomes much easier for an employee to rationalize receiving gifts. According to one interviewee, many executives "wouldn't think twice about it because you don't intend to do anything wrong." However, employees are generally not aware of your *intent*. They see the actions and make inferences based upon them.

Communicating About Ethics and Values

Many executives are uncomfortable talking about ethics and wonder about those who do. In our interviews, some executives expressed concern about the leader who talks about ethics too much: "I distrust people who talk about it all the time. I think the way you do it [ethical leadership] is to demonstrate it in action. . . . The more a person sermonizes about it, the more worried I am. . . . Sometimes you have to talk about it, but mostly you don't talk about it, you just do things." However, moral managers need to talk about ethics and values not in a sermonizing way, but in a way that explains the values that guide important decisions and actions. If people do not hear about ethics and values from the top, it is not clear to employees that ethics and values are important. You may not feel comfortable talking about ethics if it means discussing the intricacies of Aristotle or Kant. However, talking about ethics with your employees does not mean that at all. It means talking about the values that are important to you and the organization. It is a bit like teaching children about sex. Parents can choose to avoid the uncomfortable subject, hoping that their children will learn what they need to know in school, or they can bring an expert home who knows more than they do about the physiology of the human reproductive system. However, what parents really want their children to know about and adopt is a set of values the family believes in, such as love, respect, and responsibility. To be most effective, that message must come from parents, in words and in actions. Similarly, the message about the values guiding decisions and actions in business should come from senior leaders.

The Reward System

Using rewards and discipline effectively may be the most powerful way to send signals about desirable and undesirable conduct. That means rewarding those who accomplish their goals by behaving in ways that are consistent with stated values. One manager explained, "The most senior executive should reward the junior executive, the manager, the line people who make these [ethical] decisions. . . . Reinforcement is very important."

It also means clearly disciplining employees at all levels when they break the rules. A financial industry executive provided the following two examples:

> If there's a situation within the corporation of sexual harassment where [the facts are] proven and management is very quick to deal with the wrongdoer, . . . that's leadership. To let the rumor mill take over, to allow someone to quietly go away, to resign, is not ethical leadership. It is more difficult, but you send the message out to the organization by very visible, fair, balanced behavior. That's what you have to do.

> If someone has taken money, and they happen to be a twenty-five-year employee who has taken two hundred dollars over the weekend and put it back on Monday, you have to . . . fire that person. [You have to make] sure everybody understands that Joe took two hundred dollars on Friday and got [fired]. . . . [They must also] be assured that I did have a fact base, and that I did act responsibly and I do care about twenty-five-year people.

Another financial industry executive talked about how he was socialized early in his career:

> When I was assigned . . . to train under a tough, but fair partner of the firm, . . . he [said]there are things expected from you, . . . but if you ever

make a transaction in a client's account that you can't justify to me was in the best interest of the customer, you're out. Well, that kind of gets your attention.

An airline executive said:

We talk about honesty and integrity as a core value; we communicate that. But then we back it up. . . . Someone can make a mistake. They can run into the side of an airplane with a baggage cart and put a big dent in it, . . . and we put our arm around them and retrain them. . . . If that same person were to lie to us, they don't get a second chance. . . . When it comes to honesty, there is no second chance.

The moral manager consistently rewards ethical conduct and disciplines unethical conduct at all levels in the organization, and these actions serve to uphold the standards and rules. The above reward system examples represent clear signals that will be noticed and that demonstrate clearly how employees are held accountable and how the leader backs up words with actions.

In summary, to develop a reputation for ethical leadership, one must be strong on both dimensions: moral person and moral manager. The ethical leader has a reputation for being both a substantively ethical person and a leader who makes ethics and values a prominent part of the leadership agenda.

WHAT DOES ETHICAL LEADERSHIP ACCOMPLISH?

The executives we talked with said that ethical leadership was good for business, particularly in the long term, and prevents legal problems: "It probably determines the amount of money you're spending in lawsuits and with corporate attorneys. . . . You save a lot of money in regulatory fees and lawyer fees and settlement fees." They also said that ethical leadership contributes to employee commitment, satisfaction, comfort, and even fun: "People enjoy working for an ethical organization," and it helps the organization attract and retain the best employees: "If the leadership of the company reflects [ethical] values, . . . people will want to work for that company and will want to do well." Finally, employees in an organization led by an executive ethical leader will imitate the behavior of their leader and therefore the employees will be more ethical themselves.

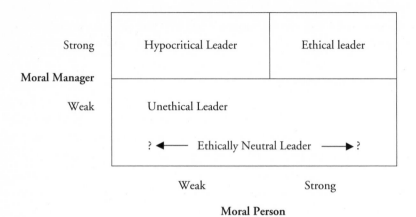

FIGURE 4.2   Executive Reputation and Ethical Leadership

Next, we combine the two pillars of ethical leadership into a 2 × 2 matrix that can help us think about the kinds of reputation an executive can develop (see Figure 4.2). As noted, the combination of strong moral person and strong moral manager produces a reputation for ethical leadership. However, what happens if the leader falters in one of these areas? The matrix suggests the following possibilities: One may develop a reputation as an unethical leader, a hypocritical leader, or an ethically neutral leader.

The Unethical Leader

A leader who is perceived to be weak on both dimensions will develop a reputation for unethical leadership. A number of executives we spoke with named Al Dunlap as a prime example of someone with a reputation for unethical executive leadership. *Business Week* recently published excerpts from John Byrne's book about Dunlap entitled *Mean Business*.[2] The article describes Dunlap as the "no-nonsense executive famous for turning around struggling companies—and sending their shares soaring in the process." However, Dunlap was also known for tirades against employees, "which could reach the point of emotional abuse"; "He was condescending, belligerent and disrespectful"; "At his worst, he became viciously profane, even violent. Executives said he would throw papers or furniture, bang his hands on his desk, and shout so ferociously that a manager's hair would be blown back by the stream of air that rushed from Dunlap's mouth." He used the promise of huge rewards to get "employees to do things they might not otherwise do." In order to make the numbers that Dunlap demanded, creative accounting techniques were employed and "dubious techniques were used to boost sales." He also lied to Wall Street analysts. "Despite the chaos inside the company, Sunbeam's chief kept up a steady drumbeat of optimistic sales and earnings forecasts, promises of tantalizing new products, and assurances that the Dunlap magic was working." In the end, the lies could no longer cover up what was really going on. Wall Street abandoned the company, and the board of directors fired Dunlap. Sunbeam was left crippled, and the company continues to struggle today.

On the moral person dimension, Dunlap was found to be dishonest, he treated people horribly, and he made decisions based upon the financial bottom line only, disregarding the interests of multiple stakeholders in the process. On the moral manager dimension, his own behavior, his communications, and the reward system were used to send a single consistent message: The bottom line was the only thing that mattered.

The Hypocritical Leader

A leader who is not perceived to be a strong ethical person but who attempts to put ethics and values at the forefront of the leadership agenda is likely to be perceived as a hypocritical leader who "talks the ethics talk" but does not "walk the ethics walk." In such cases, people tend to see the talk only as window dressing. They watch for actions to match the words, and if there is a mismatch, the words are dismissed. As suggested above, some executives expressed concern about the leader who talks about ethics too much. In terms of the leader's reputation for ethical leadership, communicating about ethics and values, without the actions to match, is probably worse than doing nothing at all because talk without action places a spotlight on the issue that would not otherwise be there. As a result, employees become cynical and distrust everything the leader says. They also figure that they, too, can ignore ethical standards if they perceive that the leader does so.

The Ethically Neutral Leader

This category generated a lot of comment. Half the executives rejected it out of hand. The other half recognized its existence, and almost all of the twenty corporate ethics officers we talked with readily acknowledged it. On the moral person dimension, it is most appropriate to say that this person is perceived to be *not clearly unethical,* but also not strongly ethical. Consider what people say about ethically neutral leaders. In terms of traits, the ethically neutral leader is seen as more self-centered than other-centered. In terms of behaviors, ethically neutral leaders are less open to input from others and they care less about people. They are less compassionate. In terms of decisionmaking, ethically neutral executive leaders are thought to have a narrower view than do ethical leaders. They focus on financial ends more than the means that are of interest to ethical leaders. They also are more likely to base decisions upon the short-term bottom line, and they are less concerned with leaving the organization or the world a better place for the future. Interestingly, much of the emphasis seems to be on what the ethically neutral leader is *not* (not open to input, not caring, not focused on means, not concerned about leaving a legacy). This is important because it means that to perceive ethical leadership, followers need evidence of positive ethical traits, behaviors, and decision processes. Lack of awareness of these positive characteristics leads to the perception that the leader is ethically neutral. Clearly, employees must be aware of these positive attributes in order for them to infer the existence of ethical leadership.

When asked to talk about ethically neutral leaders, people said virtually nothing about moral managing (role modeling, communicating, the reward system). Given that employees make sense of the messages they do get, the ethically neutral leader's focus on the short-term bottom line gets employees' attention by default. If that is what the leader is focusing on, it must be the only thing that is important. One executive said, "Ethics hasn't been on the scorecard for what's important here. . . . It's kind of like quality. Quality is something that we slipped away from and someone had to say, 'It's important.' Maybe the same is true of ethics . . . We need a Deming . . . to remind us of how important it is."

Perhaps the most important outcome of ethically neutral leadership is that employees think that ethics is not particularly important to the leader, as one leader said, "So they're left deciding on their own what's important in a particular situation." This means that they are acting without clear guidance about the ethics and values of the organization. The leader has not demonstrated this guidance, has not thought through it, has not given an example of it, has not talked about it, and has not discussed it in an open forum.

CULTIVATING A REPUTATION FOR
ETHICAL LEADERSHIP

Given the importance of ethical leadership, we offer the following practical steps executives can take to cultivate a reputation for ethical leadership.

Share Your Values: Who Are You as an Ethical Person?

One manager explained, "Ethical leadership is not easy. . . . The temptations and the rewards for unethical behavior are great. So, ethical leadership requires a discipline, a mental and personal discipline that is not easy to come by." Some senior executives arrive in their leadership positions with all of the necessary cognitive and emotional tools to be an active ethical leader. Part of the reason many of them ascend to senior leadership positions is that they have a reputation for integrity, for treating people well, and for doing the right thing. They have very likely had a lifetime of personal and work-related mentors and experiences that have molded and reinforced their values. By the time they reach the executive level, these values are so solid that, when challenged, the leader holds to them without question.

On the other hand, senior executive positions have a way of challenging values in ways they may not have been challenged before. If you think that this aspect of your leadership needs work, devote energy to developing this side of yourself. Read books. Attend workshops and seminars with other senior executives who share your concerns. Work with a personal coach. Talk with your spiritual adviser about how your values can be applied in your work.

It then becomes particularly important to share this side of yourself. Find out what employees know about you and how they think of you in ethical leadership terms. You may be a strong ethical person, but your employees may have no way of knowing that. Most people do not have an accurate view of how others see them, especially when it comes to ethics. Surveys consistently find that most people think of themselves as above average and more ethical than their peers. However, the only way to honestly assess where you stand in terms of others' perceptions is to ask for candid input. A leader should "always have someone who can tell the emperor that he or she has no clothes." So, ask those closest to you. You can also survey your employees to find out how much they know about you as an ethical leader. Be open to what you learn, and do not be surprised if employees say they simply do not know. For example, if you have not been outspoken on ethics and values issues, or you have not managed a highly public crisis that provided an opportunity for employees to learn about your values, you may be surprised to learn that employees do *not* know much about this aspect of your leadership. They may even see you as "neutral" on the ethics dimension. Talk to your communications people and your ethics officer, if you have one, about how you might successfully convey your values to employees on a regular basis. Figure out a way to open the lines of two-way communication on ethics and values issues. Ask employees to share the ethical dilemmas they face and to let you know what kind of guidance they would like from you.

Assume the Role of Moral Manager: Chief Ethics Officer of Your Organization

One manager said:

> Ethical leadership means that the person, the leader, who is exercising that leadership is well grounded in a set of values and beliefs that we would view as being ethical. However, in a leadership sense . . . it means that the leader sets an example because ethical leadership doesn't just mean that leader; it means the entire organization. If there isn't an observed ethical leadership at the top, you won't find it in the organization.

As noted, moral management requires overt action on the part of the executive to serve as a role model for ethical behavior in highly visible ways, to communicate about ethics and values, and to use the reward system to hold people accountable. James Burke, former CEO of Johnson & Johnson, provided an excellent example of highly visible action that gets everyone's attention. Soon after Burke assumed the presidency of Johnson & Johnson, he brought together twenty-eight senior managers to challenge the age-old corporate credo. He asked them to talk about whether they could really live by the document that had been hanging on corporate walls for years. "If we can't live by this document then it's an act of pretension and we ought to tear it off the walls, get rid of it. If we can live with it but want to change it that's okay, too, if we can agree on what the changes should be. And, we could also leave it the way it is." According to Burke, people "stayed up all night screaming at each other." When they were done, they had updated the credo. They then took it to J&J sites around the world, released a revised credo in 1979, and committed the organization to it. Less than three years later, the Tylenol poisoning occurred, and lots of folks were waiting to see whether management would live up to the credo values. As every student of business ethics and corporate crisis management knows, they did, and the case is now held up as a premier example of good business ethics. Burke does not take credit for J&J's success in handling the corporate crisis. He attributes the success to the value system that had been articulated. However, clearly he was responsible for guiding the organization through the values articulation process and for making the credo prominent in the corporate culture and consciousness. As another executive put it, "All the written statements in the world won't achieve ethics in an organization unless the leader is perceived as being very serious and committed."

Following the Tylenol crisis, in 1985 Burke launched the credo survey process. All employees were surveyed regarding the company's performance with respect to the credo. Based upon the results, managers held feedback and problem-solving sessions with their employees and developed action plans to address problems. The survey process continues today on a biannual schedule under Burke's successor, Ralph Larsen, and remains a valuable way to keep attention focused on the credo and the values it represents.

To better integrate the credo into the reward system, Larsen instigated a "standards of leadership" program that holds leaders at all levels accountable to the credo values:

> At the important succession planning meetings, when upward mobility in the company is discussed, "Credo Values" is first on the agenda. "Business Results" is next in line. The following behaviors associated with Credo values are noted: "Behaving with honesty and integrity. Treating others with dignity and respect. Applying Credo values. Using Credo survey results to improve business. Balancing the interests of all constituents. Managing for the long term."[3]

Finally, violations of credo policy are handled swiftly and clearly. In one incident that involved infiltration of a competitor's sales meeting, President Larsen wrote the following to his management:

> Our behavior should deeply embarrass everyone associated with Johnson & Johnson. Our investigation revealed that certain employees had engaged in improper activities that violated our policies. These actions were wrong and we took steps, immediately, to discipline those involved and guard against a recurrence of this kind of activity.[4]

CONCLUSION

Being an ethical leader requires developing a reputation for ethical leadership. Developing a reputation for ethical leadership depends upon how others perceive the leader on two dimensions: as a moral person and as a moral manager. Being a moral person encompasses who you are, what you do, and what you decide as well as making sure that others know about this dimension of you as a person. Being a moral manager involves being a role model for ethical conduct, communicating regularly about ethics and values, and using the reward system to hold everyone accountable to the values and standards. Ethical leadership pays dividends in employee pride, commitment, and loyalty—all particularly important in a full-employment economy in which good companies strive to find and keep the best people.

ENDNOTES

1. C. Barnard, *Functions of the Executive* (Cambridge: Harvard University Press, 1938 and 1968), p. 279.

2. J. A. Byrne, "Chainsaw," *Business Week*, October 18, 1999, pp. 128–149.

3. L. Foster, *Robert Wood Johnson* (State College, PA: Lillian Press, 1999), pp. 645–646.

4. Ibid., p. 646.

5

~

Crisis, Culture, and Charisma: The New Leader's Work in Public Organizations

Matthew Valle

This paper argues that the changing nature of public service requires new leadership and that the primary goal of leaders in public organizations today should be the development of, as the organization's primary core competence, an adaptive organizational culture. The changing nature of public service will be discussed in terms of the external and internal environmental forces impacting public organizations, the expanded and diverse missions that make up the work of the members of these organizations, and the style of leadership appropriate in order to take steps to create the organizational energy necessary for action. The model presented emphasizes the interaction of the environment, the followers, and the leader and describes this interaction as a combination of crisis, culture, and charisma.

In an era of increasing public pressure and dwindling budgets, the challenge of leadership in public organizations grows more acute each day. Given the pervasive stereotypes about public leaders,[1] the increasingly uncertain regulatory environments in which they operate,[2] and the constraints, controls, and processes of public management,[3] leaders in public organizations are faced with substantial, if not insurmountable, obstacles to effective management. It may go without saying that tomorrow's regulatory and

Reprinted with permission of *Public Personnel Management*, published by IPMA-HR, Alexandria, VA.

administrative problems will differ markedly from today's. Consider, for example, the changing landscape of public administration: The number of stakeholder groups has swelled and all groups are becoming increasingly vocal; demographic changes are causing shifts in federal, state, and local responsibilities; there is increasing downward pressure on the ability of public organizations to levy taxes, often in combination with an increase in the level of unfunded mandates; and the continuing pervasive and interactive nature of the global economy and global markets injects a higher degree of chaos than was previously experienced.[4] In such an environment, it is not so difficult to explain the exodus of high-quality leaders,[5] and the drain of managerial talent may continue unabated unless some mechanism exists for new leaders in public organizations to create environments that facilitate mission accomplishment, personal growth and productivity, and a rebirth of organizational energy.

Public organizations today need leaders capable of coping with continual environmental change, but the real work of new leaders in public organizations is to prepare the members of their organizations to cope with, and adapt to, changes of mission, environment, and/or direction. Such leadership will require individuals who have the ability to correctly assess current environmental threats and opportunities, both within and outside the organization, and take steps to create the organizational energy necessary for action.[6] In this paper, I will argue that leaders in public organizations must focus their efforts on developing, as the organization's primary core competence, an adaptive organizational culture. It is through such a culture that public organizations, and their leaders, will learn how to succeed in the face of constantly changing responsibilities.

THE CENTRAL ROLE OF CRISIS IN PUBLIC ORGANIZATIONS

Intuitively, we know that leadership in public organizations today is different, primarily because of the increasingly turbulent nature of the environments in which public organizations operate.[7] Changes in environment require corresponding changes in the methods by which the organization plans, organizes, and directs its energies toward mission accomplishment. Such is the province of leadership. The primary function of leadership is to guide the organization and its members toward their objectives, but those objectives have become more elusive and dynamic in public organizations.

Leadership under these circumstances requires continual environmental scanning that assesses threats and opportunities. The environment in which public service organizations operate today more closely mirrors the private sector, with constantly evolving technological focus and the interplay of local and global market forces. Actually, the turbulent nature of the environment surrounding most public organizations can be more accurately described as one of crisis.

One normally associates crisis with severe societal, economic, or political upheaval, but there are crises continually impacting organizations that are relatively pervasive but less severe.[8] Crisis may be perceived if the current situations the organization faces are of such a varied nature that simple resolution based upon reference to past actions or procedures becomes problematic. Affective reactions based upon such perceptions may include increased levels of perceived stress and decreased levels of personal satisfaction for organizational members. Behavioral reactions to crisis situations may include detrimental physical effects and increases in absenteeism and turnover. The response of the organization to these new realities is determined, in great part, by the ability of organization leaders to guide members toward the successful resolution of the crisis. The methods leaders use to guide members are the result of a series of choices that reflect how leaders and followers interact.

LEADERSHIP AND CULTURE IN PUBLIC ORGANIZATIONS

In the past, leaders in public organizations have placed great emphasis on developing stable and predictable organizational structures and work processes.[9] The purpose of leadership in such organizations was (and still may be) to train employees to anticipate problems by focusing on specific rules, procedures, and policies for handling matters requiring organizational action. This type of leadership is often referred to as *transactional*. A transactional leader guides and motivates followers by clarifying role and task requirements so that goals may be acheived.[10] Rewards accrue to those who follow the rules. Transactional leaders take corrective action only when there is a deviation from the rules or procedures. What is perhaps unintentionally made clear to employees in this type of system is that thinking and acting "outside the box" have no place in this organization. Effectiveness is measured by adherence to standards, rules, and procedures. Such an approach may prove efficient and effective if the tasks required of the organization are

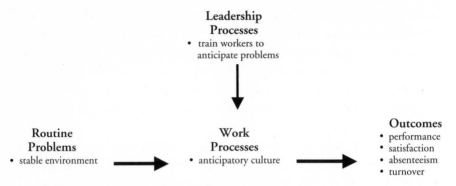

FIGURE 5.1   Leadership Processes in Stable Environments

stable and predictable and can be completed with reference to specified rules. In manufacturing organizations, rules and procedures (i.e., work processes) enhance standardization, which consequently impacts efficiency and the quality of the effort and output. Discipline is required in such organizations to produce outputs that conform to specifications. However, if the problems faced by public organizations are not routine, work processes may degenerate to fitting square pegs in round holes, no matter how square they may be.

The culture that develops under this "rule-driven" organizational system may be referred to as *anticipatory*.[11] An anticipatory system is one that takes present action based upon an expected future state. The term refers to any system in which decisions are made by reference to an established algorithm or problem-solving guide. By nature, anticipatory cultures are passive and reactive. Work processes emphasize learning the rules and procedures to guide decisions. Employees develop a reactive stance toward problems; workers engage in a deterministic search for the correct application of standards to problematic issues. The identification and exploitation of opportunities (unforeseen problems) may not even occur in such organizations. Remember, action is taken only on expected future states. Figure 5.1 shows the relationship between routine problems, leadership, and the anticipatory culture of these organizations.

If the majority of the problems public organizations face could be classified as routine, then such a system of anticipation would be the most efficient form in which to conduct the work of the organization. In some systems leaders try to isolate the technical core (i.e., the workers) from their external environment by sorting, classifying, and filtering until what arrives

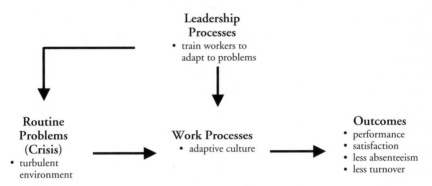

FIGURE 5.2   Leadership Processes in Turbulent Environments

for disposition is a neatly packaged, clearly solvable "problem." Much of the work done by transactional leaders is along those lines. Increasingly, however, leaders in public organizations are not able to isolate their technical core from the chaos of their environments. Therefore, if public organizations are operating in increasingly turbulent environments, is it possible to structure work processes to achieve stability when the parameters for stable operation are constantly shifting? What is the appropriate fit of organizational structure and environment in these new circumstances? And, perhaps a more practical question, do leaders in public organizations have the ability to restructure their organizations to achieve a good fit? The good news is that such a reorganization is implicit in the cultural change leaders must initiate in public organizations in order to cope with, and adapt to, the increasing complexity of their environments. And it is posited that such a change can occur without the physical shift of personnel and resources that is normally associated with organizational change.

THE NEW LEADER'S WORK

Public organizations that are subject to continual crises, whether acute or chronic, severe or less severe, need to develop mechanisms to cope with the demands of their ever-changing situations. Figure 5.2 suggests a new model for leadership in public organizations that focuses on the relationships between the culture of the subordinates in the organization; the situational context, or environment, in which the organization operates (i.e., crisis); and the leadership essential to facilitate effectiveness. This model emphasizes the interaction of leader, follower, and situation in understanding how leaders in public organizations may accomplish their expanded missions in the face of pressure from increasing numbers of stakeholders.

The primary means by which leaders facilitate the successful resolution of organizational tasks in turbulent environments is to build a culture with a core competence that values and excels at adaptation. In manufacturing terms, such a distinctive competency would be referred to as *flexibility*, and that description holds for service operations in general and public organizations specifically.[12] There is no flexibility in a system that requires rote adherence to written procedures. If crises by nature are varied and of random impact and importance, basic transactional leadership does not go far enough toward providing the necessary guidance concerning comprehensive plans of action for every possible contingency. Some famous public servants recognized this limitation of leadership in rapidly changing environments. U.S. general George Patton was fond of saying, "Never tell people how to do things, tell them what to do and they will surprise you with their ingenuity."[13] Adaptive cultures foster innovation and creative solutions, and Patton's armies were known to be highly adaptive, and dramatically successful.

An organizational culture that values adaptation, of necessity, makes use of a wider range of skills by more members. In order to accomplish the substantial tasks of information gathering and evaluation in complex environments, adaptive organizational cultures must seek information and support from diverse elements within their structure. Also, of necessity, organizational members are forced to share information, resources, and ideas. Job scope and subsequent responsibilities for outcomes are expanded. Organizational units, which previously acted as separate units (i.e., coacting groups), must now interact in order to accomplish the mission. And whereas the structure of the organization may appear on charts as functional and stable, the operation of the organizational elements may be perceived as more "teamlike" and dynamic. A structure that was developed to operate mechanistically can become organic for problem identification and resolution and revert to mechanistic processes in executions.[14] Such an ambidextrous approach allows for the "virtual" shift of people and resources. It is not necessary to physically restructure the organization with teams in mind if the de facto practice is for the members within the organization to operate as members of rapidly forming and adjourning teams.

This process is by no means as simple as it sounds. Real culture change is a slow and tedious process. Most organizational cultures are the result of critical incidents at founding and during the entrepreneurial stage of development. Leaders in public organizations do not often have the luxury of starting anew. The requirements of the new work of public organizations dictate that we have new workers, but in most cases, it is not necessary to search outside the organization for those people. Most experts agree that culture change can be managed in one of two ways:[15] (1) By using a symbolic approach, leaders attempt to influence cultural norms and values by shaping surface elements (e.g., symbols, stories, ceremonies) and continually managing meaning, and (2) by using organizational development interventions (e.g., process consultation, team development), leaders can help guide members through the stages of identifying and accepting new norms and values. Shaping team players requires careful selection, training, and rewards. For those organizational members who cannot adapt to the realities of the new organization, transfer, relocation, or perhaps termination (as a last resort) may be necessary. Most likely, organizational members can be taught to be team players. Training in problem-solving skills, communication, negotiation, conflict management, and so on can help turn individuals into team players. Team-building training is a slow process, but it is a necessary and ultimately worthwhile intervention if workers are to engage in the kind of interaction required of units to "do more with less." And finally, regardless of how egalitarian the concept of workplace teams may appear to be, unless the reward systems are structured to reinforce appropriate group and team behaviors (e.g., interaction and cooperation), the mission will never be adequately accomplished. Appropriate reward structures ensure the proper match between actions and outcomes.

Leaders who communicate new meanings to be shared (i.e., crisis becomes "challenge") forge a common vision that guides the interacting teams.[16] Such challenges will most likely arise in the external environment, but it is also possible for crises to be internally generated.[17] The link between leadership and crisis in the model shown as Figure 5.2 is meant to indicate that leaders can also generate or highlight crises. Research suggests that some executives create states of nonequilibrium as a means of achieving organizational self-renewal and creativity.[18] By being proactive in the selection of relevant or advantageous crises to address, the leader can shape the situation to his or her advantage. In doing so, the leader moves his or her organization from a reactive stance to a proactive stance. Leaders may even go so far as to change the contingencies of the environmental context, or to create their own environments.[19]

The new work of leaders in public organizations does not stop with creating the appropriate adaptive culture or resolving situational crises. There are new personal requirements imposed on the leader as a result of the shift in focus. Given the nature of the new environmental realities, the leader must rely less on concrete task and performance direction, and more on framing and guiding the work tasks so that they align with the organization's mission and focus. Such work entails exhibiting those characteristics and emulating the behaviors associated with charismatic or transformational leaders.[20] These leaders should be able to provide their followers with a compelling vision or sense of purpose, and should be able to communicate that vision clearly.[21] Vision formation and communication serve as guides to action (e.g., the "what" but not necessarily the "how," as Patton suggested).[22] Charismatic or transformational leaders can positively transform and empower their followers[23] and achieve many positive organizational changes.[24] By verbalizing a focused vision leaders contribute to the integration of activities. Osborne and Gaebler suggested in their book *Reinventing Government* that leaders in public organizations should stick to steering (purpose and problem definition) as opposed to rowing (developing solutions).[25] Instead of rules and procedures guiding action, the vision and goals espoused by the leadership of the organization serve as the coordination and control mechanisms. Table 5.1 provides a listing of useful guidelines for creating and communicating organizational vision.[26]

Charisma is not something endowed by divine forces, as was once believed.[27] Charisma is an attribute. It is a manifestation of the belief among followers that the leader possesses or exhibits charismatic qualities. And even though it seems that charisma, as an all-or-nothing quality, is overused in daily conversations about leaders and leadership, it is possible for formerly noncharismatic individuals to be trained to act more charismatically.[28] Charismatic leaders are not necessarily boastful or flamboyant. Sam Walton exercised a style of quiet leadership that was perceived to be very charismatic (and successful). For followers to attribute charisma to an individual, they must hold a particularly strong emotional reaction to, identification with, and belief in that person.[29]

Followers of charismatic leaders have been found to accept the leader without question, trust in the leader's beliefs, show willing obedience to the leader, identify with the leader, and try to emulate him or her.[30] The bond that develops between the leader and followers, if nurtured, can produce some pretty substantial changes. Individuals working under a charismatic

TABLE 5.1 Guidelines for Creating and Communicating Organizational Vision

Understand the design and use of forums. Forums allow organizational members the chance to discuss ideas and plans in an attempt to develop shared meanings. Many leaders underestimate the value of these informal discussion sessions.

Seize opportunities to provide interpretation and give direction in difficult and uncertain situations. This is your chance to change the interpretation of crises, threats, and problems into challenging tasks for the organization. It is at these times that visionary leadership is most in demand.

Reveal and name real needs and real conditions. Make sense out of difficult problems by framing issues in terms that organizational members can understand.

Help followers frame and reframe issues and strategies. Name and explain the "what" of the problems, but let the followers suggests the "how" part of solving the problems.

Offer compelling visions of the future. Give organizational members a scenario of how the problem will unfold and how it will eventually be solved.

Champion new and improved ideas. Gather ideas from many sources. Foster an environment that values innovation and experimentation.

Detail actions and expected consequences. Explain what the consequences of the difficulties are, and give the members a plan of action for solving those problems.

Adapted from Bryson, J. M., 1995. *Strategic Planning for Public and Nonprofit Organizations: A Guide to Strengthening and Sustaining Organizational Achievement,* pp. 221–224. San Francisco: Jossey-Bass.

leader have been found to have higher task performance, task adjustment, and adjustment to the leader and the group.[31] The attribution of charisma depends on the simultaneous interaction of the situational context (i.e., crisis), the characteristics of the followers (i.e., norms, values, culture), and the qualities exhibited by the leader. The charismatic bond may ultimately represent a manifestation of the need of followers during times of crisis for centralized authority.[32] In return for obedience and service, the followers expect that charismatic leaders will provide direction and focus. Such "framing" or guidance may serve as a stress reduction mechanism and could, perhaps, lead to less absenteeism and turnover. There may be great danger in such bonds in that some leaders may abuse the relationship by pursuing leader-driven instead of follower-driven goals,[33] and that is always a possibility. However, power that is controlling or coercive will eventually destroy the bonds between leader and follower. When charismatic leadership is directed toward the accomplishment of organizational goals and to the benefit of the organization, increases in productivity, performance, and satisfaction will be the result.[34] Remember, it is not the person alone who engenders the attribution of charisma, but the vision the person communicates (i.e., the path out of crisis) that is responsible for the charismatic bond between leader and followers.

IMPLICATIONS FOR PUBLIC ORGANIZATIONS

Public organizations have been characterized as diverse and fragmented.[35] Perhaps it is time to rethink our conception of the basic work of public organizations. Upheaval and change are becoming the standard operating procedure for many public organizations, yet these organizations continue to focus on the mechanics of rule interpretation and application instead of developing the distinctive competence of adaptation in their human resources. The problem is not change itself, but the lack of leadership for change.

New leaders in public organizations must first recognize the realities of their changing environments. Public administration is no longer a stable industry; nor is it a place for those who cannot innovate and inspire. Leadership in public organizations must be fundamentally customer oriented and purposefully entrepreneurial. When leaders view their subordinates as their immediate customers, they enact an environment of reciprocity. The subordinates, in turn, can then figure out how best to serve their external customers. Entrepreneurism can be stimulated by the creation of crisis. Identifying new missions and programs can help generate new ideas and insights concerning public service.

What is certain is that no one element alone can bring about the needed changes. The new leadership is a combination of some pretty old but effective ideas. It is about what all leadership is about—the interaction of environment, followers, and the leader; and crisis, culture, and charisma. Vision is the glue that binds the three elements. A clear vision can be translated into action, policy, and job-related behavioral guidelines.[36] Without clear vision, the stimulation or identification of crisis will only lead to further fragmentation and dilution of effort. Without effective communication, the vision remains nothing more than an unfulfilled idea. Motivation is nothing without direction, and even the best organizations can suffer failure unless the path to the communicated goals is made clear. And without crisis and a corresponding vision, there is little chance that charismatic qualities will be attributed to the leader. Without such an attribution, leaders can never hope to lead their organizations to perform beyond expectations, no matter how much they might wish to.

In the absence of increased budgets for equipment and resources, public organizations have but one resource left with which to accomplish their expanded and diverse new missions: people. If we are to continue to experience the same kind of productivity gains in service operations (like public government) that we have experienced in recent years in the manufacturing sector, we must increasingly rely on improvements in human productivity. Selection, training, and appropriate reward systems can help leaders build adaptive organizational cultures, which will not only succeed in crisis environments, but excel. In biological terms, such organizations will survive because they represent successful adaptations to their environment. Leadership is the key to the survival of the fittest public organizations. Unless leaders in public organizations engage in the new work of adaptive culture formation and training, the only practical outcome is extinction.

This discussion of the new work of leaders in public organizations has only scratched the surface and outlined the "what" to do and not the "how" to do it. As with any complex and formidable task, the first and primary step is for someone to decide that the work must be done. Harnessing the interactive elements of crisis, culture, and charisma presents new leaders in public organizations with a powerful strategic weapon for survival, but beyond that, these tools help in the broader, yet unchanging, mission of providing high-quality public service at the lowest cost possible. It appears to be time for some new leaders to take the first and requisite step.

ENDNOTES

1. Lipset, S. M., and Schneider, W. 1987. *The Confidence Gap: Business, Labor, and Government in the Public Mind.* Baltimore: Johns Hopkins University Press.

2. Bryson, J. M. 1995. *Strategic Planning for Public and Nonprofit Organizations: A Guide to Strengthening and Sustaining Organizational Achievement.* San Francisco: Jossey-Bass; Rainey, H. G. 1991. *Understanding and Managing Public Organizations.* San Francisco: Jossey-Bass.

3. Chase, G., and Reveal, E. C. 1983. *How to Manage in the Public Sector.* Reading, MA: Addison-Wesley.

4. Bryson, J. M. 1995. *Strategic Planning for Public and Nonprofit Organizations: A Guide to Strengthening and Sustaining Organizational Achievement.* San Francisco: Jossey-Bass.

5. Volcker Commission. 1989. *Leadership for America: Rebuilding the Public Service.* Lexington, MA: Heath.

6. Prahalad, C. K., and Bettis, R. 1988. "The dominant logic: A new link between diversity and performance," *Strategic Management Journal*, 7: 485–501.

7. Chase, G., and Reveal, E. C. 1983. *How to Manage in the Public Sector*. Reading, MA: Addison-Wesley; Rainey, H. C. 1991. *Understanding and Managing Public Organizations*. San Francisco: Jossey-Bass.

8. Madsen, D., and Snow, P. G. 1991. *The Charismatic Bond: Political Behavior in Time of Crisis*. Cambridge: Harvard University Press.

9. Bryson, J. M. 1995. *Strategic Planning for Public and Nonprofit Organizations: A Guide to Strengthening and Sustaining Organizational Achievement*. San Francisco: Jossey-Bass.

10. Burns, J. M. 1978. *Leadership*. New York: Harper & Row; Bass, B. M. 1985. *Leadership and Performance Beyond Expectations*. New York: Free Press; Bass, B. M. 1990. "From transactional to transformational leadership: Learning to share the vision," *Organizational Dynamics*, Winter: 19–31.

11. Rosen, R. 1985. *Anticipatory Systems*. New York: Pergamon Press.

12. Porter, M. E. 1990. "The competitive advantage of nations," *Harvard Business Review*, 90(2): 73–93.

13. Puryear, E. F. 1987. *19 Stars: A Study in Military Character and Leadership*. Novato, CA: Presidio Press.

14. Duncan, R. B. 1976. "The ambidextrous organization: Designing dual structures for innovation," in Ralph H. Killman, Louis R. Pondy, and Dennis Slevin (Eds.), *The Management of Organization*, 1: 167–188. New York: North Holland.

15. Wagner, J. A., and Hollenbeck, J. R., III. 1998. *Organizational Behavior: Securing Competitive Advantage*. Upper Saddle River, NJ: Prentice Hall.

16. Lipton, M. 1996. "Demystifying the development of an organizational vision," *Sloan Management Review*, Summer: 83–92.

17. Avolio, B. J., and Bass, B. M. 1988. "Transformational leadership, charisma and beyond," in J. G. Hunt, B. R. Baliga, H. P. Dachler, and C. A. Schreisheim (Eds.), *Emerging Leadership Vistas*. Lexington, MA: Lexington Press; Boal, K. B., and Bryson, J. M. 1988. "Charismatic leadership: A phenomenological and structural approach," in J. G. Hunt, B. R. Baliga, H. P. Dachler, and C. A. Schreisheim (Eds.), *Emerging Leadership Vistas*. Lexington, MA: Lexington Press; Kets de Vries, M. F. R. 1989. *Prisoners of Leadership*. New York: Wiley.

18. Hughes, G. D. 1990. "Managing high-tech product cycles," *Academy of Management Executive*, 4(2): 44–55.

19. Weick, K. E. 1979. *The Social Psychology of Organizing*. Reading, MA: Addison-Wesley.

20. Avolio, B. J., and Bass, B. M. 1988. "Transformational leadership, charisma and beyond," in J. G. Hunt, B. R. Baliga, H. P. Dachler, and C. A. Schreisheim (Eds.), *Emerging Leadership Vistas*. Lexington, MA: Lexington Press; Boal, K. B., and Bryson, J. M. 1988. "Charismatic leadership: A phenomenological and structural approach," in J. G. Hunt, B. R. Baliga, H. P. Dachler, and C. A. Schreisheim (Eds.), *Emerging Leadership Vistas*. Lexington, MA: Lexington Press.

21. Bennis, W. 1984. "The four competencies of leadership," *Training and Development Journal*, 15–19.

22. Lipton, M. 1996. "Demystifying the development of an organizational vision," *Sloan Management Review*, Summer: 83–92.

23. House, R. J., Spangler, W. D., and Wyocke, J. 1991. "Personality and charisma in the U.S. presidency: A psychological theory of leadership effectiveness," *Administrative Science Quarterly*, 36: 364–396; Block, R. 1993. *Stewardship: Choosing Service over Self-Interest.* San Francisco: Berrett-Koehler.

24. House, R. J., Spangler, W. D., and Wyocke, J. 1991. "Personality and charisma in the U.S. presidency: A psychological theory of leadership effectiveness," *Administrative Science Quarterly*, 36: 364–396.

25. Osborne, D., and Gaebler, T. 1992. *Reinventing Government.* Reading, MA: Addison-Wesley.

26. Bryson, J. M. 1995. *Strategic Planning for Public and Nonprofit Organizations: A Guide to Strengthening and Sustaining Organizational Achievement*, pp. 222, 223. San Francisco: Jossey-Bass.

27. Weber, M. 1947. *The Theory of Social and Economic Organizations.* (A. M. Henderson and T. Parsons, trans.). New York: Free Press.

28. Howell, J. M., and Frost, P. J. 1989. "A laboratory study of charismatic leadership," *Organizational Behavior and Human Decision Processes*, 43(2): 243–269.

29. Bass, B. M. 1985. *Leadership and Performance Beyond Expectations.* New York: Free Press; Conger, J. A., and Kanungo, R. N. 1987. "Towards a behavioral theory of charismatic leadership in organizational settings," *Academy of Management Review*, 12(4): 637–647.

30. House, R. J., and Baetz, M. L. 1979. "Leadership: Some empirical generalizations and new research directions," in B. M. Staw (Ed.), *Research in Organizational Behavior.* Greenwich, CT: JAI.

31. Howell, J. M., and Frost, P. J. 1989. "A laboratory study of charismatic leadership," *Organizational Behavior and Human Decision Processes*, 43(2): 243–269.

32. Madsen, D., and Snow, P. G. 1991. *The Charismatic Bond: Political Behavior in Time of Crisis.* Cambridge: Harvard University Press.

33. Howell, J. M. 1988. "The two faces of charisma: Socialized and personalized leadership in organizations," in J. A. Conger and R. N. Kanungo (Eds.), *Charismatic Leadership: The Elusive Factor in Organizational Effectiveness.* San Francisco: Jossey-Bass.

34. Howell, J. M., and Frost, P. J. 1989. "A laboratory study of charismatic leadership," *Organizational Behavior and Human Decision Processes*, 43(2): 243–269; House, R. J., and Baetz, M. L. 1979. "Leadership: Some empirical generalizations and new research directions," in B. M. Staw (Ed.), *Research in Organizational Behavior.* Greenwich, CT: JAI.

35. Rainey, H. G. 1991. *Understanding and Managing Public Organizations.* San Francisco: Jossey-Bass.

36. Lipton, M. 1996. "Demystifying the development of an organizational vision," *Sloan Management Review*, Summer: 83–92.

LEADERSHIP LEGACIES

Histroy provides lessons that we often ignore or discount. Many books and papers have been written about political, military, religious, and business leaders, as well as other individuals, who made a significant impact on an organization or society. We are fortunate to have many archives available to allow us to know and understand our leadership legacy. We should recognize that these are real stories about real people who chose to accept the challenge of leadership in times of crisis, turbulent change, and great stress and were successful even though they possessed normal human shortcomings.

The earliest efforts to describe leaders and develop a general theory of leadership were related to the bibliographic study of past leaders. The "Great Man" theory emerged after scholars reviewed the many histories and attempted to put together a composite set of personal and physical characteristics believed common to the most successful and revered leaders of the past.

Increased attention to military, religious, and business leadership resulted in the first attempts to apply scientific methods to understand the causes and effects of leadership styles, behaviors, and effectiveness. As scholars began to create research agendas that explored leadership and leadership effectiveness, the methods changed and more sophisticated techniques were developed. In the late 1900s, academic researchers in a variety of disciplines addressed the study of leadership with gusto.

Why did leadership emerge as a popular topic of study? One reason may be that our prosperity and access to education gave individuals many choices in their lives. At the same time the rate of information exchange increased at exponential rates. People and organizations were overwhelmed and looked to others to explain and help them deal with the chaos in their lives. The focus was shifted to leaders. Demonstrated leadership effectiveness became a criterion for recognition and a requisite for students competing for honors, workers competing for promotion, and candidates competing for key positions in public- and private-sector organizations.

Interestingly, there are combinations of history and recently developed theory that provide fascinating perspectives on leadership effectiveness. We have a fondness for history but often ignore its lessons, forgetting that history can be the lens through which we can best understand the phenomenon of leadership.

LEADERSHIP PERSPECTIVES

In "The Greatness That Cannot Be Taught" (Chapter 6), David Halberstam questions whether leadership can be taught or transferred. He suggests that leadership development is a natural process that results from people knowing their fields of endeavor, those around them, and themselves. He argues that emerging leaders are extremely well prepared and push themselves hard. He observes that leaders often don't become serious until mid-career, because their own talent surprises them.

Mark J. Kroll, Leslie A. Toombs, and Peter Wright examine hubris as a common reason for leadership failure in "Napoleon's Tragic March Home from Moscow: Lessons in Hubris" (Chapter 7). Hubris is defined as the insolence or arrogance resulting from excessive pride or passion. A classic example was Napoleon's Russian campaign in 1812, in which he lost his army and, eventually, his empire. The authors compare the hubris of Napoleon with that reflected in the actions of contemporary business executives who often rush to make acquisitions at any price and stretch legal and ethical limits of accepted business conduct. They suggest that introspection, listening to those who oppose, listening to alter egos, and modeling behavior to best practices are issues relevant to leaders today. Although hubris is not characteristic of all organizations, its study provides yet another classic lesson.

Leadership in the broad context is described by Albert R. Hunt in "The Greatest Man Churchill and Truman Ever Met" (Chapter 8). Insights into General George C. Marshall highlight the importance of self-knowledge, self-confidence, and compelling modesty. Vision and integrity characterized General Marshall. At the same time, Hunt reflects on the miscalculations of this great person to suggest that the most effective leaders have, at one time or another, failed, but they have learned from their failures. Marshall was a politician, but he did not promote himself. Winner of the Nobel Peace Prize, Marshall served in key military and civilian roles and was one of few people who were successful leaders in very different environments.

We conclude this part with John W. Gardner's essay from 1965, "The Antileadership Vaccine" (Chapter 9), in which he discusses the dispersion of power and our failure to cope with the "big question." This is a meaningful contemporary review even though four decades have passed since Gardner wrote it. In his opinion, the antileadership vaccine is administered by our educational systems and by the structure of our society, causing people to lose the confidence they need to assume leadership roles. Gardner notes that in training people for leadership, we have neglected the broader moral view of shared values, thus inhibiting vision, creativity, and risk taking. We appear to be approaching a point, he argues, at which everyone will value the technical expert who advises the leader or the intellectual who stands off and criticizes the leader, but no one will be concerned with the development of leadership itself.

6

~

The Greatness That
Cannot Be Taught

David Halberstam

I am highly wary of the self-conscious American cult of leadership. It's not unlike the American cult of dieting. Almost everyone in this county, I expect, would like to be thinner. And even more than thinner, I suspect that everyone would like to be a leader—every man and woman his or her own Jack Welch.

We are the great learn-it-yourself, do-it-yourself society. Everything in life can be gleaned during a short course, or from reading a book. And who teaches at these traveling leadership seminars and writes these leadership books? Successful football and basketball coaches, prominent American military officers, and what might be called the "super CEO." That's a CEO who is so successful and so charismatic that he belongs not merely to the business world but to the world of popular culture, like Welch, or Lee Iacocca before him. (Somewhere out there on the sidelines, there's also that great wannabe-but-never-was Donald Trump, selling himself in good times and bad as the exemplar of the great American dream—although he's really more like Brazil. He owes the banks so much they dare not let him fail. Say this for Trump: He's always out there hustling. Maybe someday there will be at least one grown-up in the country who takes him seriously.)

The problem with our become-a-leader-in-thirty-days craze is that what worked for Welch and Iacocca is not readily transferable, nor are the

Reprinted with permission from *Fast Company Magazine* 86 (September 2004), pp. 62–64. Copyright 2004 Gruner & Jahr, USA.

secrets of their success easily passed on in a book. I knew Iacocca in his Chrysler days, and he was not only very good at what he did but also equally good—indeed brilliant—at personalizing his success. He wove a national success story, America's comeback against the Japanese, into his own personal autobiography. America's resurgence was Lee, and Lee was America. But I doubt that anyone who was not Lee could learn to be Lee by reading his book. To be Lee, you would need his talent, his superb skills at marketing, his almost unmatchable ego, and his rage to succeed as an Italian-American in the face of the prejudice he encountered as a young man (a rage that, by the way, also helps explain the success of another great figure of the cult of leadership, Vince Lombardi). I think you had to be Lee in order to be like Lee; I don't think you could be Lee through study. And I doubt that Lee's brand of leadership is readily transported to other business situations.

That's also true for the generals we lionize as leaders. The lessons that men such as Norman Schwarzkopf and Colin Powell drew upon came from careers spent studying other men who had gone before them in their own profession. (The tough, hands-on Schwarzkopf is the lineal descendant of Grant and Patton. If he were a manufacturer, he'd be right there on the factory floor. The cool, controlled Powell, so subtle in estimating others and so careful to make sure that everyone is on the same page, is the direct heir of Eisenhower.) When it was their moment in the crucible, they tested those lessons on location, in very practical ways.

I suspect that little of what they learned has much validity in the broader, less hierarchical culture, in which you cannot give orders and assume that they will be obeyed. Even more so today: We have always been the least obedient of societies, and we are a good deal less obedient now than we were half a century ago. People are better educated, and the truly talented ones, the ones you want to motivate, have many more options of their own. They're not likely to sit around and take orders from a harsh drill-sergeant-like superior. In business, this means that talented young executives, if they are treated like foot soldiers, will simply walk out the door.

I have similar doubts about coaches making the leadership tour—especially football coaches. It's our most hierarchical sport, and football players, more than most athletes and most Americans, are accustomed to doing what coaches tell them. A good football coach is not necessarily a born leader. He's simply a good football coach. In professional football today, that's less about leadership than about estimating talent, handling the salary cap, and being lucky because your players sustain a minimal number of injuries. In college football, it's more often than not about recruiting and having an amenable admissions director working with you.

So if leadership can't be taught or transferred, how do you foster it? Where do you find leaders, and how do you create them? The truth is that in most fields, it's a natural process. Leaders are men and women who have chosen the right profession. They're good at it, and because they're good at it, they like it, and because they like it, they're even better at it. They're so good at it that they'd rather work than play. They're naturals, and excelling comes naturally as well. They've understood their field from the start, and they've studied it without even knowing they've studied it. They could look around from the day they joined an organization and understand the talents of those who went before them, understand the people around them, and know when and just how hard to push them.

What they have is precious—nothing less than a gift. They may realize when they're relatively young that they have a genuine talent and that they can go quite far, much farther than they originally thought. But often, they don't become serious until mid-career, because their own talent surprises them—they were not that brilliant when they were in college or just starting out. Academic excellence, after all, rarely translates into professional success, and the special intelligence that makes leaders thrive in their field is not necessarily an intelligence that transfers well to other fields. They are extremely well prepared, and they push themselves hard. Most crucial to leadership, they give off a unique aura, the sum of their confidence, their tone of voice, their feeling for command. They are not people you want to fail.

So with the bar set so high, who is a great leader? For a remarkable example of leadership in a terrible time, I would cite one of my great personal heroes, General Matthew Bunker Ridgway, during the Korean War. Ridgway took over a bedraggled, disheartened American fighting force that had just been hammered by the Chinese up near the Yalu River in one of America's worst military defeats. In the brief period of several months, he turned it into what it was supposed to be: a proud combat-ready force, more than able to hold its own in a difficult, bitter war.

Let me set the scene. In the fall of 1950, General Douglas MacArthur had just executed his brilliant Inchon landing behind North Korean lines. Trapped, the North Korean army hastily retreated north. Thanks to Inchon, MacArthur, a general who always put himself above the normal chain of command, was at the pinnacle of his success. No one dared question him as his armies started pursuing the enemy across the 38th parallel. But President Truman and the Joint Chiefs of Staff were properly nervous as MacArthur went farther north, because just across the Korean-Chinese border were hundreds of thousands of Chinese troops. The one thing Truman and the Joint Chiefs feared was a larger, wider war with the Chinese. In mid-October Truman flew to Wake Island and met with MacArthur. Speaking as a general and a self-appointed expert on the mind of the Oriental, MacArthur assured Truman the Chinese would not enter the war, but that if they did, the result would be the greatest slaughter in history.

And so MacArthur, exceeding his orders, sent his forces farther north, pushing them to race to the Chinese border so that they could be home by Christmas. In late November, his troops—most wearing summer-weight uniforms in Arctic temperatures, fighting in terrible terrain with their lines of communication vastly overextended—were hit by surprise by hundreds of thousands of Chinese. The American units, terribly vulnerable to this assault, largely fell apart (though the U.S. Marines' fighting withdrawal from the Chosin Reservoir is one of our most valorous moments).

A month later, in late December, with MacArthur alternating between talk of using the atom bomb and getting off the Korean peninsula completely, Ridgway took command of the Eighth Army in Korea. He was nothing less than a miracle worker. Today he would be called the real deal. He was already known as a great soldier, having led the airborne jump behind German lines on D-Day. A friend of mine in the CIA briefed him during the Korean War and later told me that he had never dealt with anyone as demanding, as probing, and as relentless as Ridgway. He was highly intelligent and ferociously focused. He needed to know everything, especially about the enemy. He was furious with commanders who did not know their men and who did not know exactly where the enemy was. He pushed his troops hard, but he was always out there at the front, sharing as much as possible in their hardships. He wanted his troops warmly clothed, well fed, and well led by tough field officers whom he did not fear to relieve if he felt they weren't getting the job done. There would be no more retreating, he told his command upon his arrival. They would turn around and start moving north again— hence his nickname, "Wrongway Ridgway."

Ridgway was courageous, but he is also instructive to us as a reflection of a new kind of military leader. In retrospect, MacArthur, the man he would soon replace as allied commander in the Far East, seems like a leader from another century: He was always busily engaged in cultivating his own personal mystique as the great man, the Great MacArthur who was head and shoulders above all other generals. The idea was that because he was such a great general, those he led were also great and would now fight well because he was leading them.

Ridgway was very different, a leader for the new, modern era. His leadership was of a more egalitarian kind, premised on letting the men fighting under him find something within themselves that made them tough and combat-ready. The point of his leadership was not that they would think that he was a great general—although in time they did—but that they would fight well because they were now more confident about who they were and what their mission was, and confident, too, that they were tough and well prepared. And in a stunningly short time, he turned the Eighth Army around and made it a remarkable fighting force, one that could stalemate the vastly superior number of Chinese.

Don't just take my word for it. Listen to the normally taciturn General Omar Bradley, then chairman of the Joint Chiefs, talk of that moment and of the role played by Ridgway: "It is not often in wartime that a single battlefield commander can make a decisive difference, but in Korea, Ridgway would prove to be the exception. His brilliant, driving, uncompromising leadership would turn the battle like no other general's in our military history."

That was leadership at its best: a truly great man rising to the heights during an unforeseen, desperate occasion, lifted by his talents and his instincts, and imposing the force of his will on so many disheartened others. It was as if he had prepared for this moment during his entire career—and maybe he had. You won't find the secrets of it in any of his books. He did what he did because to do anything else would have been less than who he was.

7

~

Napoleon's Tragic March Home from Moscow: Lessons in Hubris

Mark J. Kroll
Leslie A. Toombs
Peter Wright

Napoleon, supreme egoist that he was, ignored the significance of the omens until he and his host were completely and irrevocably committed to an undertaking that was doomed. Never did the gods punish hubris more severely.

M. de Fezensac[1]

In June 1812, Napoleon Bonaparte was ruler of the Empire of France, king of Italy, and master of the European continent. At the head of the Grand Army, numbering over 500,000 men, the largest force ever assembled at that point in history, he set out to conquer the one nation in Europe he had not yet subjugated—Imperial Russia. In December of the same year, less than 20,000 of those men would make it home alive, and as a practical matter, all that Emperor Napoleon had accomplished in his meteoric career would soon be lost. The tragedy of the Russian campaign, the loss of life, and the horrible suffering of those on the march back from Moscow have been a source of fascination for historians ever since. Explanations for the disaster include poor planning, unusually bad weather, insightful leadership

Reprinted with permission from *Academy of Management Executive* 14: 1 (February 2000), pp. 117–127. Copyright 2000 Academy of Management.

on the opposing side, and plain bad luck. But as indicated by our epigraph, almost all accounts of the campaign include a recognition of the role played by hubris.[2]

Hubris has been defined as exaggerated pride, self-confidence, or arrogance, frequently resulting in retribution.[3] Hubris may be blamed for the resounding failure of Napoleon's campaign because Napoleon possessed all its symptoms: unbounded confidence given his past successes and the accompanying narcissism, the adulation that fed that narcissism, and his callous indifference to the rules that governed nineteenth-century geopolitics. As a result, Napoleon was able to convince himself that, despite all of the obvious obstacles, he could, through force of will, succeed in bringing Russia, and especially Emperor Alexander I, the sole power on the continent that refused to pay him homage, to their knees. His campaign was much less about the need to thwart the hostile intentions of a rival power, and more about the need to satisfy a hubris-infected personality with an arrogant confidence about what great feats could be accomplished.

One frequently cited explanation for hubris is that leaders often hunger for reassurance and applause from others. This hunger may first arise when a child's narcissistic displays are fondly received by parents.[4] As a result leaders grow and become a part of groups or organizations; however, they may seek the same adulation from organization members in response to their displays of skill.

Those who excel in select skills may receive positive feedback from others as they produce beneficial results. Napoleon clearly excelled in the skills of warfare, as he planned and implemented winning campaigns. Before the Russian attack, Napoleon had amassed a record of thirty-five wins versus only three losses. The losses were either early in his career, and then forgotten, or were only very temporary setbacks from which he quickly recovered. Through these warfare experiences, he developed a distinctive approach to command, along with considerable confidence in that approach. By the time of the Russian campaign, however, this confidence had turned into arrogance and a sense of invincibility. Worse, given his record, he appears to have believed that the unique problems of a war with Russia were minor details that the force of will could surmount.

In the contemporary corporate arena, actions such as takeovers, corporate expansion programs, and blatant disregard of the rules of the game may reflect the presence of hubris. These actions sometimes suggest that the firm's management believes that the world, and the major forces in it, including financial markets, government regulators, and competitors, are wrong, and that they are right and are not governed by the same forces. Like Napoleon's Grand Army, corporate hubris is often punished severely. We will take a look at three circumstances in which hubris may set businesses and their leaders down a perilous path: corporate acquisitions, unbridled growth for its own sake, and disregard for the rules. Parallels are drawn with Napoleon's circumstances.

CORPORATE ACQUISITIONS

Well before the invasion of Russia, Napoleon's top lieutenants argued that the chances of failure and the cost in lives and matériel would be high. Napoleon rejected their warnings, pointing out that his plans called for a quick, decisive, and therefore low-cost campaign. He had conducted such campaigns before and saw no difference this time.[5] Richard Roll has suggested that all too frequently takeover attempts result from an executive's belief that he or she can greatly improve the target firm's efficiency. The executive rejects feedback from others and, in particular, the wisdom of the financial markets,[6] even though it is generally recognized that the securities markets provide accurate feedback by doing a fairly effective job of valuing publicly traded firms.[7] The premiums executives sometimes pay over target firms' prevailing market prices often reflect a Napoleonic logic: "I will be able to overcome all the obstacles and make the acquired business far more successful than its incumbent management; I can turn a profit on the deal in spite of the high price I am paying."

However, compelling research evidence shows that corporate acquisitions driven by managerial hubris are often financially harmful for the shareholders of acquiring firms.[8] It also appears that as the level of managerial hubris rises, so does the likelihood that a firm will grossly overpay for an acquisition.[9] Compounding the problem of overpayment is the possibility that managerial hubris will undermine the process of integrating the acquired and acquiring firms. There is the very real threat that the acquiring firm's management, imbued with a sense of conquest, will treat the acquired firm's management and employees as conquered supplicants. This is especially likely if the acquiring firm is perceived as having a better track record than the acquired firm.[10] The inevitable results are a failure to achieve potential synergies and a loss of talent from the acquired firm. Both outcomes will exacerbate the initial overpayment problem.

An example of potential corporate hubris in an acquisition is the buyout of WordPerfect by Novell in March 1994. Novell's CEO, Raymond Noorda, offered $1.4 billion for WordPerfect, in what industry observers suggested was an attempt to build a software empire comparable to Microsoft's. Following the acquisition, Novell reportedly ran roughshod over WordPerfect's management and culture, creating a hemorrhage of managerial and technical talent and a significant deterioration in the performance of WordPerfect. In early 1996, Novell was forced to sell WordPerfect for about $124 million, or less than 10 percent of what it had paid for the firm in 1994.[11]

UNBRIDLED GROWTH FOR ITS OWN SAKE

Hubris can also manifest itself in a drive to dominate others and engage in empire building for its own sake. Napoleon's determination to invade Russia was driven not only by a desire to take over that country, but also by a burning ambition to dominate Czar Alexander. The czar was the only European monarch Napoleon had not subjugated, and by doing so Napoleon would have become the sole master of Europe. The same need for domination and empire building may surface in the corporate world. It is generally recognized that individual executives infected with hubris have narcissistic requirements that demand they control fiefdoms of such large scale as to justify their own importance.[12] An executive infected with hubris is likely to see growth as a means of building a bureaucracy of sufficient size to reflect his or her prominence. For instance, the rise and fall of the Saatchi & Saatchi advertising empire in the 1990s reflected the ambition of a pair of brothers who no longer concerned themselves with building a profitable advertising business.[13] Instead, they aspired to dominance by building an advertising empire that was the very biggest, only to be forced out of the business they had built. Similarly, Barclay's Bank under CEO Sir John Quinton went on a quest to become Britain's largest bank in the early 1990s. This attempt also failed and Sir John was forced to abdicate.[14]

BLATANT DISREGARD OF THE RULES

Napoleon rose to power during the French Revolution, having been an officer in the army of the First Republic.[15] After establishing a winning record at the head of the Grand Army, he decided that he merited the

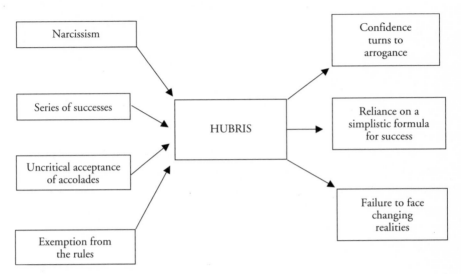

FIGURE 7.1   Sources and Implications of Hubris

title of first council or dictator and later named himself emperor. These blatant power grabs were undertaken in spite of his earlier pledges of fidelity to the republic and its democratic ideals. He evidently concluded that obligations to the French people and living up to oaths were for others to fulfill.[16]

Managers afflicted with hubris can also create a climate in which they and the organizations they govern do not play by the same rules as everyone else.[17] For example, observers have remarked on the indifference of the managers of Archer Daniels Midland Company to the laws they broke and how the longtime CEO, Dwayne O. Andreas, allowed an anything-goes culture to develop.[18] Such hubris-prone personalities are likely to perceive themselves as having made great sacrifices and contributions that entitle them to special dispensation.[19]

SOURCES OF HUBRIS

As illustrated in Figure 7.1, hubris has four sources: a personality prone to narcissism; a string of successes that feed the narcissism; blindly believing the accolades of others, particularly the media; and a history of getting away with breaking the rules. All these conditions can lead executives to believe that they are above the rules.[20]

Narcissism

Hubris derives from an overbearing sense of grandiosity, need for admiration, and self-absorption—in a word, narcissism. Narcissism is commonly found in many successful people, and it often compels them to seek leadership positions, with their accompanying power, status, and self-affirmation.[21] However, narcissism can drive executives to use their leadership roles to create a reality that further reinforces their narcissism.[22] Even very charismatic leaders may use their leadership talents to gain position and status in order to satisfy their narcissism at the expense of others.[23] In *War and Peace*, Tolstoy comments on Napoleon's narcissism: "He alone—with his ideal of glory and grandeur developed in Italy and Egypt, his insane self-adulation, could justify what had to be done."[24]

A number of business analysts have attributed Quaker Oats's disastrous acquisition of Snapple Beverages in part to the hubris of Quaker's management. Quaker's then CEO, William Smithburg, had made some very successful moves earlier in his tenure, often proving the pundits wrong. The company's Gatorade purchase won Smithburg praise in the business press. Observers believe he saw in Snapple an opportunity to surpass past triumphs and establish Quaker as a force to be reckoned with in the beverage industry. In spite of the consensus view of Wall Street analysts that Quaker was paying at least double what Snapple was worth, Quaker paid $1.7 billion for the firm. Even worse, perhaps owing to their extreme confidence in their ability to turn things around, Quaker's management went ahead with the purchase in spite of strong indications that Snapple was in the process of imploding. On the day the deal was announced, Quaker's stock dropped $7.38, or over 10 percent.[25]

It is possible that the need to create a reality that fits an executive's narcissistic vision, even though it materially departs from actual facts, may often lead to organizational underperformance. Narcissism may be reinforced by subordinates who, having little sense of control over the world around them, look to and idolize a leader they believe can deal with the helplessness they feel.[26] The leader's apparent confidence and pride fulfill the needs of followers for someone to bring order and stability to their lives.[27] They in turn feed the leader's narcissism and thus transform his or her self-confidence into arrogance.[28] Napoleon arrived on the French political stage in the midst of the confusion of postrevolutionary France. The population, exhausted by ten years of violence and uncertainty, undoubtedly saw in Bonaparte the firm hand that could at last take the helm. Napoleon fed on that need. Having taken great pains to rid themselves of a royal monarchy in 1789, many French people embraced Napoleon as another type of monarch, consul for life, further contributing to his narcissism and hubris.

Series of Successes

Narcissism and hubris feed on further successes. As an executive accumulates a record of accomplishment, his or her susceptibility to hubris tends to grow.[29] Indeed, a consistent theme that runs through the various accounts of Napoleon's career is the inclination for his narcissism and hubris to grow with each successful campaign.[30] Following his successes in Italy, for instance, he remarked to one of his officers:

> They haven't seen anything yet, and the future holds successes for us far beyond what we have so far accomplished. Fortune is a woman, and the more she does for me, the more I will demand from her. In our day no one has conceived anything great; it is for me to give an example.[31]

In the context of contemporary business, the relationship between hubris and prior success and subsequent egoism makes particular sense when one recognizes that the executives of most organizations take disproportionate credit for high firm performance.[32] The valuable stock options and the lofty salaries American executives receive (mean executive total compensation in 1998 for the top eight hundred chief executives in the United States was $6.5 million) tend to reinforce the credit executives take for corporate performance.[33] Napoleon similarly took full credit for all the victories of the Grand Army. When Napoleon set off for Moscow at the head of an army of half a million soldiers, he had compiled an extraordinary win-loss record. In one sixteen-month period, beginning in November 1805, he had won the battles of Ulm, Austerlitz, Auerstadt, Eylau, and Freidland against the Austrians, Russians, and Prussians, so he was the toast of Paris. This inclination on the part of most leaders to attribute successes primarily to their own actions[34] may be a natural one. Leaders may visualize how their own behavior brought about success and they may see a clear and linear connection between the two. If they had not initiated certain actions, accordingly, the desirable outcomes attained would probably not have occurred.

Uncritical Acceptance of Accolades

The third source of hubris is a natural outgrowth of the first two: Leaders come to believe the exaggerated accolades they receive from others. Praise from others, particularly the press, is likely to intensify hubris because it confirms and legitimizes an executive's narcissism and reinforces the executive's own feelings of grandiosity. As his or her fame spreads, especially in the media, the executive's hubris is in effect ratified.[35] Napoleon was widely heralded as a military genius of the first order. If he did not think of himself as the master of Europe early in his career, the newspapers of the day certainly helped him perpetuate this image. For instance, the *Journal de Paris* reported in 1807 that "he [Napoleon] was invincible, grateful to God, forceful, modest, clever, magnanimous . . . and he combined the qualities of all the great men of history."[36]

Contemporary leaders may become more susceptible to hubris as the press increasingly focuses on them. The press, however, may not present a balanced view of leaders.[37] An excellent example of someone who recognized the extremes in which the press can portray individuals is James Carville, a key strategist in President Clinton's 1992 campaign. Shortly after the 1992 election, Carville was heralded as a political strategy genius. He acknowledged the accolades but also pointed out that he had managed failing campaigns and had received a heavy dose of criticism in the press. He said he knew he was not as good as the press made him out to be following Clinton's election, just as he knew he was not as bad as the press had portrayed him in his defeats.[38]

Exemption from the Rules

Finally, those possessed by hubris tend to be part of a group that Freud referred to as "the exceptions" to the rules, people with a history of breaking the rules, inflicting sacrifice on others, and getting away with it.[39] Narcissistic personalities are predisposed to break the rules because they tend to possess a sense of independence from the norms that govern others. This sense of independence from norms may be accompanied not only by a willingness to exploit others, but also by a lack of empathy for them.[40]

Napoleon's behavior dramatically illustrates these inclinations. He consistently broke all of the eighteenth-century rules limiting the scope of destructiveness of warfare. He encouraged his troops to loot the countries through which they passed rather than rely on provisions from France. During the 1796 Italian campaign, he invaded the neutral Duchy of Parma in order to escape a trap laid by the Austrians. Having overrun the duchy for convenience, he also took hostage the governor of the capital city of Piacenze to make it easier to loot the city.[41] Following the Russian campaign, with loss of life in the hundreds of thousands, he issued his famous Twenty-ninth Bulletin, blaming the massive losses on the weather, but adding, "His Majesty's health has never been better."[42] On returning to Paris, Napoleon ordered lavish receptions and balls. An officer who attended one gala later commented, "I felt I was dancing on tombs."[43]

Breaking the rules has its counterpart in contemporary business. For instance, in August 1991, Salomon Brothers, a major bond-trading house, admitted to a host of U.S. Treasury Department rule violations. These revelations caused the Treasury Department to suspend the firm's trading privileges and forced the resignation of the top three officers. From the accounts of both insiders and outsiders familiar with the firm, the violations were a direct result of what acting Salomon chairman Warren Buffett referred to as the firm's "macho and cavalier culture." Salomon's bond traders regularly flouted Treasury Department regulations designed specifically to rein in Salomon's excesses. Salomon's traders simply did not agree with the rules. This cultural deficiency appears to have been tolerated by Salomon's former CEO, John Gutfreund, who once told *The Economist* he was out for "the money, the power and the glory."[44]

IMPLICATIONS OF HUBRIS

When senior managers succumb to hubris, they are likely to engage in behavior that reflects that hubris: confidence to the point of arrogance, relying on simplistic formulas for success, and failing to face changing realities.[45] All of these can be very costly to the firm in various ways.

Confidence Turns to Arrogance

Individuals possessed with hubris have an overbearing confidence in their abilities to make events conform to their will in spite of contrary external evidence. They believe that whatever external problems might arise will be easily and willfully overcome.[46] For example, Napoleon was advised by several of his senior officers that an attack on Russia was foolhardy. In fact, Napoleon's close friend and one-time ambassador to the Russian court, General Armand Louis de Caulaincourt, recounted to Napoleon Czar Alexander's explanation of how Russia would defeat him:

It will not be a one-day war. Your [emperor] will be obliged to return to Paris to manage his affairs [after a long absence], and every advantage will be with the Russians. Then the winter, the cruel climate, and most important of all, my determination and avowed intention to prolong the struggle, and not, like so many monarchs, have the weakness to sign a peace treaty in my own capital. All these will take their toll.[47]

To this prophetic report, Napoleon responded with complete indifference, dismissing Czar Alexander's observations with the comment, "One good battle will knock the bottoms out of my friend Alexander's fine resolutions. He is fickle and feeble."[48]

This pattern of behavior is also evident in modern corporate takeovers. As mentioned earlier, the acquisition of Snapple by Quaker Oats appears to have been largely the result of management's assumption that it possessed unique talents that could breathe new life into Snapple. This high level of confidence appears to have been so strong that even a rapidly deteriorating situation at Snapple and an exorbitant price tag could not dissuade the Quaker Oats managers. The net result was Quaker's later having to divest Snapple and write off a $1.4 billion loss.[49]

Relying on a Simplistic Formula for Success

Another ramification of hubris is the tendency for leaders to develop what they perceive as their own unique and ingenious formulas for success. Such formulas, having served well in the past, are reapplied in many situations. In effect, leaders may reduce their strategy formulation and implementation to predictable action plans.[50] Napoleon's Russian campaign clearly reflected a reliance on what had worked well in the past, to the point that former innovations became standard operating procedure. This predictability served the Russians well, as General Michael Barclay de Tolly and Major General Prince Golenishchev-Kutuzov both consistently refused to play by Napoleon's established rules of warfare.

In an attempt to repeat past successes, Napoleon had sought to quickly engage the Russians early in the campaign in order to divide and destroy their army with overwhelming, decisive force. Quick and decisive engagements had worked well for Napoleon in Austria, Italy, and Prussia. Knowing this, both Russian commanders, and especially Kutuzov, baited the enemy with rearguard attacks, followed by further retreats into Russia. These compelled Napoleon to follow the Russians, in the hope that perhaps at the next major city the sought-after engagement would occur. These pursuits progressively stretched his lines of supply and communication thinner.

Reliance on a simple formula has its counterpart in the world of business. A famous example is the strategy of General Motors in the 1970s. Company executives were committed to their big car, rear-wheel-drive formula for success despite the industry's changing around them. Well into the 1970s, and even after several oil shocks, GM's managers still clung to the belief that the land yacht products of the 1950s and 1960s would again prevail.[51] The commitment to this formula resulted in GM's market share dropping from 49 percent to 28 percent over two decades.[52]

Failure to Face Changing Realities

Another ramification of hubris is the tendency to create a simplified scanning process, selectively screening for external environmental cues that were previously relevant in implementing a time-tested formula for success. This screening process tends to exclude those environmental factors that have previously not been critical to implementing the formula for success. One of Napoleon's previous experiences had been that local populations often viewed him as a liberator. This reaction allowed him to provision his army and avoid attacks by partisans. Because Russia was a feudal society, he anticipated the same reaction from local peasants. Instead, he was subject to incessant attacks by roving bands of Cossack partisans.

Senior executives of General Motors similarly exercised an external scanning process so simple that they did not even consider it necessary to establish a consumer market research department until 1985.[53] In fact, GM's competitive analysis in the early 1970s consisted largely of assessing the threats that its own Pontiac and Buick divisions posed for each other. Rarely did the analysis scrutinize the threats posed by Ford and Chrysler, much less by the Japanese automakers.[54]

Given the obvious dangers hubris represents to a successful firm's future success, we will look at remedies for both the individual executive and the board of directors.

WHAT EXECUTIVES CAN DO TO GUARD AGAINST HUBRIS

A sincere self-examination of an executive's leadership behaviors may be the best place to start. Asking questions such as "Am I willing to take the counsel of others when those ideas are counter to my own views of circumstances?" and "What do I need to do to improve my abilities to help the organization move forward?" will be helpful in this self-examination process.

Reflect on One's Own Performance

Managers sometimes exhibit the natural human tendency to attribute successes to their own actions, while blaming failures on external forces.[55] Those managers who have the capacity to recognize their own culpability in poor firm performance, however, tend to be more successful in the long term.[56] Thus, to combat the tendency to blame externalities, managers need to confront their own failures. For instance, Daimler-Benz was an organization that by the 1980s had experienced enough success to infuse its managers with hubris. By the 1990s, according to industry observers, the firm had fallen victim to its managers' arrogance, as demonstrated by its deteriorating performance. Jurgen Schrempp had presided over the unbridled growth of Daimler's aerospace division before becoming the CEO. However, Schrempp was reflective enough to realize that the decline in Daimler-Benz's fortunes was due as much to internal problems as to the downturn in Europe's economy. Schrempp began reinventing Daimler-Benz, including taking such personally painful steps as owning up to his failure with the aerospace division and his allowing it to go into bankruptcy. The result was a 45 percent appreciation in Daimler's share price over a twelve-month period.[57]

Listen to Naysayers

Executives exhibiting hubris tend to fall into the trap of listening only to people whose opinions are compatible with their own. Indeed, such executives tend to build teams with members whose conception of the desirable closely resembles their own. Such behavior tends to promote "groupthink," which normally leads to inferior alternatives and decisionmaking.[58] Alternatively, such managers may surround themselves with sycophants who echo what they believe the leader likes to hear, even if they inherently consider the leader's choices flawed. In sixteenth-century Italy, Machiavelli observed, "Courts are always full of flatterers; men take such pleasure in their own concerns, and are so easily deceived, that this plague of flattery is hard to escape."[59]

To combat the limitations of groupthink and sycophants, senior executives need to make sure that their team is composed of members with diverse backgrounds as well as functional areas. Just as important, the members chosen must have the integrity and courage to argue for alternatives that may differ from those preferred by the senior executives. In fact, superior alternatives and strategizing are often the outcomes of groups whose members have dissimilar opinions and who are allowed to openly discuss their views without retribution.[60] Senior executives, however, not only must allow but also should encourage open discussions. Otherwise, even people of integrity and courage may be thwarted from fully contributing to discussions. Unfortunately, leaders often discourage open discourse. Napoleon's first wife, Josephine, for example, recorded in her memoirs, "In his presence, no one had the right to hazard the slightest [contrary] observation."[61]

Appoint an Alter Ego

Senior executives may also benefit from an alter ego who can tell them when they are wrong.[62] This is especially important in organizations where personnel are inclined to nominally go along with the leader. The person who plays the role of alter ego should also serve as a mediator and a sounding board. Preferably, such a person should be nonthreatening to the senior executive, having developed a relationship of mutual trust. This alter ego must be respected by the top leader and not criticized for expressing different opinions.

Not only Napoleon's confidant Caulaincourt but most of his lieutenants offered a host of reasons why Napoleon should not invade Russia. Napoleon invariably accused them of being timid, weak, and incapable of seeing what could be accomplished. However, following Napoleon's departure from Russia, Caulaincourt found him far more willing to listen to what he had to say about the Russian campaign. Caulaincourt was in fact amazed by how frankly he could talk to the emperor compared with the period before the campaign. Unfortunately, this willingness to listen came only after an estimated 570,000 casualties.[63]

Model Behavior That Is in the Organization's Best Interest

Senior managers serve as role models for others employed by the company. Consequently, they should display behavior that contributes to firm performance. Herb Kelleher, former CEO of Southwest Airlines, is a maverick who, by example, has created a culture in which employees can do things differently. In 1971, Southwest had three planes serving three Texas cities. Today the company has over 240 aircraft serving fifty cities. This growth is largely the result of Kelleher's leadership style, which values creativity and efficiency. As Kelleher puts it,

We've always [encouraged that] work be done differently. You know, we don't assign seats. Used to be we only had about four people on the whole plane, so the idea of assigned seats just made people laugh. Now the reason is you can turn airplanes quicker at the gate. And if you can turn an airplane quicker, you can have it fly more routes each day. That generates more revenue, so you can offer lower fares.[64]

WHAT CAN BOARD MEMBERS DO TO CONTROL HUBRIS?

Monitor Executives for Signs of Hubris

We are hearing increasing calls for boards of directors, and especially outside board members, to take on a greater monitoring role in confronting the potential hubris of senior executives.[65] The departure of Ronald Allen as CEO of Delta Airlines resulted when outside board members took such action. Allen had led Delta through a series of acquisitions and painful cost-cutting programs that made him look decisive but were costly to employees and customers. Allen had plans to buy Continental Airlines and to continue cost cutting. However, the board became disheartened by declining employee morale, which was detracting from customer service. The board also saw a need for Delta to revert to its strategy of disciplined internal growth rather than acquisitions. Allen was replaced by Leo Mullin, who promised that customers and employees would not take a back seat to the company's stockholders.[66]

Promote a Heterogeneous Corporate Culture

Boards should ensure that views that run counter to conventional wisdom are tolerated or encouraged, and they should promote the use of a more decentralized organizational structure.[67] Board members may also recommend that corporate codes of ethics and values be developed. Such codes should emphasize that firm decisions will promote the benefits of all stakeholders.

Develop a Strong Organizational Knowledge Base

As the world's economy continues to prove both turbulent and extremely competitive, the information needs of firms will continue to change rapidly. Prevailing systems have done well in gathering information within organizations.[68] But if internal reports are positive, managers may be prone to staying with simplistic formulas for success even if external conditions are changing, threatening the viability of the firm.

A CALL TO ACTION

In ancient Greece, hubris was considered a crime under Athenian law, and in Greek tragedy it was considered the greatest of sins, reflecting an arrogance growing out of a misplaced sense of one's own abilities rather than the generosity of the gods.[69] As we have seen, many historians have concluded that Napoleon fell victim to his own overinflated sense of what he could accomplish, losing an army and an empire.

Financial and managerial markets also exact their own form of retribution for corporate hubris. People afflicted with corporate hubris often find it necessary to build an organization that reflects their narcissistic requirements through such conquests as acquisitions, even though acquisitions have not uniformly proven to be the path to quick riches for shareholders. The pursuit of narcissistic gratification can also inspire growth and investment decisions that may lead to a larger, but not necessarily more profitable, organization. Finally, hubris can lead to arrogance that justifies breaking rules.

Hubris tends to appear most frequently in people already prone to narcissism. A string of successes, some good press, and subordinates willing to feed that narcissism can exacerbate hubris. As did Napoleon in a military context, corporate executives infected with hubris may come to believe they possess abilities and insights others do not have and may trivialize the wisdom and contributions of others. Predictably, such executives come to believe that their formula for success is infallible and that additional information is largely irrelevant. The results of this process are especially unfortunate in competitive arenas such as war or commerce, as behavior becomes predictable and thus susceptible to attack in ways that are not part of the executive's model of reality. Tables 7.1 and 7.2 compare examples of the sources and implications of hubris.

The most practical way for an individual to combat hubris is to be introspective enough to realize one will never have all the answers and that the counsel of others is vital. One must also realize that success in an organizational context results from a complex interplay of the organization's various resources with the environment. Although the leader may be a significant component in that success, it is dangerous to assume that the leader's role is the only factor. Executives should also work to ensure that they will have at least one confidante who is in a position to speak the truth.

TABLE 7.1   Examples of the Sources of Hubris

Sources	Napoleon	Executives
Narcissism	Napoleon's need for position and self-aggrandization to satisfy his narcissism.	Executives with hubris will seek out positions of power to satisfy their narcissism.
Recent successes	Napoleon's hubris grew as his record of battlefield victories lengthened.	A record of outstanding performance permits an executive to rationalize his or her hubris.
Exaggerated accolades of others	Napoleon's hubris fed on the adulation showered on him by the French people and press.	As executives receive praise from others and the media, their hubris is reinforced.
Exemption from the rules	Napoleon regularly broke the rules that governed 19th-century Europe, and his hubris grew as he got away with more and more.	A sense of entitlement accompanies hubris in executives as they break the rules and get away with it.

The most practical way to combat hubris in an organizational setting is to ensure that top executives are monitored by a vigilant board with a reasonable number of outside directors. In addition, organizations should work to establish cultural norms that encourage the membership to disagree without being disagreeable. Organizations should also encourage the kind of continuous environmental surveillance necessary to avoid assuming that the future will conform to the predictable patterns that allowed for past glories.

Hubris does not affect every organization, but it is important to monitor for hubris because it can lead to devastating consequences. Boards must learn to distinguish between the confidence of an executive who, in the face of opposition, pursues an entrepreneurial vision and the blind disregard of an executive suffering from hubris. Confidence and arrogance may be intertwined, as in the case of Napoleon, who was both a military genius and a slave to his own narcissism. However, the lesson of history is clear: All too often, successful leaders with many positive qualities become their own worst enemies by succumbing to their narcissistic inclinations and allowing hubris to cloud their vision. When an organization and its leader have

TABLE 7.2   Examples of the Implications of Hubris

Implications	Napoleon	Executives
Confidence turns to arrogance	When Napoleon's officers pointed out the perils of the Russian campaign, he called them timid and weak.	Executives with hubris appear to undertake mergers that are overpriced out of a sense that they know better than others what is best.
Relying on a simplistic formula	Napoleon assumed the quick, hard-hitting attacks that had worked before would subdue Russia.	Once executives believe they alone know the formula for success, they repeatedly trot out the same strategy regardless of circumstances.
Unwillingness to see the obvious	Napoleon systematically refused to recognize the differences between the Russian campaign and earlier campaigns.	Once absorbed with hubris, and convinced of infallibility, executives may become blind to signals of environmental change.

achieved their ambitions, they must not allow hubris to erode their hard-earned accomplishments.

ENDNOTES

1. De Fezensac, M., translated by Lee Kennett. 1970. *The Russian campaign, 1812.* Athens: University of Georgia Press: viii.

2. Our discussion of the 1812 Russian campaign and the geopolitical situation at the time of the campaign is based on numerous sources. To avoid the bias of any single historian or account of the events, we have avoided taking any positions that are not reflected in at least two of the works listed here: Aldington, R. 1943. *The Duke: Being an account of the life and achievements of Arthur Wellesley, First Duke of Wellington.* New York: Viking; Aubry, O. 1938. *Napoleon: Soldier and emperor.* New York: Lippincott; Ballard, C. R. 1971. *Napoleon, an outline.* New York: Books for Libraries; Barnett, C. 1978. *Bonaparte.* New York: Hill & Wang; Carr, A. 1941. *Napoleon speaks.* New York: Viking; Cate, C. 1985. *The war of the two emperors.* New York: Random House; Duffy, C. 1973. *Borodino and the War of 1812.* New York: Scribner's; De Fezensac, op. cit.; Fournier, A. 1913. *Napoleon I.* New York: Holt; Nicolson, N. 1985. *Napoleon 1812.* New York: Harper & Row; Tarle, E. 1942. *Napoleon's invasion of Russia 1812.* New York: Oxford University Press; Tolstoy, L. N., translated by Louise and Aylmer Maude. 1970. *War and Peace.* London: Oxford University Press.

3. Hayward, M. L. A., and Hambrick, D. C. 1997. Explaining the premiums paid for large acquisitions: Evidence of CEO hubris. *Administrative Science Quarterly,* 42:103–127; Kets de Vries, M. F. R. 1990. The organizational fool: Balancing a leader's hubris. *Human Relations,* 43:751–770; Wilson, A. The Classics Pages, at http://www.globalnet.co.uk-loxias.

4. Kohut, H. 1978. Creativeness: Charisma group psychology. In P. Omstein (Ed.), *The search for the self,* Vol. 2. New York: International Universities Press.

5. Cate, op. cit.: 9–11.

6. Roll, R. 1986. The hubris hypothesis of corporate takeovers. *Journal of Business,* 59:197–216.

7. Fischer, D. E., and Jordan, R. J. 1995. *Security analysis and portfolio management,* 6th ed. Upper Saddle River, N.J.: Prentice-Hall: 556.

8. Berkovitch, E., and Narayanan, M. P. 1993. Motives for takeovers: An empirical investigation. *Journal of Financial and Quantitative Analysis,* 28:347–362; Bradley, M., Desai, A., and Kim, E. H. 1988. Synergistic gains from corporate acquisitions and their division between the stockholders of target and acquiring firms. *Journal of Financial Economics,* 21:3–40; Jarrell, G. A., and Paulsen, A. B. 1989. The returns to acquiring firms in tender offers: Evidence from three decades. *Financial Management,* Autumn:12–19; Limmack, R. J. 1993. Bidder companies and defended bids: A test of Roll's hubris hypothesis. *Managerial Finance,* 19:25–36.

9. Hayward and Hambrick, op. cit.: 103–127. Hitt, M., Harrison, J., Ireland, R. D., and Best, L. 1998. Attributes of successful and unsuccessful acquisitions of U.S. firms. *British Journal of Management,* 9:91–114.

10. Hambrick, D. C., and Cannella, A. A., Jr. 1993. Relative standing: A framework for understanding departures of acquired executives. *Academy of Management Journal,* 36:733–762.

11. How sweet a deal for Novell? 1994. *Business Week,* April 4:38; Software firm fights to remake business after ill-kited merger. 1996. *Wall Street Journal,* January 12:AI–A8.

12. Kets de Vries, M. F. R., and Miller, D. 1985. Narcissism and leadership: An object relations perspective. *Human Relations,* 38:583–601.

13. Goldmam, K. 1997. *Conflicting accounts: The creation and crash of the Saatchi & Saatchi advertising empire.* New York: Simon & Schuster; Hubris redeemed. 1997. *Forbes,* January 13:42–44.

14. The shake-up in the Barclay's boardroom. 1992. *The Economist,* April 25:83–84.

15. Barnett, op. cit.: 36–53.

16. Lefebvre, G. 1969. *Napoleon 1799–1807.* New York: Routledge Kegan Paul: 141.

17. Kets de Vries, M. F. R. 1991. Whatever happened to the philosopher-king? The leader's addiction to power. *Journal of Management Studies,* 28:339–351.

18. Archer Daniel's cleanup: Don't stop now. 1996. *Business Week,* January 29:37.

19. Frances, A. (Task Force Chair). 1994. *Diagnostic and statistical manual of mental disorders,* 4th ed. Washington, D.C.: American Psychiatric Association: 658–661; Miller, A. 1981. *Prisoners of childhood.* New York: Basic Books: 33–34.

20. The four sources of hubris we identify are derived from several works (which are listed here). As Hayward and Hambrick observed, there is no definitive set of factors that must always be present in significant amounts in order to engender hubris. However, there are clearly common threads that run through much of the hubris-related literature. We have distilled

from that literature the four sources we have discussed. It would of course be unrealistic to assume that hubris can exist only in an intense presence of all four of the sources we discuss. However, it seems reasonable to conclude that greater degrees of the four sources of hubris will lead to elevated levels of hubris. Also see Brockner, J. 1988. *Self-esteem at work: Research, theory and practice.* Lexington, MA: Lexington Books; Hayward and Hambrick, op. cit.: 103–127; Kets de Vries, The organizational fool, op. cit.: 751–770; Kets de Vries and Miller, op. cit.: 583–601; Salancik, G. R., and Meindl, J. R. 1984. Corporate attributions as strategic illusions of management control. *Administrative Science Quarterly,* 29:238–254.

21. Kets de Vries, The organizational fool, op. cit.: 764. Frances, op. cit.: 658–661.

22. Sankowsky, D. 1995. The charismatic leader as narcissist: Understanding the abuse of power. *Organizational Dynamics,* Spring:57–71.

23. O'Connor, J., Mumford, M. D., Clifton, T. C., and Gessner, T. L. 1995. Charismatic leaders and destructiveness: An historiometric study. *Leadership Quarterly,* 6:529–555.

24. Tolstoy, op. cit.: 427.

25. Crunch time at Quaker Oats. 1996. *Business Week,* September 23:71; Putting the snap back in Snapple. 1996. *Business Week,* July 22:40; Snapple is now up to Smithburg. 1995. *Advertising Age,* October 30:8; Quaker Oats to buy Snapple for $1.7 billion. 1994. *Wall Street Journal,* November 3:A3; He who laughs last. 1996. *Forbes,* January 1:42–43; Snapped up. 1997. *Beverage World,* April 15:92; Quaker acts—At last. 1997. *Fortune,* European edition, May 26:30.

26. Kets de Vries, The organizational fool, op. cit.: 765.

27. Kets de Vries and Miller, op. cit.: 583–601.

28. Ibid., 589.

29. Brockner, op. cit.

30. Barnett, op. cit.: 45.

31. De Raguse, D. 1857. *Memoires I.* Paris: 297.

32. Meindl, J. R., and Ehrlich, S. B. 1987. The romance of leadership and the evaluation of organizational performance. *Academy of Management Journal,* 30:91–109. Also see Staw, B. M., McKechnie, P., and Puffer, S. M. 1983. The justification of organizational performance. *Administrative Science Quarterly,* 28:582–600; Bettman, J. R., and Weitz, B. A. 1983. Attributes in the board room: Causal reasoning in corporate annual reports. *Administrative Science Quarterly,* 28:165–183.

33. The scorecard. 1999. *Forbes,* May 17:216–286.

34. Clapham, S. E., and Schwenk, C. R. 1991. Self-serving attributions, managerial cognition, and company performance. *Strategic Management Journal,* 12:219–229.

35. Chen, C. C., and Meindl, J. R. 1991. The construction of leadership images in the popular press: The case of Donald Burr and People Express. *Administrative Science Quarterly,* 36:521–551; Hayward and Hambrick, op. cit.: 109; Meindl, J. R., Ehrlich, S. B., and Dukerich, J. M. 1985. The romance of leadership. *Administrative Science Quarterly,* 30:78–102.

36. Holtman, R. 1969. *Napoleonic propaganda.* New York: Greenwood Press: 33.

37. Chen and Meindl, op. cit.: 521–551; Meindl, Ehrlich, and Dukerich, op. cit.: 78–102.

38. James Carville. Speech given before the student body and faculty of Louisiana State University, broadcast by CSPAN, November 1992.

39. Freud, S. 1957. Some character-types met with in psychoanalytic work. In J. Starchey (Ed.), *The Standard Edition of the Complete Psychological Works of Sigmund Freud,* Vol. 14. London: Hogarth Press and Institute of Psychoanalysis.

40. Kets de Vries, Philosopher-king, op. cit.: 342.

41. Barnett, op. cit.: 45.

42. Ibid., 182.

43. Nicolson, op. cit.: 180.

44. Salomon brothers: Life after Gutfreund. 1991. *The Economist,* August 24:67–68; Who should run Salomon Brothers? 1991. *Institutional Investor,* September:11–14.

45. While the three behaviors we discuss here are not the only ones manifested by a hubris-infected executive, for the sake of brevity we address these three as they are likely to have the greatest strategic consequences for the firm. Another behavior not discussed that may manifest itself in someone imbued with hubris is abuse of authority that leads to the alienation and departure of valued employees. A charismatic leader who is also consumed with hubris may use his or her talents to achieve a position of leadership and trust, only to betray that trust when it becomes expedient to do so in order to satisfy his or her personal needs. Throughout his career, Napoleon betrayed those to whom he had made commitments when it became expedient to do so, including his first wife, Empress Josephine. Please see Sankowsky, op. cit.: 57–71.

46. Kets de Vries and Miller, op. cit.; Kets de Vries, The organizational fool, op. cit.

47. Nicolson, op. cit.: 17.

48. Ibid.: 18.

49. Snapped up, op. cit.: 92.

50. Miller, D. 1993. The architecture of simplicity. *Academy of Management Review,* 18:116–138.

51. Keller, M. 1989. *Rude awakening.* New York: Harper Perennial.

52. Slip slidin' away at General Motors. 1998. *Business Week,* March 23:38.

53. Keller, op. cit.: 21.

54. Ibid.: 51.

55. Clapham and Schwenk, op. cit.: 227.

56. Ibid.

57. A tough deadline. 1996. *Forbes,* April 22:165–174; Mercedes-Benz's bold niche strategy. 1997. *Forbes,* September 8:68–76; Neutron Jurgen? 1996. *The Economist,* March 16:72; Schrempp, J. E. 1997. Thriving on global economic changes, address delivered to the Economic Club of Detroit, January 6; Neutron Jurgen ignites a revolution at DaimlerBenz. 1997. *Fortune,* November 10:144–152; The bulldozer at Daimler-Benz. 1997. *Business Week,* February 10:52.

58. Filley, A. C., House, R. J., and Kerr, S. 1976. *Managerial process and organizational behavior.* Glenview, Ill.: Scott, Foresman: 57–62; Janis, I. L. 1972. *Victims of groupthink.* Boston: Houghton Mifflin: 13–15.

59. Kets de Vries, The organizational fool, op. cit.: 757.

60. Filley et al., op. cit.: 353; Janis, op. cit.

61. Le Normand, M. A. 1895. *The historical and secret memoirs of the Empress Josephine.* London: 229.

62. Kets de Vries, The organizational fool, op. cit.: 757.

63. Nicolson, op. cit.: 162. The attentive reader may wonder at the 570,000 casualty figure, given that Napoleon entered Russia with an army of 500,000 and about 20,000 recrossed the Neiman River and escaped alive. However, several supplemental regiments of reinforcements joined the army at various points during the retreat, thus increasing the absolute number of men involved in the campaign. In addition to the 570,000 official casualties, there were many thousands of noncombatant casualties. Many of the officers brought with them wives, children, and personal servants who were not officially part of the army but suffered the same fates as their husbands, fathers, and masters. In addition, early-nineteenth-century armies were often accompanied by merchants who sold various items to the troops along the way, as well as by women camp followers, many of whom faired poorly. Ibid., 172.

64. Kelleher, Herb. http://www.iflyswa.com/herb/herbie.html.

65. It is worth noting that some scholars have argued that subordinate insiders will check the behavior of the CEO as they are natural competitors for control of the firm and their fortunes are tied to the firm's. For these reasons, they will act to cause the replacement of the CEO by influencing outside board members when the CEO's behavior is truly harmful to the firm. See Fama, E. F. 1980. Agency problems and the theory of the firm. *Journal of Political Economy,* 88:288–307.

66. Bailing out of Delta. 1997. *Business Week,* May 26:62; Delta Air's Allen to quit three top posts. 1997. *Wall Street Journal,* May 13.

67. As organizations become more decentralized and move toward the use of self-directed work teams, decisionmaking occurs at lower levels in the organization. This is especially true in organizations where empowerment exists. In such organizations, hubris at the corporate level may be less of an issue in that control of decisionmaking is reduced.

68. Drucker, P. F., Dyson, E., Handy, C., Saffo, P., and Senge, P. M. 1997. Looking ahead: Implications of the present. *Harvard Business Review,* September-October:22.

69. Wilson, op. cit.

8

⁓

The Greatest Man Churchill and Truman Ever Met

Albert R. Hunt

In a time when anniversaries from the monumental to the mundane are celebrated, today marks one of the more important, if little noticed, in modern American history: It was fifty-five years ago that George Catlett Marshall became U.S. Army chief of staff.

For the next dozen years General Marshall, as chief of staff, secretary of state, and secretary of defense, left a legacy rivaled by few public servants in this century: He built and shaped the military machine that won World War II, launched the economic plan that put postwar Europe back on its feet, and reinforced the supremacy of civilian control when he recommended the firing of General Douglas MacArthur. Dwight Eisenhower, Winston Churchill, Harry Truman, and countless others considered him the greatest man they'd ever met.

It's unclear whether this man of such vision and integrity would have been able to adapt to the exigencies of contemporary politics and statecraft. But Forrest Pogue's magnificent four-volume biography of General Marshall should be required reading for today's practitioners.

When George Marshall took over as chief of staff on September 1, 1939, there were two stark realities: Hitler's powerful army had overrun Poland that day and was on the verge of dominating the continent of Europe to an extent not seen since Napoleon; and the U.S. Army numbered fewer than 200,000 soldiers, rating behind sixteen other nations. In less than five years General Marshall built an army of 8.3 million, the most powerful fighting machine the world had ever seen.

As secretary of state and later as secretary of defense, General Marshall was President Truman's right hand; no one played a larger role in constructing the policy that contained the menace of communism. The author of the Marshall Plan was the first military man to win the Nobel Peace Prize in peacetime.

The issues were so awesome, and General Marshall's involvement was so central, that he made major mistakes. He didn't adequately anticipate a Japanese attack on Pearl Harbor in 1941; arguably, along with General Eisenhower and others, he underestimated Soviet intentions in 1945; and he was on the wrong side of the debate over recognizing Israel in 1948. But as big as these miscalculations are, they are dwarfed by his contributions.

The Marshall vision and sense of duty never were deterred by the prevailing political winds. It's easy to forget what a Herculean task he performed in building the army, overcoming initial public resistance. In 1938 a majority of the House voted for a constitutional amendment to require a national referendum before the United States could go to war. In 1941, less than four months before Pearl Harbor, the extension of the draft passed by one vote; without General Marshall's enormous influence on Capitol Hill it would have failed decisively.

The aftermath of World War II ushered in another new world order; despite the Soviet threat there was a strong tendency to look inward. But General Marshall and President Truman not only proposed the multi-billion-dollar rescue of Europe but persuaded a Republican Congress to approve it.

General Marshall, an unusually secure man, spotted bright subordinates and then delegated huge responsibilities. In the army, General Eisenhower, Omar Bradley, Matthew Ridgway, and George Patton all were Marshall men. The army chief of staff had no use for yes-men. At the end of his first week, General Bradley once recalled, he summoned his top aides and expressed strong disappointment: "You haven't disagreed with a single thing I have done all week."

He was a military leader with a special sensitivity. When some expressed surprise that an army general won the Nobel Peace Prize, he noted in his acceptance speech that "the cost of war is constantly spread before me, written neatly in many ledgers whose columns are gravestones. I am greatly moved to find some means or method of avoiding another calamity of war." Working with industrialists and Congress he made sure that his army was the best supplied and best cared for in the world.

This son of the Virginia Military Institute lacked the charisma of MacArthur or even Eisenhower, but he possessed a powerful presence that commanded trust and respect. Churchill, notoriously condescending to military commanders, quickly realized that George Marshall was different. Although he eschewed conventional politics he was a superb politician. During the war he was at the epicenter of an extraordinary collection of powerful personalities and egos: Churchill and Roosevelt, the Machiavellian commanders in chief with their own notions of military strategy, and in his own army, MacArthur and Patton. Yet the single domineering military figure was George C. Marshall.

He loathed self-promotion. An oft-quoted Marshall dictum is that there's no end to what can be accomplished if you credit others; it's not clear whether he actually said it, but he certainly practiced it.

The most remarkable example of his character was when the time came to choose the supreme Allied commander for the invasion of Europe; most everyone, from Churchill to the entire American military establishment, thought General Marshall the perfect choice. Yet when President Roosevelt pressed him for a recommendation, General Marshall, with a devout belief in civilian control, refused to lift a hand on his own behalf, insisting the president must be free to make the choice. FDR said he would sleep better with General Marshall in Washington; General Eisenhower thus led what became the Normandy invasion. General Marshall never expressed any regret and reveled in his subordinate's success.

Yet as Forrest Pogue says, George Marshall was humble only "if you use the term correctly. He was quite aware of his ability to run the Army and the war better than anyone else." And he was secure enough not to react when he was viciously attacked by Joe McCarthy and the Republican right in the early 1950s.

Would General Marshall succeed as easily today? Mr. Pogue suspects not, worried that he would despise television's penchant for the instantaneous passions of the moment, the overreliance on polls, and the constant negative drumbeat about public service.

Whether it's politicians or generals or athletes, there is an irresistible temptation to suggest we don't make them like we used to. In that vein, it's good to remember that in 1888 Lord Bryce wrote his famous essay about American politics entitled "Why Great Men Are Not Elected President." Americans, over the next sixty years, then proceeded to elect Teddy Roosevelt, Woodrow Wilson, Franklin Roosevelt, and Harry Truman.

Perhaps there's a George Marshall on the horizon. Let's hope so.

9

~

The Antileadership Vaccine

John W. Gardner

It is generally believed that we need enlightened and responsible leaders—at every level and in every phase of our national life. Everyone says so. But the nature of leadership in our society is very imperfectly understood, and many of the public statements about it are utter nonsense.

This is unfortunate because there are serious issues of leadership facing this society, and we had better understand them.

THE DISPERSION OF POWER

The most fundamental thing to be said about leadership in the United States is also the most obvious. We have gone as far as any known society in creating a leadership system that is not based on caste or class, nor even on wealth. There is not yet equal access to leadership (witness the remaining barriers facing women and Negroes), but we have come a long, long way from the family- or class-based leadership group. Even with its present defects, ours is a relatively open system.

The next important thing to be said is that leadership is dispersed among a great many groups in our society. The president, of course, has a unique, and uniquely important, leadership role, but beneath him, fragmentation is the rule. This idea is directly at odds with the notion that the society is run by a coherent power group—the Power Elite, as C. Wright Mills called it, or the Establishment, as later writers have named it. It is hard not to believe

---

The Antileadership Vaccine, by John W. Gardner, president's essay reprinted from the 1965 Carnegie Corporation of New York Annual Report.

that such a group exists. Foreigners find it particularly difficult to believe in the reality of the fluid, scattered, shifting leadership that is visible to the naked eye. The real leadership, they imagine, must be behind the scenes. But at a national level this simply isn't so.

In many local communities and even in some states there is a coherent power group, sometimes behind the scenes, sometimes out in the open. In communities where such an "establishment," that is, a coherent ruling group, exists, the leading citizen can be thought of as having power in a generalized sense: He can bring about a change in zoning ordinances, influence the location of a new factory, and determine whether the local museum will buy contemporary paintings. But in the dispersed and fragmented power system that prevails in the nation as a whole one cannot say "So-and-so is powerful," without further elaboration. Those who know how our system works always want to know, "Powerful in what way? Powerful to accomplish what?" We have leaders in business and leaders in government, military leaders and educational leaders, leaders in labor and in agriculture, leaders in science, in the world of art, and in many other special fields. As a rule, leaders in any one of these fields do not recognize the authority of leaders from a neighboring field. Often they don't even know one another, nor do they particularly want to. Mutual suspicion is just about as common as mutual respect—and a lot more common than mutual cooperation in manipulating society's levers.

Most of the significant issues in our society are settled by a balancing of forces. A lot of people and groups are involved and the most powerful do not always win. Sometimes a coalition of the less powerful wins. Sometimes an individual of very limited power gets himself into the position of casting the deciding ballot.

Not only are there apt to be many groups involved in any critical issue, but their relative strength varies with each issue that comes up. A group that is powerful today may not be powerful next year. A group that can cast a decisive vote on question A may not even be listened to when question B comes up.

THE NATURE OF LEADERSHIP

People who have never exercised power have all kinds of curious ideas about it. The popular notion of top leadership is a fantasy of capricious power: The top man presses a button and something remarkable happens; he gives an order as the whim strikes him, and it is obeyed.

Actually, the capricious use of power is relatively rare except in some large dictatorships and some small family firms. Most leaders are hedged around by constraints—tradition, constitutional limitations, the realities of the external situation, rights and privileges of followers, the requirements of teamwork, and most of all the inexorable demands of large-scale organizations, which do not operate on capriciousness. In short, most power is wielded circumspectly.

There are many different ways of leading, many kinds of leaders. Consider, for example, the marked contrasts between the politician and the intellectual leader, the large-scale manager and the spiritual leader. One sees solemn descriptions of the qualities needed for leadership without any reference at all to the fact that the necessary attributes depend on the kind of leadership under discussion. Even in a single field there may be different kinds of leadership with different required attributes. Think of the difference between the military hero and the military manager.

If social action is to occur, certain functions must be performed. The problems facing the group or organization must be clarified, and ideas necessary to their solution formulated. Objectives must be defined. There must be widespread awareness of those objectives, and the will to achieve them. Often those on whom action depends must develop new attitudes and habits. Social machinery must be set in motion. The consequences of social effort must be evaluated and criticized, and new goals set.

A particular leader may contribute at only one point to this process. He may be gifted in analysis of the problem, but limited in his capacity to communicate. He may be superb in communicating, but incapable of managing. He may, in short, be an outstanding leader without being good at every aspect of leadership.

If anything significant is to be accomplished, leaders must understand the social institutions and processes through which action is carried out. And in a society as complex as ours, that is no mean achievement. A leader, whether corporation president, university dean, or labor official, knows his organization, understands what makes it move, comprehends its limitations. Every social system or institution has a logic and dynamic of its own that cannot be ignored.

We have all seen men with lots of bright ideas but no patience with the machinery by which ideas are translated into action. As a rule, the machinery defeats them. It is a pity, because the professional and academic man can play a useful role in practical affairs. But too often he is a dilettante. He dips in here or there; he gives bits of advice on a dozen fronts; he never gets his hands dirty working with one piece of the social machinery until he knows it well. He will not take the time to understand the social institutions and processes by which change is accomplished.

Although our decentralized system of leadership has served us well, we must not be so complacent as to imagine that it has no weaknesses, that it faces no new challenges, or that we have nothing to learn. There are grave questions to be answered concerning the leadership of our society. Are we living up to standards of leadership that we have achieved in our own past? Do the conditions of modern life introduce new complications into the task of leadership? Are we failing to prepare leaders for tomorrow?

Here are some of our salient difficulties.

FAILURE TO COPE WITH THE BIG QUESTIONS

Nothing should be allowed to impair the effectiveness and independence of our specialized leadership groups. But such fragmented leadership does create certain problems. One of them is that it isn't anybody's business to think about the big questions that cut across specialties—the largest questions facing our society. Where are we headed? Where do we want to head? What are the major trends determining our future? Should we do anything about them? Our fragmented leadership fails to deal effectively with these transcendent questions.

Very few of our most prominent people take a really large view of the leadership assignment. Most of them are simply tending the machinery of that part of society to which they belong. The machinery may be a great corporation or a great government agency or a great law practice or a great university. These people may tend it very well indeed, but they are not pursuing a vision of what the total society needs. They have not developed a strategy as to how it can be achieved, and they are not moving to accomplish it.

One does not blame them, of course. They do not see themselves as leaders of the society at large, and they have plenty to do handling their own specialized role.

Yet it is doubtful that we can any longer afford such widespread inattention to the largest questions facing us. We achieved greatness in an era when changes came more slowly than now. The problems facing the society took shape at a stately pace. We could afford to be slow in recognizing them, slow in coping with them. Today, problems of enormous import hit us swiftly. Great social changes emerge with frightening speed. We can no longer afford to respond in a leisurely fashion.

Our inability to cope with the largest questions tends to weaken the private sector. Any question that cannot be dealt with by one of the special leadership groups—that is, any question that cuts across special fields—tends to end up being dealt with by government. Most Americans value the role played by nongovernmental leadership in this country and would wish it to continue. In my judgment it will not continue under the present conditions.

The cure is not to work against the fragmentation of leadership, which is a vital element in our pluralism, but to create better channels of communication among significant leadership groups, especially in connection with the great issues that transcend any particular group.

FAILURE OF CONFIDENCE

Another of the maladies of leadership today is a failure of confidence. Anyone who accomplishes anything of significance has more confidence than the facts would justify. It is something that outstanding executives have in common with gifted military commanders, brilliant political leaders, and great artists. It is true of societies as well as of individuals. Every great civilization has been characterized by confidence in itself.

Lacking such confidence, too many leaders add ingenious new twists to the modern art that I call "How to reach a decision without really deciding." They require that the question be put through a series of clearances within the organization and let the clearance process settle it. Or take a public opinion poll and let the poll settle it. Or devise elaborate statistical systems, cost-accounting systems, information-processing systems, hoping that out of them will come unassailable support for one course of action rather than another.

This is not to say that leadership cannot profit enormously from good information. If the modern leader doesn't know the facts he is in grave trouble, but rarely do the facts provide unqualified guidance. After the facts are in, the leader must in some measure emulate the little girl who told the teacher she was going to draw a picture of God. The teacher said, "But, Mary, no one knows what God looks like," and Mary said, "They will when I get through."

The confidence required of leaders poses a delicate problem for a free society. We don't want to be led by Men of Destiny who think they know all the answers. Neither do we wish to be led by Nervous Nellies. It is a matter of balance. We are no longer in much danger, in this society, from Men of Destiny. But we are in danger of falling under the leadership of men who lack the confidence to lead. And we are in danger of destroying the effectiveness of those who have a natural gift for leadership.

Of all our deficiencies with respect to leadership, one of the gravest is that we are not doing what we should to encourage potential leaders. In the late eighteenth century we produced out of a small population a truly extraordinary group of leaders: Washington, Adams, Jefferson, Franklin, Madison, Monroe, and others. Why is it so difficult today, out of a vastly greater population, to produce men of that caliber? It is a question that most reflective people ask themselves sooner or later. There is no reason to doubt that the human material is still there, but there is excellent reason to believe that we are failing to develop it—or that we are diverting it into nonleadership activities.

THE ANTILEADERSHIP VACCINE

Indeed, it is my belief that we are immunizing a high proportion of our most gifted young people against any tendencies to leadership. It will be worth our time to examine how the antileadership vaccine is administered.

The process is initiated by the society itself. The conditions of life in a modern, complex society are not conducive to the emergence of leaders. The young person today is acutely aware of the fact that he is an anonymous member of a mass society, an individual lost among millions of others. The processes by which leadership is exercised are not visible to him, and he is bound to believe that they are exceedingly intricate. Very little in his experience encourages him to think that he might someday exercise a role of leadership.

This unfocused discouragement is of little consequence compared with the expert dissuasion the young person will encounter if he is sufficiently bright to attend a college or university. In those institutions today, the best students are carefully schooled to avoid leadership responsibilities.

Most of our intellectually gifted young people go from college directly into graduate school or into one of the older and more prestigious professional schools. There they are introduced to—or, more correctly, powerfully indoctrinated in—a set of attitudes appropriate to scholars, scientists, and professional men. This is all to the good. The students learn to identify themselves strongly with their calling and its ideals. They acquire a conception of what a good scholar, scientist, or professional man is like.

As things stand now, however, that conception leaves little room for leadership in the normal sense; the only kind of leadership encouraged is that which follows from the performing of purely professional tasks in a superior manner. Entry into what most of us would regard as the leadership roles in the society at large is discouraged.

In the early stages of a career, there is a good reason for this: Becoming a first-class scholar, scientist, or professional requires single-minded dedication. Unfortunately, by the time the individual is sufficiently far along in his career to afford a broadening of interests, he often finds himself irrevocably set in a narrow mold.

The antileadership vaccine has other more subtle and powerful ingredients. The image of the corporation president, politician, or college president that is current among most intellectuals and professionals today has some decidedly unattractive features. It is said that such men compromise their convictions almost daily, if not hourly. It is said that they have tasted the corrupting experience of power. They must be status seekers, the argument goes, or they would not be where they are.

Needless to say, the student picks up such attitudes. It is not that professors propound these views and students learn them. Rather, they are in the air and students absorb them. The resulting unfavorable image contrasts dramatically with the image these young people are given of the professional who is almost by definition dedicated to his field, pure in his motives, and unencumbered by worldly ambition.

My own extensive acquaintance with scholars and professionals on the one hand and administrators and managers on the other does not confirm this contrast in character. In my experience, each category has its share of opportunists. Nevertheless, the negative attitudes persist.

As a result the academic world appears to be approaching a point at which everyone will want to educate the technical expert who advises the leader, or the intellectual who stands off and criticizes the leader, but no one will want to educate the leader himself.

ARE LEADERS NECESSARY?

For a good many academic and other professional people, negative attitudes toward leadership go deeper than skepticism concerning the leader's integrity. Many have real doubts, not always explicitly formulated, about the necessity for leadership.

The doubts are of two kinds. First, many scientific and professional people are accustomed to the kinds of problems that can be solved by expert technical advice or action. It is easy for them to imagine that any social enterprise could be managed in the same way. They envisage a world that does not need leaders, only experts. The notion is based, of course, upon a false conception of the leader's function. The supplying of technically correct solutions is the least of his responsibilities.

There is another kind of question that some academic or professional people raise concerning leadership: Is the very notion of leadership somehow at odds with the ideals of a free society? Is it a throwback to earlier notions of social organization?

These are not foolish questions. We have in fact outgrown or rejected several varieties of leadership that have loomed large in the history of mankind. We do not want autocratic leaders who treat us like inferior beings. We do not want leaders, no matter how wise or kind, who treat us like children.

But at the same time that we were rejecting those forms of leadership we were evolving forms more suitable to our values. As a result our best leaders today are not out of place in a free society—on the contrary, they strengthen our free society.

We can have the kinds of leaders we want, but we cannot choose to do without them. It is in the nature of social organization that we must have them at all levels of our national life, in and out of government—in business, labor, politics, education, science, the arts, and every other field. Since we must have them, it helps considerably if they are gifted in the performance of their appointed task. The sad truth is that a great many of our organizations are badly managed or badly led. And because of that, people within those organizations are frustrated when they need not be frustrated. They are not helped when they could be helped. They are not given the opportunities to fulfill themselves that are clearly possible.

In the minds of some, leadership is associated with goals that are distasteful—power, profit, efficiency, and the like. But leadership, properly conceived, also serves the individual human goals that our society values so highly, and we shall not achieve those goals without it.

Leaders worthy of the name, whether they are university presidents or senators, corporation executives or newspaper editors, school superintendents or governors, contribute to the continuing definition and articulation of the most cherished values of our society. They offer, in short, moral leadership. So much of our energy has been devoted to tending the machinery of our complex society that we have neglected this element in leadership. I am using the word *moral* to refer to the shared values that must undergird any functioning society. The thing that makes a number of individuals a society rather than a population or a crowd is the presence of shared attitudes, habits, and values, a shared conception of the enterprise of which they are all a part, shared views of why it is worthwhile for the enterprise to continue and to flourish. Leaders can help in bringing that about. In fact, it is required that they do so. When leaders lose their credibility or their moral authority, then the society begins to disintegrate.

Leaders have a significant role in creating the state of mind that is the society. They can serve as symbols of the moral unity of the society. They can express the values that hold the society together. Most important, they can conceive and articulate goals that lift people out of their petty preoccupations, carry them above the conflicts that tear a society apart, and unite them in the pursuit of objectives worthy of their best efforts.

— III —

THE FOLLOWER FACTOR

All over this country, corporations and government agencies, there are millions of executives who imagine that their place on the organization chart has given them a body of followers. And of course it hasn't. It has given them subordinates. Whether subordinates become followers depends on whether the executives act like leaders.

John Gardner

Whether we ask successful leaders to describe the relationship they want with their followers or ask successful followers to describe the relationship they want with their leaders, we get essentially the same description. Our experience is that when followers are asked what attributes they want most from a leader, the response is, most often, honesty, respect, and a sense of belonging. Each understands the perspective of the other and both recognize that they can be successful in the long term only if they share success. However, leadership theory and practical applications derived from theory focus, all too often, on the role of the leader in creating success, thereby undervaluing the role of the follower. In far too many organizations, the leadership role is seen as the only avenue to personal success, and therefore it is developed, encouraged, appreciated, and rewarded, whereas followership is not.

Contemporary organizations can no longer depend upon the leader alone. The trend to form work teams so that a diversity of knowledge and skills is used to confront complex situations characterizes the environment today. We must study and appreciate the role of the follower in the dynamics of group and organizational success. Most of us are followers more often than we are leaders. Nearly every leader also serves as a follower. Followership dominates our lives and our organizations, and leaders come from the ranks of the followers. In fact, few leaders can be successful without first having learned the skills of following. Aristotle's *Politics,* Plato's *Republic,* Homer's *Odyssey,* and Hegel's *Phenomenology of Mind* affirm the mastery of followership as the sine qua non of leadership: Qualities that we associate with effective followers are the same qualities that we find in effective leaders. The experience of following also gives leaders perspective and enables them to share vision, communicate with empathy, treat people as individuals, and empower followers to achieve shared goals and objectives. Effective leaders realize that they are also followers and purposefully set the example when performing that role. Thus, a major tenet of developing effective leadership is understanding, experiencing, and modeling effective followership.

In organizations where good followership is appreciated, effective followers and leaders are very comfortable moving from one role to the other. Fortunately, more and more organizations are recognizing that good followership leads to a strategic advantage and have begun to develop and reward effective followers.

In an attempt to get around the stereotypes associated with followership, many organizations refer to their followers with terms such as *constituents, associates, members,* or *colleagues.* The term *subordinate* has begun to fade from the vocabularies. However, what we call people in our organizations matters much less than how we treat them. No matter what they are called, followers who are treated with disdain by those in charge are clearly regarded as subordinates.

Followers want to feel a sense of partnership with the leader in accomplishing goals and defining a path to the future. Social, economic, and technological conditions have encouraged a better-educated and more sophisticated constituency; superior education, skills, and access to information are no longer the sole purview of leaders. As a result of the blurred differences between followers' abilities and their own, leaders must more actively involve followers in organizational processes.

If leaders are to develop good followers, they must encourage participation in the creation of the vision, mission, and goals while allowing their ideas to be modified and "owned" by everyone. Separating the individual from leadership creates "we," building a true sense of involvement and empowerment among followers. Hence a requisite leadership communication skill is listening, and the necessary followership communication skill is courageously speaking up.

Failure to recognize interdependencies between leader and follower can have serious consequences for both. These interdependencies are critical to a leader's success and ensure an ongoing pattern of leadership development. In many ways, leaders serve followers—certainly a reversal of traditional perceptions. But effective leaders create opportunities, help provide necessary resources, delegate authority, and vigorously support the decisions made and actions taken. Often, leaders must watch while others do things differently than they would have. Helping people learn by allowing them to make mistakes takes true courage and results in organizational learning. This is how leaders develop effective followers who, in turn, are learning the elements of effective leadership.

Many leaders thrive on having followers revere them. Unfortunately, the organization becomes completely dependent upon that leader—everything happens because of her or him. Truly effective leaders have people around them who are bright, critical, courageous, and independent. Decisions are made at the organizational level having the most information. Followers are given the means and responsibility to do the job; creativity and innovation are prized. Thus, leaders are best evaluated on the basis of organizational success as well as how well they develop their followers.

LEADERSHIP PERSPECTIVES

In Chapter 10, "Followership: It's Personal, Too," Robert Goffee and Gareth Jones posit that people seek, admire, and respect leaders who produce within them the three emotional responses of a feeling of significance, a feeling of community, and a feeling of excitement. Followers are not empty vessels waiting to be led or even transformed by the leader.

Warren Bennis takes a radical position in "The End of Leadership: Exemplary Leadership Is Impossible Without Full Inclusion, Initiatives, and Cooperation of Followers" (Chapter 11). The paradox presented is that exemplary leadership and organizational change are not possible without a partnership with followers. The author describes the preeminence of top-down leadership, which is maladaptive, leading ultimately to failure. His notion of the end of leadership is truly a redirection, translated as a partnership between leaders and followers. Second, the leader must continue reminding people in the organization of what is important. Third, the leader must generate and sustain trust throughout the organization. Fourth, the leader and followers must emerge as intimate allies. Thus, Bennis sees that great groups and organizations make great leaders.

In Chapter 12, Earl H. Potter III and William E. Rosenbach present their conceptual model of followership in "Followers as Partners: The Spirit of Leadership." They describe effective followers as partners who are committed to taking the initiative for high performance and healthy relationships with their leaders. The authors argue that leaders who encourage partnerships as well as followers who seek to be partners characterize leaders and followers whose organizations thrive in the rapidly changing global environment.

10

~

Followership: It's Personal, Too

Robert Goffee
Gareth Jones

To be adequately understood, leadership must be seen for what it is: part of a duality or a relationship. There can be no leaders without followers.

So let's look at this incendiary topic through the follower's eyes. We're lucky; the sociological and psychological literature on the follower's experience is rich indeed. It tells us what people seek, admire, and respect; that is, they follow leaders who produce within them three emotional responses.

The first is a feeling of significance. Followers will give their hearts and souls to authority figures who say, "You really matter," no matter how small the followers' contributions may be. This dynamic, of course, comes from the human drive to be valued. We yearn to not live and die in vain. When leaders, then, herald the significance of an individual's work, they are rewarded with loyalty, even obedience. They have given meaning to a follower's life, and as a basis for a relationship, that is not just sturdy; it is as solid as cement.

The second emotional response followers want from their leaders is a feeling of community. Now there's a messy concept: community. The library is filled with books trying to define it. But for our purposes, let's say community occurs when people feel a unity of purpose around work and, simultaneously, a willingness to relate to one another as human beings. It is the rare business executive who can create such an environment. But you can be sure that when a feeling of community is successfully engineered, it is so deeply gratifying that followers will call the person who created it their leader.

Finally, followers will tell you that a leader is nearby when they get a buzzing feeling. People want excitement, challenge, and edge in their lives. It makes them feel engaged in the world. And so, despite all the literature that tells you a leader needn't be charismatic, followers will sooner feel leadership from someone who is extroverted and energetic than from someone who isn't. Right or wrong, that's how followers feel.

Some traditional theories of leadership portray the follower as an empty vessel waiting to be led, or even transformed, by the leader. Other theories suggest that followers require nurturing and need to be persuaded to give of themselves. But these theories would have us believe that followers are passive. Yes, followership implies commitment, but never without conditions. The follower wants the leader to create feelings of significance, community, and excitement—or the deal is off.

After all, to the follower, as much as it is to the person who stands above him in the organizational hierarchy, leadership is entirely personal.

11

~

The End of Leadership: Exemplary Leadership Is Impossible Without Full Inclusion, Initiatives, and Cooperation of Followers

Warren Bennis

I've never fully approved of formal debates. The very premise of a debate, where issues are egregiously oversimplified, can't help but lose the subtly nuanced distinctions we academics relish and thrive on. So when I was asked not long ago to participate in this kind of foolishness, I was naturally resistant to participate, especially when the "resolution before the house" was phrased as follows: "All successful organizational change must originate at the top." To make matters worse, the organizers of the debate insisted that I take the opposite position of the "resolution of the house," casting me "against type," so to speak. I would have felt far more comfortable being on the side of strong leadership, a position more compatible with most of my recent writing. I did agree, however, despite my strong reservations, primarily because the organizers were colleagues and I wanted an expense-paid trip to the East Coast. In accepting, I was reminded of an old *New Yorker* cartoon showing Charles Dickens in his publisher's office, being told rather sternly by his editor, "Well, Mr. Dickens, it's either the best of times OR the worst of times. It can't be both."

What I discovered was that getting impaled on the horns of a false dichotomy was rather more fun than I anticipated. More important, in

---

Reprinted by permission of *Organizational Dynamics* 28: 1 (Summer 1999), pp. 71–80.

preparing for the debate, I arrived at an unexpected conclusion, close to an epiphanic event. I came to the unmistakable realization that top-down leadership was not only wrong, unrealistic, and maladaptive but also, given the report of history, dangerous. And given certain changes taking place in the organizational landscape, this obsolete form of leadership will erode competitive advantage and destroy the aspirations of any organization that aims to be in the phone book beyond the year 2002.

I think it is now possible to talk about the end of leadership without the risk of hyperbole. Some of this change is organic and inevitable. But much of it is the legacy of our times, ignited by that dynamic duo: globalization and relentlessly disruptive technology.

THE ENCOMPASSING TENDENCY

The idea of traditional top-down leadership is based on the myth of the triumphant individual. It is a myth deeply ingrained in the American psyche and unfortunately fostered and celebrated in the daily press, business magazines, and much of academic and popular writing. My own work, at times, has also suffered from this deification of the icons of American business: the Welches, the Barneviks, the Gateses—fill in your own hero. Whether it is midnight rider Paul Revere or basketball's Michael Jordan or, more recently, Mark McGwire, we are a nation enamored of heroes—rugged self-starters who meet challenges and overcome adversity. Our contemporary views of leadership are entwined with our notions of heroism, so much so that the distinction between "leader" and "hero" (or "celebrity," for that matter) often becomes blurred.

In our society leadership is too often seen as an inherently individual phenomenon. It's Oprah and Michael (Jordan or Eisner) and Bill (Clinton or Gates) and Larry and Hillary and Monica. We are all victims of or witnesses to what Leo Braudy calls the "frenzy of renown," the "peoplification" of society. Think of it: Can you imagine a best-selling magazine as popular as *People* called *System*?

And yet we do understand the significance of systems. After all, it is systems that encourage collaboration and systems that make change not only effective but possible. A shrinking world in which technological and political complexity increase at an accelerating rate offers fewer and fewer arenas in which individual action, top-down leadership, suffices. And here is the troubling disconnect. Despite the rhetoric of collaboration, we continue to live in a "byline" culture where recognition and status are conferred on individuals, *not teams of people* who make change possible.

But even as the lone hero continues to gallop through our imaginations, shattering obstacles with silver bullets, leaping tall buildings in a single bound, we know that that's a falsely lulling fantasy and that is not the way real change, enduring change, takes place. We know there is an alternative reality.

What's surprising is that this should surprise us. In a society as complex and technologically sophisticated as ours, the most urgent projects require the coordinated contributions of many talented people working together. Whether the task is building a global business or discovering the mysteries of the human brain, it doesn't happen at the top; top-down leadership can't hope to accomplish it, however gifted the person at the top is. There are simply too many problems to be identified and solved, too many connections to be made. So we cling to the myth of the Lone Ranger that great things are accomplished by a larger-than-life individual shouting commands, giving direction, inspiring the troops, sounding the tocsin, decreeing the compelling vision, leading the way, and changing paradigms with brio and shimmer.

This *encompassing tendency* is dysfunctional in today's world of blurring, spastic, hyperturbulent change and will get us into unspeakable troubles unless we understand that the search engine, the main stem winder for effective change, is the workforce and their creative alliance with top leadership.

A personal case in point. My colleague David Heenan and I wrote a book about the role of Number Twos in organizations, how they work and don't work. We thought it an original idea, one that was significant and astonishingly neglected in the literature. We entitled the book *Second Banana* and had chapters on some of the most famous and successful partnerships between Ones and Twos in corporate life, for example, the fabled relationship between Warren Buffet and his Number Two, Charles Munger, known for containing Buffet's enthusiasm about investments and referred to by Buffet as the "Abominable No Man." And there was a chapter called "Banana Splits," on infamously unsuccessful partnerships such as the widely publicized split between Michael Eisner and Michael Ovitz. All twelve of the publishers who reviewed the book declined. One put it rather nicely. He said, "Warren, no one in America wants to be Number Two." He also quoted Leonard Bernstein, who once proclaimed that "the hardest instrument to play in a symphony orchestra is second fiddle."

So David and I changed the title to *Co-Leaders* and added a subtitle, *The Power of Great Partnerships*. With that new title and a shift in emphasis away from being Number Two, it was published this year by John Wiley.

I give this example not to plug the book but to illustrate the power of this encompassing tendency of the Great Man to dominate our thinking and pervert our understanding of organizational life and how leading change really works.

THE ARGUMENT

I will present my argument in an unorthodox way by drawing on sources a little out of the ordinary for management scholars: examples and analogies from poetry, history, and theater, as well as the more traditional sources of experimental studies and business anecdotes. I'll start with an excerpt from a poem by Bertolt Brecht, the Marxist playwright.

Questions from a Worker

Who built the town of Thebes of Seven Gates?
The names of kings are written in the books.
Was it the kings who dragged the slab of rock?
And Babylon, so many times destroyed,
Who built her up again so many times?
Young Alexander conquered India.
All by himself?
Caesar beat the Gauls.
Not even a cook to help him with his meals?
Philip of Spain wept aloud when his Armada
Went down. Did no one else weep?
Frederick the Great won the Seven Years War.
Who else was the winner?
On every page a triumph.
Who baked the victory cake?
In every decade a great man. Who picked up the check?
So many reports.
So many questions.

"In every decade a great man." That encompassing tendency again. And it shows up throughout history. In Plutarch's great biography of Cato the Elder, he wrote, "Rome showed itself to be truly great, and hence worthy of great leaders." What we tend to forget is that greatness lies within nations and organizations themselves as much, if not more, than their leaders. Could Gandhi have achieved his greatness without staying close to the people and representing their greatness of spirit? So many questions.

Now for a contemporary business example. I wrote an article in which I quoted one of my favorite management philosophers, the Great One, Wayne Gretzky, saying, " It's not where the puck is, it's where the puck will be." Soon after, I received a rather sour letter from the chairman and CEO of one of our largest *Fortune* 100 companies, who wrote:

> I was particularly interested in what you characterize as the Gretzky factor. I think I know where the puck is going to be—the problem is, we've got thousands and thousands of folk who don't want the puck to go there, would rather that it wasn't going there, and in the event that it is going there, aren't going to let us position ourselves to meet it until after we've skated past. *In plain English, we've got a bunch of people who want the world to be the way it used to be—and are very disinclined to accept any alternative forecast of the future.* (Emphasis mine.)

Now what's interesting about this "leader" is that (1) he was regarded as one of the most innovative and creative CEOs in his industrial sector and (2) his unquestionable "genius" was totally useless because he lacked a critical mass of willing followers. And he had no followers because he was unable to generate and sustain a minimum degree of trust with his workforce, widely known to be resistant to and—no exaggeration—*dyspeptic* about his pre-Copernican ego and macho style.

If there is one generalization we make about leadership and change, it is this: No change can occur without willing and committed followers.

Let us turn now to social movements and how they are led and mobilized. Mohandas Gandhi's singular American apostle was Dr. Martin Luther King, Jr., who was introduced to his teachings as a graduate student in Boston University's Divinity School in the early 1950s. I had gone to college with Coretta Scott and got acquainted with her future husband while she attended the New England Conservatory of Music and I was in graduate school at MIT. Recently, upon reading John Lewis's book *Walking with the*

Wind, I recalled how back then, light years ago, Coretta seemed the charismatic one and Martin shy and bashful. Lewis, one of King's acolytes in the civil rights movement of the 1960s, now a congressman from Atlanta and one of the most respected African-American leaders, tells us in his book how much of the movement was a team effort, a "band of brothers and sisters," and how Dr. King "often joined demonstrations late or ducked out early." (I should add that Lewis was and is a devoted admirer of King.) Gary Wills wrote that

> he tried to lift others up and found himself lifted up in the process. *He literally talked himself into useful kinds of trouble.* King's oratory urged others on to heroic tasks and where they went he had to follow. Reluctant to go to jail, he was shamed into going—after so many young people responded to his speeches and found themselves in danger. (Emphasis mine.)

Don't be misled here. I'm not just reiterating one of those well-worn bromides about leadership—you know, where leaders carefully watch where their followers are going and then follow them. I'm saying something quite different. I'm saying that exemplary leadership and organizational change are impossible without the full inclusion, initiatives, and cooperation of followers.

I mentioned earlier that top-down leadership tendency is also *maladaptive,* and I think it's time to return to that now. It's become something of a cliché to discuss the extraordinary complexity and ambiguity and uncertainties of our current business environment. As one of my CEO friends put it, "If you're not confused, you don't know what's going on." At the risk of oversimplifying his important work on leadership, Ron Heifetz asserted that with relatively simple, "technical problems," leadership is relatively "easy"; that is, top-down leadership can solve them. But with "adaptive" problems, complex and messy problems, like dealing with a seriously ill cancer patient or cleaning up an ecological hazard, many stakeholders must be involved and mobilized. The truth is that adaptive problems require complex and diverse alliances. Decrees, orders, and so on *do not work.*

An elegant experiment dreamed up by one of the most imaginative, and least acknowledged, social psychologists of his day, Alex Bavelas, dramatizes, if not proves, this point. Imagine a simple, wooden, circular dining-room table, about ten feet in diameter with plywood partitions walling off the five participants from visible sight of each other. The table is constructed so that

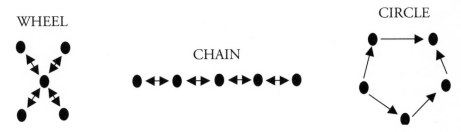

FIGURE 11.1   Organizational Networks

subjects can communicate only by passing messages written on 3 × 5 cards through narrow slots in the partitions. The cards are all color-coded so that you can count how many messages are sent to whom and by whom. Also, the table is constructed so that different organizational forms can be simulated. For example, you can create a rough example of a typical bureaucratic, command-and-control organization by restricting the flow of messages to only one central person. We used three kinds of organizational models, the wheel, which more-or-less resembles the typical organizational pyramid; the chain, a slight modification of the wheel; and the circle, where everyone could communicate with the two participants adjacent to them—not quite a completely connected network, but one of equality (see Figure 11.1).

The problem to be solved was relatively simple. Each subject was given a pillbox that contained six different-colored marbles. They were what we used to call purees, pure white, pure blue, pure green, pure red, and so on and were easily identifiable. For each experimental trial, there was only one color that each subject had in common. On one trial, for example, it was the red, on another it was the green, and so on, randomly varied. There were fifteen trials. As soon as the subject thought he had the correct color, he would drop the marble down a rubber tube in the table so that the experimenter could not only measure the accuracy for the group but also how long it took all five subjects to deposit the marble. Our predictions were not surprising and they were confirmed. The wheel, the form most like the top-down leadership model, was the most accurate and the most efficient; they were very, very quick. We did notice that in our postexperiment questionnaire, the central person reported having the highest morale and was wildly enthusiastic about his role whereas the other group members were, to be polite, pissed. Expectable and not particularly exciting results.

So we decided to change the task to a more "adaptive" problem and substituted for the primary colors, the so-called purees, ambiguously colored marbles: cat's eyes, ginger ale-ish, bluish-green, or greenish-blue, all sorts of dappled-colored marbles. Again, our predictions were confirmed. Now, under ambiguous and changing conditions, the circle was the most efficient and accurate, and all members claimed relatively high morale. On only one occasion, and we repeated this particular experiment about fifty times, did the wheel perform better. In this one case, the central person was an exceptionally gifted artist and writer. She was also taking a minor in art history. Genius happens, once in a blue moon.

The connection between that antediluvian experiment and the messy, changing business environment barely needs stating. But it dramatically illustrates my point that none of us is as smart as all of us, that the top-down model, in the present business context, is dysfunctional, maladaptive, and, as I'll get to now, dangerous.

The dangers of top-down leadership, vivid examples of colossal folly and disaster, are so numerous that one doesn't know where to begin. Stalin's communal farms? Niemeyer's Brasilia? Hitler's Holocaust? Chainsaw Al's Follies? Napoleon's Russian campaign? LBJ's Vietnam? Mao's Cultural Revolution? Maggie Thatcher's poll tax? Perhaps the best source to turn to in this respect is Barbara Tuchman's *March of Folly*, an ignored treasure for students of organizational behavior.

Tuchman argues that folly occurs when a governmental leader pursues policies contrary to the self-interest of the nation. But to be real folly, the policy must have been perceived as counterproductive *in its own time*, not merely in hindsight. Second, there are always feasible alternative means that were available. She takes her notion of folly and refracts it through the prism of four major epochal events: the Trojan Horse escorted through the gates of Troy, led innocently (and stupidly) by Priam's own warriors (who had heard from Cassandra, among others, that it was probably a Greek ploy); the Renaissance popes and how their actions brought about the Protestant Reformation; George III and the loss of the "colonies"; and LBJ and the Vietnam War. Tuchman wrote:

Wooden-headedness, the source of self-deception, is a factor that plays a remarkable role in individuals. It consists in assessing a situation in terms of preconceived fixed notions while ignoring or rejecting any contrary signs. It is acting according to wish while not allowing oneself to be deflected by the facts. It is epitomized in a historian's statement about Philip II of Spain, the surpassing wooden-head of all sovereigns: "No experience of the failure of the policy could shake his belief in its essential excellence."

THE NEW LEADERSHIP

So where does all of this lead us in terms of the current organizational context? What should be clear by now is that postbureaucratic organization requires a new kind of alliance between leaders and the led. Today's organizations are evolving into federations, networks, clusters, cross-functional teams, temporary systems, ad hoc task forces, lattices, modules, matrices—almost anything but pyramids with their obsolete top-down leadership. The new leader encourages healthy dissent and values those followers courageous enough to say no. Respect will go to the leader who exults in cultural differences and knows that diversity is the best hope for long-term survival and success. The title of this article was deliberately provocative but, I hope, not too misleading. It's not quite the *end* of leadership, actually, but it clearly points the way to a new, far more subtle and indirect form of influence for leaders to be effective. The new reality is that intellectual capital, brain power, know-how, and human imagination have supplanted capital as the critical success factor, and leaders will have to learn an entirely new set of skills that are not understood, not taught in our business schools, and, for all of those reasons, rarely practiced. I am going to suggest that there are four competencies that will determine the success of new leadership.

1. The New Leader Understands and Practices the Power of Appreciation and Is a Connoisseur of Talent, More a Curator than a Creator

We all pay lip service to acknowledgment and appreciation. To generalize just a tad, most organizations are woefully neglectful of bestowing either. And it is one of the most powerful motivators, especially for knowledge workers. To take only one example out of numberless cases, many years ago, I sent my first book to the dean and, in turn, received a perfunctory, dictated note saying that he would take the book on his next plane trip and read it then. That was it. That was the last word I ever heard from him about something I had spent over three years working on. Not very motivating or energizing, to say the least.

What I'm also getting at is that the leaders are rarely the best or the brightest in the new organizations. The new leaders have a smell for talent, an imaginative rolodex, are unafraid of hiring people better than they are, and are often more curators than creators. In my book *Organizing Genius*, I looked at the leadership of Great Groups, and in most cases, the leader was rarely the cleverest or the sharpest. Peter Schneider, president of Disney's colossally successful Feature Animation studio, leads a group of twelve hundred animators. He can't draw to save his life. Bob Taylor, former head of the Palo Alto Research Center, where the first commercial PC was invented, wasn't a computer scientist. J. Robert Oppenheimer, head of the fabled Manhattan Project, which produced the first nuclear device, while a brilliant physicist, never matched the accomplishments of the future Nobel laureates working for him at Los Alamos. It goes on and on. Perhaps a story about two of Britain's most famous nineteenth-century British prime ministers illustrates this point. It was said about William Ewart Gladstone that when you had dinner with Mr. Gladstone, you felt that he was the world's most brilliant and provocative, the most intelligent and wittiest conversationalist you had ever met. But when you were dining with Mr. Disraeli, you felt that *you* were the world's most brilliant and provocative, the most intelligent, and so on.

Max DePree put it best when he said that good leaders "abandon their ego to the talents of others."

2. The New Leader Keeps Reminding People of What's Important

Organizations drift into entropy and the bureaucratization of imagination when they forget what's important. Simple to say, but that one sentence is one of the few pieces of advice I suggest to leaders: Remind your people of what's important. Even in my profession of teaching I will occasionally hear a colleague say, usually in half jest, that the university would be a great place to work if only there weren't students around. What else is there but helping students to become successful at life? What can be more ennobling?

A powerful enough vision can transform what would otherwise be routine drudgery into collectively focused energy—even sacrifice. Witness again the Manhattan Project. The scientists there were willing to put their careers on hold and to undertake what was, in essence, a massive engineering feat because they believed the free world depended on their doing so. Reminiscing about Los Alamos, Richard Feynman, the irreverent future Nobel laureate, told a story that illustrates how reminding people of "what's important" can give meaning and value to work. The U.S. Army had recruited talented engineers from all over the United States for special duty on the project. They were assigned to work on the primitive computers of the period (1943–1945), doing energy calculations and other tedious jobs. But the army, obsessed with security, refused to tell them anything specific about the project. They didn't know that they were building a weapon that could end the war or even what their calculations meant. They were simply expected to do the work, which they did slowly and not very well. Feynman, who supervised the technicians, prevailed on his superiors to tell the recruits what they were doing and why. Permission was granted to lift the veil of secrecy, and Oppenheimer gave them a special lecture on the nature of the project and their own contribution.

"*Complete* transformation," Feynman recalled. "*They* began to invent ways of doing it better. They improved the scheme. They worked at night. They didn't need supervising in the night, they didn't need anything. They understood everything; they invented several of the programs we used." Ever the scientist, Feynman calculated that the work was done "nearly ten times as fast" after it had meaning.

Meaning—Charles Handy has it right in his book *The Hungry Spirit*. We are all hungry spirits craving purpose and meaning at work, to contribute something beyond ourselves, and leaders can never forget to stop reminding people of what's important.

3. The New Leader Generates and Sustains Trust

We're all aware that the terms of the new social contract of work have changed. No one can depend on lifelong loyalty or commitment to any organization. Since 1985, 25 percent of the American workforce has been laid off at least once. That's about a half million people on average each year. In 1998, when the unemployment rate was the lowest in thirty years, roughly 110,000 workers were downsized. At a time when the new social contract makes the times between organizations and their knowledge workers tenuous, trust becomes the emotional glue that can bond people to an organization. *Trust* is a small word with powerful connotations and is a hugely complex factor. The ingredients are a combination of competence, constancy, caring, fairness, candor, and authenticity—most of all the latter. And that is achieved by the new leaders when they can balance successfully the tripod of forces working on and in most of us: ambition, competence, and integrity. Authenticity, as Groucho Marx joked, cannot be faked. To be redundant, it's real. The current cliché is "Walk your talk." But it's far more than that. The best and perhaps the only way I know to illustrate (as opposed to define) authenticity is to quote from Robert Bolt's preface to his play *A Man for All Seasons*:

> At any rate, Thomas More, as I wrote about him, became for me a man with an adamantine sense of his own self. He knew where he began and left off, what area of himself he could yield to the encroachments of his enemies, and what to the encroachments of those he loved. It was a substantial area in both cases, for he had a proper sense of fear and was a busy lover. Since he was a clever man and a great lawyer, he was able to retire from those areas in wonderfully good order, but at length he was asked to retreat from that final area where he located his self. And there this supple, humorous, unassuming and sophisticated person set like metal, was overtaken by an absolutely primitive rigor, and could no more be budged than a cliff.

4. The New Leader and the Led Are Intimate Allies

Earlier I referred to how Dr. King's followers shamed him into going to jail because so many young people responded to his speeches and found themselves in danger. They were the unsung heroes. People you've never heard of: James Bevel, Diane Nash, Otis Moss, and many others. All heroes. John Lewis tells us in his book how much of the civil rights movement was a heroic team effort, referring to Shakespeare's Henry V's "band of brothers."

It's not too much of a stretch to consider Jakob Schindler, the protagonist of an epochal story immortalized in Stephen Spielberg's film *Schindler's List*. The power of Spielberg's film is the transformation of Schindler from a sleazy, down-at-the-heels small-time con man who moves to Poland in order to harness cheap Jewish labor to make munitions that he can then sell to the Germans at low cost. The compelling narrative of the film is his transformation, and it comes about over a period of time when Schindler interacts with his Jewish workers, most of all the accountant, Levin, but also frequent and achingly painful moments when he confronts the evil of the war, of the Holocaust, of the suffering, of the injustice. In the penultimate scene, when the war is over and the Nazis have evacuated the factory, but before the American troops arrive, the prisoners give him a ring, made for him, from the precious metals used by the workers. As he tries to put the ring on, he begins crying, "Why, why are you doing this? With this metal, we could have saved three, maybe four, maybe five more Jews." And he drives off in tears.

I find it hard to be objective about a scene that tears at my soul, but I want to argue that though this was a unique event, it portrays what new leadership is all about: Great leaders are made by great groups and by organizations that create the social architecture of respect and dignity. And through some kind of weird alchemy, some ineffable symbiosis, great leadership brings that about. Without each other, the leader and the led are culturally impoverished. Only a poet could sum up the majesty of this alchemy:

We are all angels with only one wing.
We can only fly while embracing each other.

These new leaders will not have the loudest voices, but the most attentive ears. Instead of pyramids, the postbureaucratic organizations will be structures built of energy and ideas, led by people who find their joy in the task at hand, while embracing each other—and not worrying about leaving monuments behind.

SELECTED BIBLIOGRAPHY

There are several books I referred to in the article that would more likely be found on the bookshelf of a history or English professor than a management scholar or practitioner but two of them, *Frenzy of Renown* by Leo Braudy (Oxford, 1986) and Barbara Tuchman's *March of Folly* (Alfred Knopf, 1984), deserve to be. They are just terrific books on leadership. Braudy's is the first and only history of celebrity and is brilliantly written as might be expected but often found lacking in academic treatises. I've said enough about Tuchman in the text; I use her book in my undergraduate leadership class, and it's very useful. What historian Tuchman refers to as folly or wooden-headedness, we might refer to as cognitive dissonance. John Lewis's book *Walking with the Wind* (Simon & Schuster, 1998) is a splendid personal memoire of the civil rights movement, written by one of the most important African-American leaders. In Jim O'Toole's *Leading Change* (Jossey-Bass, 1995), the frontispiece, which I reproduced here, underlines, with great wit and clarity, the basic premise of this important work; that is, leaders better learn how to enroll willing followers. It could have also been written by a humanities professor, which he basically is, except with brio and a deep philosophical lens, he has written one of the most provocative and important books on leadership. Ronald Heifetz's book *Leadership Without*

Easy Answers (Belknap, 1994) more than lives up to its name and is not an easy read, as the title suggests. But it is deep and complex and goes way beyond the domain of corporate America, though he doesn't exclude that, into areas of community leadership and doctor-patient relationships, among others. Gary Wills's book *Certain Trumpets* (Simon & Schuster, 1994) is already a classic. It has a lot in common with Howard Gardner's *Leading Minds* (Basic Books, 1995), which I should have referenced as well. Wills goes at leadership as a political scientist cum historian would, whereas Gardner is a cognitive psychologist. They both rely on fascinating narratives, but their choices of leaders, at the margins anyway, give away their worldview, their range, and their informed biases. So whereas Wills chooses to focus on Cesare Borgia or King David, Gardner takes up Robert Maynard Hutchins or Jean Monet. At the same time, they often choose the same icons, like Martha Graham, Gandhi, Eleanor Roosevelt, and Pope John XXIII. Two recent books I coauthored, one with Patricia Biederman, *Organizing Genius* (Perseus, 1997), and one with David Heenan, *Co-Leaders* (Wiley, 1999), provided some of the conceptual background for this article but try to put the spotlight not so much on leadership as on great groups and partnerships.

I'll end this bibliographic narrative with Bertolt Brecht, who always liked to have the last word anyway. He was incapable of collaboration or partnership except for his brilliantly wicked work with Kurt Weill *(Threepenny Opera)*. The poem I used came from Georg Tabori's book *The World of Brecht* (Samuel French, 1964).

12

~

Followers as Partners: The Spirit of Leadership

Earl H. Potter III
William E. Rosenbach

The recognition that the person on the front line often has the best solution to a difficult problem is at the heart of the entrepreneurial thinking. Freedom to uncover new ideas and create an environment that encourages followers to share their best thinking with their leaders is essential to innovation and change.

For example, Andy Hartman, an airline mechanic, came up with an idea to fix engine parts for seventy-five cents instead of getting replacements from a vendor for more than four thousand dollars. The parts are the mount bushings on an oil cooler flap actuator. The oil cooler cools the engine's oil, the flap actuator regulates a flap that brings airflow to the oil cooler, and the mount bushings hold the parts together. "I figured out what size the old bushings were and had the machine shop make up some stock material (for a bushing) to see if it would work, and I sent it off to the engineers, and they approved it," said Hartman. His idea was instituted for all oil cooler flap actuators throughout the company.

Telling this story encourages others to try their own ideas and also reminds leaders to look for good ideas among their followers. Such problems are objective; there are clear criteria for judging merit and time to evaluate the merit. However, this may not be the case in situations where the risks are higher and the tempo of operations is greater. Yet, the notion that a follower may have the best solution can still be true.

U.S. policy toward Cubans seeking refuge in the United States has changed since the mid-1990s. Where the U.S. Coast Guard had been directed to "rescue" refugees and bring them to port, where they would be processed via the laws of the United States, the Coast Guard now has orders to stop Cubans attempting to reach the United States before they are "feet dry" and return them to Cuba. The Cubans know this and are increasingly resorting to desperate measures to elude interdiction.

On February 4, 2004, eleven Cubans attempted to reach Florida in a 1950s Buick converted into a "tail-finned boat." The year before, Marciel Basanta Lopez and Luis Grass Rodriguez had tried to reach the United States in a 1951 Chevrolet pickup suspended between pontoons made from empty fifty-five-gallon oil drums. The Coast Guard intercepted Lopez and Rodriguez, sank their "boat," and returned the men to Cuba. In this instance, four women and five children were placed inside the boat/car, the windows were blacked out, the doors were sealed to keep the water out, and the men sat on the roof.

Under normal circumstances the Coast Guard would fire disabling shots into a boat's engine and board the boat when it stopped. In this situation, however, the vessel was powered by the original V-8 engine under the car's hood. The men refused to stop, and Coast Guard officials feared that the frail vessel would sink if aggressive tactics were used to stop it. Coast Guard captain Phil Heyl, commanding officer of Coast Guard Group Key West, then in charge of the operation, had his own ideas about how the vessel should be stopped, but before he gave an order, he asked his team for their ideas. There were several suggestions, and among them was one offered by a chief petty officer, who suggested that they put sugar in the gas tank. This was not Captain Heyl's idea and he had doubts that it would work, but he accepted the suggestion. It worked. The boat's engine stalled, the Coast Guard boarded, and all personnel aboard were removed safely and returned to Cuba.

In a recent consulting opportunity with the chair of a science department in a major research university, we worked with a leader who wanted to create a "self-managed" work team among his administrative staff. He was tired of establishing work schedules, resolving conflicts, and approving routine requests. He had a research agenda on the front burner. Moreover, there was an existing self-managed team among his lab technicians, and he liked the way it worked. In this case, however, he was unable to move his employees.

They wanted no part of increased responsibility, preferring security to freedom. Their average age was twenty-six!

This leader knew what he wanted and by all evidence was able to work effectively with employees as partners. Still, he was unable to teach, enable, and encourage his employees to accept a more complete partnership. He didn't have a model that he could use to frame the expectations he had of his employees, and he didn't have a strategy that would get him to where he wanted to go. The model we will describe offers both.

Leadership experts have long argued for consultation among leaders and followers when conditions permit, usually when the problem is complex, expertise is widely distributed among the members of a group, and there is time for deliberation. Then, there are the times when the pace of action is fast and orders are called for. The challenge these days is that the tempo of operations has increased in general. It is too easy to believe that every situation is one in which there is no time for consultation and no place for alternative ideas. Yet, the evidence is clear that followers often have information and ideas that are essential to the success of operations. In fact, the failure to bring all perspectives to bear on an operation can have disastrous consequences.

On January 28, 1980, the Coast Guard cutter *Blackthorn* sank in Tampa Bay after colliding with an inbound freighter. Twenty-six lives were lost. In the subsequent investigation, investigators determined that each of the six persons in the pilothouse that day had information vital to the well-being of the ship, but that information was not shared. An environment that encouraged the sharing of information did not exist, and some personnel "on the bridge" had disengaged from the operation.

Dr. Robert Ginnett of the Center for Creative Leadership has studied airline crews in order to describe the behavior of the most effective pilots in command. Ginnett found that the most effective leaders were those who engaged the entire crew as partners, with the result that each was fully involved in and attentive to the ongoing mission. Moreover, the leader had created an environment in which crew members were enabled to behave as partners, sharing information as they got it, offering alternative perspectives without fear, and actively seeking ways to improve operations at all times.

Partners are those who have the competence and energy to do the job that they are assigned but who are also attentive to the purpose of the organization. At any time partners understand the goals of their leader and use this understanding to focus their own efforts. Such followers seek to master the skills required for their job and maximize their own accomplishments while seeking also to understand their boss's agenda and the strategy for accomplishing that agenda. Partners understand how to get ideas into play when the tempo of operations is high and when it is time to do what they are told.

If an organization is characterized by strong relationships among leaders and followers at all levels, purpose and direction are transmitted throughout the chain of command. Purpose informs and guides every choice, and contradictions between observed actions and purpose are apparent to all. Questions arise when members can see a deviation from purpose. Seniors welcome questions because they see the question as either an opportunity for improved operations or an opportunity to educate followers in order to increase their understanding of how the command operates to achieve the mission.

The most effective leaders develop their followers as partners by teaching them how to play this role. But not all organizational members are, or need to be, partners. The role of partner is reserved for mature team members who are high performers with the experience and commitment to understand the big picture. It is a role to which all service members can aspire and is not dependent upon rank or position. Leaders and followers who behave as partners make modern organizations work at all times and under all conditions.

Sometimes the best way to staff an organization that will rely on its members' behaving as partners is to hire them. At other times, leaders will need to develop partners from those assigned to the unit. In either case, leaders who have to hire or develop partners need a model to guide their efforts. What follows is such a model.

A MODEL FOR EVALUATING FOLLOWERS AS PARTNERS

Partners and Other Followers

The most effective followers know that they cannot be fully effective unless they work in partnership, which requires both a commitment to high performance and a commitment to developing effective relationships with partners (including their boss), whose collaboration is essential to success in their own work. These followers are intent on high performance and recognize that they share the responsibility for the quality of the relationship they have with their leaders. These followers are partners, but the two dimensions that define partnership (performance initiative and relationship initiative) also describe three other follower roles that are familiar to organizational leaders: the subordinate, the contributor, and the politician.

Types of Followers

Subordinate. The subordinate is the "traditional" follower who does what he or she is told—competent at a satisfactory level but not one to whom the organization looks for leadership or to whom challenging assignments are given. The subordinate keeps a job and may rise in a seniority-driven organization but demonstrates neither a sensitivity to relationships nor a commitment to high performance. The subordinate is the only kind of valued follower in hierarchical organizations that operate only with orders from the top and obedience from the bottom. In organizational settings where this is desired behavior, "good" followers will exhibit these characteristics even when they are fully capable of and even desirous of behaving like individuals described in other quadrants of this analysis. It is also the likely style of a somewhat or completely disaffected follower who is not interested in giving anything extra, or whose job is not one of his or her primary concerns.

Contributor. This type of follower behaves in an exemplary way: works hard and is known for the quality of his or her work. This person rarely seeks to understand the perspective of the boss, however, and generally waits for direction before turning to new challenges. Although this person is thorough and creative in obtaining the resources, information, and skills that are needed to do the job, the interpersonal dynamics of the workplace are not of primary concern, and therefore, this person rarely shares her or his expertise and knowledge. These individuals can develop into full partners by gaining skills and perspectives on the relationship initiative dimension. Alternatively, their valued inclinations can be accommodated and their work value maximized by allowing them to focus on what they excel at and feel comfortable doing, and by removing or minimizing aspects of the job that call for interpersonal relationships with the boss.

Politician. The politician gives more attention to managing relationships than to maximizing performance. This person possesses valuable interpersonal qualities that are often misdirected or misunderstood. Followers such as these are unusually sensitive to interpersonal dynamics and are valuable for their ability to contribute when interpersonal difficulties have arisen or

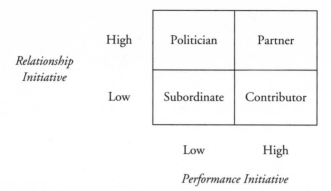

FIGURE 12.1   Follower Styles

might arise. They can provide valuable assistance to the leader because they are willing and able to give insights into group relationships. However, often these followers neglect the defined aspects of their jobs in favor of the more relationship-oriented or political aspects of their relationship with the boss. This is a particular problem when others rely on them for job performance. Politicians can become full partners by focusing on job performance and learning how to balance these two concerns, or they can be accepted as they are and given responsibilities that call primarily for the skills and inclinations they possess.

Partner.   The partner is committed to high performance and effective relationships. In fact, the energy given to the development of relationships serves the purpose of gaining the kind of understanding that leads to plans and actions that anticipate new directions and contributions that serve unmet needs. Organizations that anticipate and keep pace with change in the global environment are characterized by leaders who encourage partnership and followers who seek to be partners.

FOLLOWER BEHAVIORS

These four types of followers can be identified by their behavior on the performance initiative dimension and relationship initiative dimension.

Performance Initiative

Performance initiative refers to the follower's active efforts to do a good job. A person who demonstrates a great deal of performance initiative finds ways to improve his or her own performance in the organization, which might include improving skills, sharing resources with team members, and trying new strategies. The people at the high end of this scale understand that their future depends on the future of the organization and are not content to simply do what they were asked to do yesterday. At the low end of this scale one stills finds satisfactory performers, whereas at the high end one finds experts who lead in their fields and whose contributions strengthen the performance of the organization.

To assess this dimension of follower initiative, we need to consider the extent to which the follower thinks of ways to get his or her assigned job done, the extent to which the follower treats himself or herself as a valuable resource, how well the follower works with coworkers, and what view the follower takes toward organizational and environmental change. Followers differ in the extent to which they take positive initiatives in each of the four domains described below:

Doing the Job. Followers vary in the extent to which they strive to be as good as they can be at what they do. At one end of this continuum are the followers who go through the motions, performing the tasks that are assigned to them up to the minimum standards required to keep their jobs, and doing little or no more. At the other end of this continuum, some followers care deeply about the quality of their performance. They set their own standards, ones that are higher than the minimum prescribed by the organization, and that are focused on effective performance rather than on merely meeting defined standards. For these followers, work is an important and integral part of their lives. They take pride in what they do and apply high personal standards for performance from which they can derive personal satisfaction.

Working with Others. Another important dimension of follower performance is working with others in the organization. At one extreme is the follower who cannot work well with others and therefore is continually involved in arguments and disputes, irritating everyone in the process. These followers actually interfere with the performance of others in the organization. In contrast, some followers work alone. They do not have difficulties with others, but they do not really work with them either. Their performance is solely dependent on what they themselves do (or so they think). But many followers do take advantage of working with others, to varying degrees. When followers work effectively with others, they are able to balance their own personal interests with the interests of others, discovering a common purpose and working to achieve common goals. That means emphasizing cooperation over competition, finding success in the success of the whole group instead of in self-achievement only.

Self as a Resource.   Another important aspect of follower performance initiative lies in the extent to which the person treats herself or himself as a valuable but limited resource. Some followers pay little attention to their own well-being, neglecting physical, mental, and emotional health. Although this may yield some short-term benefits for the organization if the follower is effective in important ways, in the long run such neglect is likely to lead to burnout or stagnation (depending on the other aspects of follower performance initiative). Followers who will be effective over the long haul recognize that they are their own most valuable resource and take care to maintain their own physical, mental, and emotional health by balancing work and other interests (e.g., family and friends, community activities and relations, physical and nutritional fitness).

Embracing Change.   The other important dimension of follower initiative is the follower's orientation to change. In many cases, a follower's reaction to change is to ignore it or hide from it. Change is threatening and confusing, altering the time-honored and familiar. Some followers actively take the initiative to resist change, finding ways to prevent things from being done differently. At the positive end of this dimension are the followers who look for new and better ways to do things because they are committed to continuous quality improvement and see change as the vehicle for continuous improvement. These followers see change as an opportunity for improvement for themselves and their organizations. Such followers anticipate or look for change. They can be extremely effective as agents for change, by explaining to their coworkers the advantages of doing things differently, showing by example how different doesn't have to mean worse.

Relationship Initiative

Relationship initiative refers to the follower's active attempts to improve his or her working relationship with the leader. People who demonstrate a high degree of relationship initiative find ways to help the leader succeed because they know that "you can't succeed if your boss fails."

The other absolutely vital, but typically neglected, dimension of follower initiative that has to be understood is the follower's relationship to the leader. On the relationship initiative dimension there are several questions to be explored: To what extent does the follower understand and identify with the leader's vision for the organization? Does the follower actively try to engender mutual trust with the leader? To what extent is the follower willing to communicate in a courageous fashion with the leader? How actively does the follower work to negotiate differences with the leader? At the low end of this dimension people take the relationship that they are given. At the high end they work to increase openness and understanding in order to gain a perspective that can inform their choices as a partner. The following subscales describe relationship initiative:

Identifying with the Leader. Followers vary considerably in the extent to which they understand and empathize with the leader's perspective. Many followers simply do not. Viewing the leader as something strange and not quite human, they do not try to think about how things look from the leader's perspective or what the leader's goals or problems might be. In organizations with clear hierarchical structures and relatively strict chains of command, it is probably quite natural to see this element missing in the typical follower's approach to the leader. Followers may even be encouraged to think of their leaders as sufficiently different (i.e., superior) as to defy understanding by mere mortals. In contrast, some followers have thought more dispassionately about their leaders, understand their aspirations and styles, and have developed sufficient respect for the leader to adopt those aspirations as their own. These followers understand the leader's perspective, do what they can to help the leader succeed, and take pride and satisfaction in the leader's accomplishments.

Building Trust. Followers can also take the initiative to act in ways that will build their leader's confidence and trust in them. This means that the follower will look for and take advantage of opportunities to demonstrate to the leader that she or he is reliable, discreet, and loyal. Followers who demonstrate these qualities to their leaders will in turn be asked for their opinions and reactions to new ideas. Followers who do not seek out such opportunities for building trust, who do not understand or see as important this aspect of their relationship with their leaders, will be treated accordingly and will not be in a position to help their leaders as much as they might.

Courageous Communication.   Part of building trust includes being honest, even when that is not the easiest thing to do. This aspect of relationship initiative is important enough to consider in its own right. Some followers fear (often with good reason) being the bearer of bad news and are likely to refrain from speaking unpleasant truths. This can range from the classic notion of the yes-man to simply refraining from speaking one's mind when that might be uncomfortable for the speaker and listeners. But followers who take the initiative in their relationships with their leaders are willing to speak the truth even when others may not enjoy hearing the truth, in order to serve the goals of the organization. A follower who exhibits courageous communication takes risks in order to be honest.

Negotiating Differences.   Another aspect of relationship initiative concerns the follower's approach to differences that arise between leaders and followers. A follower who is oriented toward improving her or his relationship with the leader is in a position to negotiate or mediate these differences. In the case of a difference of opinion between a leader and follower, the follower may engage in open or hidden opposition to the leader's decisions, hiding his or her differences of opinion and quickly agreeing with the leader regardless of true personal opinion. Alternatively, the follower who is concerned about the leader-follower relationship will air these differences in order to have a real discussion that may persuade either party or lead to a compromise that is satisfactory to everyone.

DEVELOPING PARTNERS

Creating the conditions that lead followers to partnership requires first that leaders know what they are looking for in their followers. The model we have described above offers this picture. Creating the right conditions for effective followership next requires a clear understanding of practical steps that invite followers to partnership.

Sharon Moore, owner of Moore Interiors, makes a point of making room for partners in her company. When Moore Interiors reorganized and moved functions among its two buildings, the warehouse became the company's new headquarters. Sharon decided to identify the former warehouse as "Moore Interiors" in bold letters on the warehouse and gave the job of putting the name on the building to a salesman in the company. She also gave the salesman the license to figure out how to do the job, which would take a week.

As the work unfolded Sharon could see that the salesman had chosen a different approach than she originally had in mind. He was putting three-foot-tall letters six feet apart so that "Moore Interiors" would stretch across the entire face of the large building and "Beauty for Rooms" (the company's motto) would make a bold statement on the opposite side of the building. Sharon thought about redirecting the young man's efforts but then thought of the cost to personal initiative of doing so. She decided to let the salesman finish the way he had started. In the weeks after the job was done, the company received numerous compliments on the appearance of the new headquarters building. Sharon decided that the job did look better than what she had had in mind, but more important, one more salesman understood that his ideas were valued. Even more important, Sharon shared her reflections about this event with all of the employees. The wider result was that everyone understood how the owner viewed quality, initiative, and teamwork.

Those leaders who share their own thinking about why they do what they do and push their followers to think with them about why things work the way they do also push their followers to become partners. Those who encourage feedback on operations and welcome questions from their followers have a greater chance of achieving partnership. Ginnett's work shows that the difference between the best pilots in command and the others is that they directly engage each member of the crew and empower them to be active partners in the success of the mission. The best partners learn how to share what they see and think because their leaders teach them when to give their input—and when not to. Leaders who work day-to-day to create partners will find them ready when they need them, and partners who are willing to accept this role will find that they are valued by their leaders.

REFERENCES

Ginnett, R. C. 1990. "Crews as groups: Their formation and their leadership." In E. L. Wiener, B. B. Kanki, and R. L. Helmreich (Eds.), *Cockpit Resource Management*. San Diego: Academic Press.

Pain, J. 2004. "Cubans in floating Buick to be sent home." *The Oregonian*. February 5.

Rosenbach, W. E., Pittman, T. S., and Potter, E. H. 1997. "The Performance and Relationship Questionnaire." Gettysburg College, Gettysburg, PA.

— IV —

LEARNING TO LEAD

Can leadership be taught? This is the wrong question. A more relevant question is: Can leadership be learned? The answer is a resounding yes! The potential for good leadership is widely dispersed in our society, not limited to a privileged few. Learning about leadership means learning to recognize bad leadership as well as good. Learning about leadership involves understanding the dynamic relationship between leader and followers; recognizing the differing contexts and situations of the leadership landscape; and understanding the importance of the behavioral sciences, biography, the classics, economics, history, logic, and related disciplines, all of which provide the perspective so important to leadership effectiveness. Individuals committed to improving their leadership effectiveness will take advantage of opportunities to improve their skills as speakers, debaters, negotiators, problem clarifiers, and advocates. Would-be leaders will also follow Thomas Cronin's advice to "squint with their ears." Most important, the developing leader learns to appreciate her or his strengths and weaknesses. We recall Colin Powell's response to a student's question regarding how one could best prepare to be an effective leader. General Powell responded by advising students to study past and present leaders but not to get too hung up on role models because they need to be authentically themselves and to learn from their own mistakes. We strongly believe that leadership can be learned from multiple perspectives. We agree with John Gardner that what you learn after you know it all is what really matters.

What leaders do is important, but how they do it is of equal concern. Although much research has focused on identifying the one best style, no single style or personality is best for all situations. The leader acting alone can often accomplish relatively simple tasks, but the more ambiguous and complex the situation, the greater the need for a participative style. Participatory decisions, however, are time consuming; the path to consensus is often long and tedious. Thus timing as well as the situation is involved in leadership style.

When decisions must be made quickly, the leader must act alone with the available information and, very often, on intuition. Intuition is not guessing; rather, it is the recollection of experiences and knowledge without the conscious recognition of how the cumulative information was recalled. In the conflict of facts versus intuition, the latter is often the best choice for effective leadership, depending on the context.

All successful leaders have a global orientation. They must thoroughly understand not only the microcosm of their organization but also where the organization fits in the larger perspective. To create a vision of the future the leader must understand the environment in which the organization exists today and the one in which it will exist tomorrow. Leaders serve an increasingly diverse constituency and must seek and value that diversity if they are to transform their vision into action.

According to Thomas Cronin, students of leadership must develop their capacities for observation, reflection, imagination, invention, and judgment. They must also learn to communicate and listen effectively and develop their abilities to gather and interpret evidence, marshal facts, and employ the most rigorous methods in the pursuit of knowledge. They need to develop an unyielding commitment to the truth balanced with a full appreciation of what remains to be learned. Students of leadership learn from mentors who lead by example and who make desirable things happen. We agree!

Ultimately, leadership is a choice made by those who have achieved self-knowledge and self-confidence. Leadership development focuses on self-knowledge. The accumulation of self-knowledge allows us to make choices. Effective leaders seem to continue their quest for both as an ongoing activity.

LEADERSHIP PERSPECTIVES

In "What Makes a Leader?" (Chapter 13), Daniel Goleman, the premier expert on emotional intelligence, describes why emotional intelligence is the crucial component of leadership and how it is displayed in leaders. Superb leaders have very different ways of leading, and different situations call for different styles of leadership. The author has found, however, that effective leaders are alike in one crucial way: They all have a high degree of what has come to be known as emotional intelligence. Goleman discusses each component of emotional intelligence and shows how to recognize it in potential leaders and how it can be learned.

In Chapter 14, "Don't Bother Putting Leadership into People," Joseph A. Raelin argues that most leadership training that is being conducted in corporate off-sites is ill advised because the intent of most of this training is to put leadership into people so that they can transform themselves and then their organizations. Instead, Raelin suggests that leadership should be put directly into the organization, where it belongs.

In "Mentor Networks and Career Success: Lessons for Turbulent Times" (Chapter 15), Suzanne C. de Janasz, Sherry E. Sullivan, and Vicki Whiting describe how many of the key professional achievements of leaders are attributed to the guidance of mentors. Because organizational structures have changed and careers have become boundaryless, the aspiring leader today must make use of an intelligent network of multiple mentors. The authors offer five specific strategies for creating effective developmental relationships and building intelligent career networks.

Douglas A. Ready and Jay A. Conger, in Chapter 16, "Why Leadership-Development Efforts Fail," describe three pathologies: the "ownership is power" mind-set, the productization of leadership development, and make-believe metrics that cause many leadership development programs to fail. The authors then describe ways to overcome these destructive tendencies and how to create a successful pipeline of next-generation leaders.

In "Global Leadership, Education, and Human Survival" (Chapter 17), Christopher Williams describes global leadership as the pivotal point for appropriate policies and action to ensure human survival, but a fast-changing world requires learning leadership. Serving leaders have little time for formal learning and must learn on the job through reciprocal peer interaction and transactional relationships with their followers. But according to Williams, the global aspect demands another dimension, cybernetic learning, in which an awareness of global ethics is central.

13

~

What Makes a Leader?

Daniel Goleman

All businesspeople know a story about a highly intelligent, highly skilled executive who was promoted into a leadership position only to fail at the job. And they also know a story about someone with solid—but not extraordinary—intellectual abilities and technical skills who was promoted into a similar position and then soared.

Such anecdotes support the widespread belief that identifying individuals with the "right stuff" to be leaders is more art than science. After all, the personal styles of superb leaders vary: Some leaders are subdued and analytical; others shout their manifestos from the mountaintops. And just as important, different situations call for different types of leadership. Most mergers need a sensitive negotiator at the helm, whereas many turnarounds require a more forceful authority.

I have found, however, that the most effective leaders are alike in one crucial way: They all have a high degree of what has come to be known as *emotional intelligence*. It's not that IQ and technical skills are irrelevant. They do matter, but mainly as "threshold capabilities"; that is, they are the entry-level requirements for executive positions. But my research, along with other recent studies, clearly shows that emotional intelligence is the sine qua non of leadership. Without it, a person can have the best training in the world, an incisive, analytical mind, and an endless supply of smart ideas, but he still won't make a great leader.

In the course of the past year, my colleagues and I have focused on how emotional intelligence operates at work. We have examined the relationship between emotional intelligence and effective performance, especially in leaders. And we have observed how emotional intelligence shows itself on the job. How can you tell if someone has high emotional intelligence, for example, and how can you recognize it in yourself? In the following pages, we'll explore these questions, taking each of the components of emotional intelligence—self-awareness, self-regulation, motivation, empathy, and social skill—in turn.

EVALUATING EMOTIONAL INTELLIGENCE

Most large companies today have employed trained psychologists to develop what are known as *competency models* to aid them in identifying, training, and promoting likely stars in the leadership firmament. These psychologists have also developed such models for lower-level positions. And in recent years, I have analyzed competency models from eighty-eight companies, most of which were large and global and included the likes of Lucent Technologies, British Airways, and Credit Suisse.

In carrying out this work, my objective was to determine which personal capabilities drove outstanding performance within these organizations, and to what degree they did so. I grouped capabilities into three categories: purely technical skills like accounting and business planning; cognitive abilities like analytical reasoning; and competencies demonstrating emotional intelligence such as the ability to work with others and effectiveness in leading change.

To create some of the competency models, psychologists asked senior managers at the companies to identify the capabilities that typified the organization's most outstanding leaders. To create other models, the psychologists used objective criteria such as a division's profitability to differentiate the star performers at senior levels within their organizations from the average ones. Those individuals were then extensively interviewed and tested, and their capabilities were compared. This process resulted in the creation of lists of ingredients for highly effective leaders. The lists ranged in length from seven to fifteen items and included such ingredients as initiative and strategic vision.

When I analyzed all these data, I found dramatic results. To be sure, intellect was a driver of outstanding performance. Cognitive skills such as big-picture thinking and long-term vision were particularly important. But when I calculated the ratio of technical skills, IQ, and emotional intelligence

TABLE 13.1   Five Components of Emotional Intelligence at Work

	Definition	*Hallmarks*
Self-Awareness	The ability to recognize and understand your moods, emotions, and drives, as well as their effect on others	Self-confidence Realistic self-assessment Self-deprecating sense of humor
Self-Regulation	The ability to control or redirect disruptive impulses and moods The propensity to suspend judgment—to think before acting	Trustworthiness and integrity Comfort with ambiguity Openness to change
Motivation	A passion to work for reasons that go beyond money or status A propensity to pursue goals with energy and persistence	Strong drive to achieve Optimism, even in the face of failure Organizational commitment
Empathy	The ability to understand the emotional makeup of other people Skill in treating people according to their emotional reactions	Expertise in building and retaining talent Cross-cultural sensitivity Service to clients and customers
Social Skill	Proficiency in managing relationships and building networks An ability to find common ground and build rapport	Effectiveness in leading change Persuasiveness Expertise in building and leading teams

as ingredients of excellent performance, emotional intelligence proved to be twice as important as the others for jobs at all levels.

Moreover, my analysis showed that emotional intelligence played an increasingly important role at the highest levels of the company, where differences in technical skills are of negligible importance. In other words, the higher the rank of a person considered a star performer, the more emotional intelligence capabilities showed up as the reason for his or her effectiveness.

When I compared star performers with average ones in senior leadership positions, nearly 90 percent of the difference in their profiles was attributable
to emotional intelligence factors rather than cognitive abilities.

Other researchers have confirmed that emotional intelligence not only
distinguishes outstanding leaders but can also be linked to strong performance. The findings of the late David McClelland, the renowned researcher
in human and organizational behavior, are a good example. In a 1996 study
of a global food and beverage company, McClelland found that when senior
managers had a critical mass of emotional intelligence capabilities, their divisions outperformed yearly earnings goals by 20 percent. Meanwhile, division leaders without that critical mass underperformed by almost the same
amount. McClelland's findings, interestingly, held as true in the company's
U.S. divisions as in its divisions in Asia and Europe.

In short, the numbers are beginning to tell us a persuasive story about the
link between a company's success and the emotional intelligence of its leaders.
And just as important, research is also demonstrating that people can, if they
take the right approach, develop their emotional intelligence (see Exhibit 13.1).

SELF-AWARENESS

Self-awareness is the first component of emotional intelligence—which
makes sense when one considers that the Delphic oracle gave the advice to
"know thyself" thousands of years ago. Self-awareness means having a deep
understanding of one's emotions, strengths, weaknesses, needs, and drives.
People with strong self-awareness are neither overly critical nor unrealisti-
cally hopeful. Rather, they are honest—with themselves and with others.

People who have a high degree of self-awareness recognize how their feelings affect them, other people, and their job performance. Thus a self-aware
person who knows that tight deadlines bring out the worst in him plans his
time carefully and gets his work done well in advance. Another person with
high self-awareness will be able to work with a demanding client. She will
understand the client's impact on her moods and the deeper reasons for her
frustration. "Their trivial demands take us away from the real work that
needs to be done," she might explain. And she will go one step further and
turn her anger into something constructive.

Self-awareness extends to a person's understanding of his or her values
and goals. Someone who is highly self-aware knows where he is headed and
why; so, for example, he will be able to be firm in turning down a job offer

EXHIBIT 13.1   Can Emotional Intelligence Be Learned?

For ages, people have debated whether leaders are born or made. So, too, goes the debate about emotional intelligence. Are people born with certain levels of empathy, for example, or do they acquire empathy as a result of life's experiences? The answer is both. Scientific inquiry strongly suggests that there is a genetic component to emotional intelligence. Psychological and developmental research indicates that nurture plays a role as well. How much of each perhaps will never be known, but research and practice clearly demonstrate that emotional intelligence can be learned.

One thing is certain: Emotional intelligence increases with age. There is an old-fashioned word for the phenomenon: maturity. Yet even with maturity, some people still need training to enhance their emotional intelligence. Unfortunately, far too many training programs that intend to build leadership skills—including emotional intelligence—are a waste of time and money. The problem is simple: They focus on the wrong part of the brain.

Emotional intelligence is born largely in the neurotransmitters of the brain's limbic system, which governs feelings, impulses, and drives. Research indicates that the limbic system learns best through motivation, extended practice, and feedback. Compare this with the kind of learning that goes on in the neocortex, which governs analytical and technical ability. The neocortex grasps concepts and logic. It is the part of the brain that figures out how to use a computer or make a sales call by reading a book. Not surprisingly—but mistakenly—it is also the part of the brain targeted by most training programs aimed at enhancing emotional intelligence. When such programs take, in effect, a neocortical approach, my research with the consortium for Research on Emotional Intelligence in Organizations has shown they can even have a *negative* impact on people's job performance.

To enhance emotional intelligence, organizations must refocus their training to include the limbic system. They must help people break old behavioral habits and establish new ones. That not only takes much more time than conventional training programs, but it also requires an individualized approach.

Imagine an executive who is thought to be low on empathy by her colleagues. Part of that deficit shows itself as an inability to listen; she interrupts people and doesn't pay close attention to what they're saying. To fix the problem, the executive needs to be motivated to change, and then she needs practice and feedback from others in the company. A colleague or coach could be tapped to let the executive know when she has been observed failing to listen. She would then have to replay the incident and give a better response, that is, demonstrate her ability to absorb what others are saying. And the executive could be directed to observe certain executives who listen well and to mimic their behavior.

With persistence and practice, such a process can lead to lasting results. I know one Wall Street executive who sought to improve his empathy—specifically his ability to read people's reactions and see their perspectives. Before beginning his quest, the executive's subordinates were terrified of working with him. People even went so far as to hide bad news from him. Naturally, he was shocked when finally confronted with these facts. He went home and told his family—but they only confirmed what he had heard at work. When their opinions on any given subject did not mesh with his, they, too, were frightened of him.

Enlisting the help of a coach, the executive went to work to heighten his empathy through practice and feedback. His first step was to take a vacation to a foreign country where he did not speak the language. While there, he monitored his reactions to the unfamiliar and his openness to people who were different from him. When he returned home, humbled by his week abroad, the executive asked his coach to shadow him for parts of the day, several times a week, in order to critique how he treated people with new or different perspectives. At the same time, he consciously used on-the-job interactions as opportunities to practice "hearing" ideas that differed from his. Finally, the executive had himself videotaped in meetings and asked those who worked for and with him to critique his ability to acknowledge and understand the feelings of others. It took several months, but the executive's emotional intelligence did ultimately rise, and the improvement was reflected in his overall performance on the job.

It's important to emphasize that building one's emotional intelligence cannot—will not—happen without sincere desire and concerted effort. A brief seminar won't help; nor can one buy a how-to manual. It is much harder to learn to empathize—to internalize empathy as a natural response to people—than it is to become adept at regression analysis. But it can be done. "Nothing great was ever achieved without enthusiasm," wrote Ralph Waldo Emerson. If your goal is to become a real leader, these words can serve as a guidepost in your efforts to develop high emotional intelligence.

---

that is tempting financially but does not fit with his principles or long-term goals. A person who lacks self-awareness is apt to make decisions that bring on inner turmoil by treading on buried values. "The money looked good so I signed on," someone might say two years into a job, "but the work means so little to me that I'm constantly bored." The decisions of self-aware people mesh with their values; consequently, they often find work to be energizing.

How can one recognize self-awareness? First and foremost, it shows itself as candor and an ability to assess oneself realistically. People with high self-awareness are able to speak accurately and openly—although not necessarily effusively or confessionally—about their emotions and the impact they have on their work. For instance, one manager I know of was skeptical about a new personal-shopper service that her company, a major department-store chain, was about to introduce. Without prompting from her team or her boss, she offered them an explanation. "It's hard for me to get behind the rollout of this service," she admitted, "because I really wanted to run the project but I wasn't selected. Bear with me while I deal with that." The manager did indeed examine her feelings; a week later, she was supporting the project fully.

Such self-knowledge often shows itself in the hiring process. Ask a candidate to describe a time he got carried away by his feelings and did something he later regretted. Self-aware candidates will be frank in admitting to failure—and will often tell their tales with a smile. One of the hallmarks of self-awareness is a self-deprecating sense of humor.

Self-awareness can also be identified during performance reviews. Self-aware people know—and are comfortable talking about—their limitations and strengths, and they often demonstrate a thirst for constructive criticism. By contrast, people with low self-awareness interpret the message that they need to improve as a threat or a sign of failure.

Self-aware people can also be recognized by their self-confidence. They have a firm grasp of their capabilities and are less likely to set themselves up to fail by, for example, overstretching on assignments. They know, too, when to ask for help. And the risks they take on the job are calculated. They won't ask for a challenge that they know they can't handle alone. They'll play to their strengths.

Consider the actions of a mid-level employee who was invited to sit in on a strategy meeting with her company's top executives. Although she was the most junior person in the room, she did not sit there quietly, listening in awestruck or fearful silence. She knew she had a head for clear logic and the skill to present ideas persuasively, and she offered cogent suggestions about the company's strategy. At the same time, her self-awareness stopped her from wandering into territory where she knew she was weak.

Despite the value of having self-aware people in the workplace, my research indicates that senior executives don't often give self-awareness the credit it deserves when they look for potential leaders. Many executives mistake candor about feelings for "wimpiness" and fail to give due respect to employees who openly acknowledge their shortcomings. Such people are too readily dismissed as "not tough enough" to lead others.

In fact, the opposite is true. In the first place, people generally admire and respect candor. Further, leaders are constantly required to make judgment calls that require a candid assessment of capabilities—their own and those of others. Do we have the management expertise to acquire a competitor? Can we launch a new product within six months? People who assess themselves honestly—that is, self-aware people—are well suited to do the same for the organizations they run.

SELF-REGULATION

Biological impulses drive our emotions. We cannot do away with them—but we do much to manage them. Self-regulation, which is like an ongoing inner conversation, is the component of emotional intelligence that frees us from being prisoners of our feelings. People engaged in such a conversation feel bad moods and emotional impulses just as everyone else does, but they find ways to control them and even to channel them in useful ways.

Imagine an executive who has just watched a team of his employees present a botched analysis to the company's board of directors. In the gloom that follows, the executive might find himself tempted to pound on the table in anger or kick over a chair. He could leap up and scream at the group. Or he might maintain a grim silence, glaring at everyone before stalking off.

But if he had a gift for self-regulation, he would choose a different approach. He would pick his words carefully, acknowledging the team's poor performance without rushing to any hasty judgment. He would then step back to consider the reasons for the failure. Are they personal—a lack of effort? Are there any mitigating factors? What was his role in the debacle? After considering these questions, he would call the team together, lay out the incident's consequences, and offer his feelings about it. He would then present his analysis of the problem and a well-considered solution.

Why does self-regulation matter so much for leaders? First of all, people who are in control of their feelings and impulses—that is, people who are reasonable—are able to create an environment of trust and fairness. In such an environment, politics and infighting are sharply reduced and productivity is high. Talented people flock to the organization and aren't tempted to leave. And self-regulation has a trickle-down effect. No one wants to be known as a hothead when the boss is known for her calm approach. Fewer bad moods at the top mean fewer throughout the organization.

Second, self-regulation is important for competitive reasons. Everyone knows that business today is rife with ambiguity and change. Companies merge and break apart regularly. Technology transforms work at a dizzying pace. People who have mastered their emotions are able to roll with the changes. When a new change program is announced, they don't panic; instead, they are able to suspend judgment, seek out information, and listen to executives explain the new program. As the initiative moves forward, they are able to move with it.

Sometimes they even lead the way. Consider the case of a manager at a large manufacturing company. Like her colleagues, she had used a certain software program for five years. The program drove how she collected and reported data and how she thought about the company's strategy. One day, senior executives announced that a new program was to be installed that would radically change how information was gathered and assessed within the organization. While many people in the company complained bitterly about how disruptive the change would be, the manager mulled over the reasons for the new program and was convinced of its potential to improve performance. She eagerly attended training sessions—some of her colleagues refused to do so—and was eventually promoted to run several divisions, in part because she used the new technology so effectively.

I want to push the importance of self-regulation to leadership even further and make the case that it enhances integrity, which is not only a personal virtue but also an organizational strength. Many of the bad things that happen in companies are a function of impulsive behavior. People rarely plan to exaggerate profits, pad expense accounts, dip into the till, or abuse power for selfish ends. Instead, an opportunity presents itself, and people with low impulse control just say yes.

By contrast, consider the behavior of the senior executive at a large food company. The executive was scrupulously honest in his negotiations with local distributors. He would routinely lay out his cost structure in detail, thereby giving the distributors a realistic understanding of the company's pricing. This approach meant the executive couldn't always drive a hard bargain. Now, on occasion, he felt the urge to increase profits by withholding information about the company's costs. But he challenged that impulse—he saw that it made more sense in the long run to counteract it. His emotional self-regulation paid off in strong, lasting relationships with distributors that benefited the company more than any short-term financial gains would have.

The signs of emotional self-regulation, therefore, are not hard to miss: a propensity for reflection and thoughtfulness, comfort with ambiguity and change, and integrity—an ability to say no to impulsive urges.

Like self-awareness, self-regulation often does not get its due. People who can master their emotions are sometimes seen as cold fish—their considered responses are taken as a lack of passion. People with fiery temperaments are frequently thought of as "classic" leaders—their outbursts are considered hallmarks of charisma and power. But when such people make it to the top, their impulsiveness often works against them. In my research, extreme displays of negative emotion have never emerged as a driver of good leadership.

MOTIVATION

If there is one trait that virtually all effective leaders have, it is motivation. They are driven to achieve beyond expectations—their own and everyone else's. The key word here is *achieve*. Plenty of people are motivated by external factors such as a big salary or the status that comes from having an impressive title or being part of a prestigious company. By contrast, those with leadership potential are motivated by a deeply embedded desire to achieve for the sake of achievement.

If you are looking for leaders, how can you identify people who are motivated by the drive to achieve rather than by external rewards? The first sign is a passion for the work itself—such people seek out creative challenges, love to learn, and take great pride in a job well done. They also display an unflagging energy to do things better. People with such energy often seem restless with the status quo. They are persistent with their questions about why things are done one way rather than another; they are eager to explore new approaches to their work.

A cosmetics company manager, for example, was frustrated that he had to wait two weeks to get sales results from people in the field. He finally tracked down an automated phone system that would beep each of his salespeople at 5 P.M. every day. An automated message then prompted them to punch in their numbers—how many calls and sales they had made that day. The system shortened the feedback time on sales results from weeks to hours.

That story illustrates two other common traits of people who are driven to achieve. They are forever raising the performance bar, and they like to keep score. Take the performance bar first. During performance reviews, people with high levels of motivation might ask to be "stretched" by their supervisors. Of course, an employee who combines self-awareness with internal motivation will recognize her limits—but she won't settle for objectives that seem too easy to fulfill.

And it follows naturally that people who are driven to do better also want a way of tracking progress—their own, their team's, and their company's. Whereas people with low achievement motivation are often fuzzy about results, those with high achievement motivation often keep score by tracking such hard measures as profitability or market share. I know of a money manager who starts and ends his day on the Internet, gauging the performance of his stock fund against four industry-set benchmarks.

Interestingly, people with high motivation remain optimistic even when the score is against them. In such cases, self-regulation combines with achievement motivation to overcome the frustration and depression that come after a setback or failure. Take the case of another portfolio manager at a large investment company. After several successful years, her fund tumbled for three consecutive quarters, leading three large institutional clients to shift their business elsewhere.

Some executives would have blamed the nosedive on circumstances outside their control; others might have seen the setback as evidence of personal failure. This portfolio manager, however, saw an opportunity to prove she could lead a turnaround. Two years later, when she was promoted to a very senior level in the company, she described the experience as "the best thing that ever happened to me; I learned so much from it."

Executives trying to recognize high levels of achievement motivation in their people can look for one last piece of evidence: commitment to the organization. When people love their job for the work itself, they often feel committed to the organization that makes that work possible. Committed employees are likely to stay with an organization even when they are pursued by headhunters waving money.

It's not difficult to understand how and why a motivation to achieve translates into strong leadership. If you set the performance bar high for yourself, you will do the same for the organization when you are in a position to do so. Likewise, a drive to surpass goals and an interest in keeping score can be contagious. Leaders with these traits can often build a team of managers around them with the same traits. And of course, optimism and organizational commitment are fundamental to leadership—just try to imagine running a company without them.

EMPATHY

Of all the dimensions of emotional intelligence, empathy is the most easily recognized. We have all felt the empathy of a sensitive teacher or friend; we have all been struck by its absence in an unfeeling coach or boss. But when it comes to business, we rarely hear people praised, let alone rewarded, for their empathy. The very word seems unbusinesslike, out of place amid the tough realities of the marketplace.

But empathy doesn't mean a kind of "I'm okay, you're okay" mushiness. For a leader, that is, it doesn't mean adopting other people's emotions as one's own and trying to please everybody. That would be a nightmare—it would make action impossible. Rather, empathy means thoughtfully considering employees' feelings—along with other factors—in the process of making intelligent decisions.

For an example of empathy in action, consider what happened when two giant brokerage companies merged, creating redundant jobs in all their divisions. One division manager called his people together and gave a gloomy speech that emphasized the number of people who would soon be fired. The manager of another division gave his people a different kind of speech. He was up front about his own worry and confusion, and he promised to keep people informed and to treat everyone fairly.

The difference between these two managers was empathy. The first manager was too worried about his own fate to consider the feelings of his anxiety-stricken colleagues. The second knew intuitively what his people were feeling, and he acknowledged their fears with his words. Is it any surprise that the first manager saw his division sink as many demoralized people, especially the most talented, departed? By contrast, the second manager continued to be a strong leader, his best people stayed, and his division remained as productive as ever.

Empathy is particularly important today as a component of leadership for at least three reasons: the increasing use of teams, the rapid pace of globalization, and the growing need to retain talent.

Consider the challenge of leading a team. As anyone who has even been a part of one can attest, teams are cauldrons of bubbling emotions. They are often charged with reaching a consensus—hard enough with two people and much more difficult as the numbers increase. Even in groups with as few as four or five members, alliances form and clashing agendas get set. A team's leader must be able to sense and understand the viewpoints of everyone around the table.

That's exactly what a marketing manager at a large information technology company was able to do when she was appointed to lead a troubled team. The group was in turmoil, overloaded by work and missing deadlines. Tensions were high among the members. Tinkering with procedures was not enough to bring the group together and make it an effective part of the company.

So the manager took several steps. In a series of one-on-one sessions, she took the time to listen to everyone in the group—what was frustrating them, how they rated their colleagues, whether they felt they had been ignored. And then she directed the team in a way that brought it together: She encouraged people to speak more openly about their frustrations, and she helped people raise constructive complaints during meetings. In short, her empathy allowed her to understand her team's emotional makeup. The result was not just heightened collaboration among the members but also added business, as the team was called on for help by a wider range of internal clients.

Globalization is another reason for the rising importance of empathy for business leaders. Cross-cultural dialogue can easily lead to miscues and misunderstandings. Empathy is an antidote. People who have it are attuned to subtleties in body language; they can hear the message beneath the words being spoken. Beyond that, they have a deep understanding of the existence and importance of cultural and ethnic differences.

Consider the case of an American consultant whose team had just pitched a project to a potential Japanese client. In its dealings with Americans, the team was accustomed to being bombarded with questions after such a proposal, but this time it was greeted with a long silence. Other members of the team, taking the silence as disapproval, were ready to pack up and leave. The lead consultant gestured them to stop. Although he was not particularly familiar with Japanese culture, he read the client's face and posture and sensed not rejection but interest—even deep consideration. He was right: When the client finally spoke, it was to give the consulting firm the job.

Finally, empathy plays a key role in the retention of talent, particularly in today's information economy. Leaders have always needed empathy to develop and keep good people, but today the stakes are higher. When good people leave, they take the company's knowledge with them.

That's where coaching and mentoring come in. It has repeatedly been shown that coaching and mentoring pay off not just in better performance but also in increased job satisfaction and decreased turnover. But what makes coaching and mentoring work best is the nature of the relationship. Outstanding coaches and mentors get inside the heads of the people they are helping. They sense how to give effective feedback. They know when to push for better performance and when to hold back. In the way they motivate their protégés, they demonstrate empathy in action.

In what is probably sounding like a refrain, let me repeat that empathy doesn't get much respect in business. People wonder how leaders can make hard decisions if they are "feeling" for all the people who will be affected. But leaders with empathy do more than sympathize with the people around them: They use their knowledge to improve their companies in subtle but important ways.

SOCIAL SKILL

The first three components of emotional intelligence are all self-management skills. The last two, empathy and social skill, concern a person's ability to manage relationships with others. As a component of emotional intelligence, social skill is not as simple as it sounds. It's not just a matter of friendliness, although people with high levels of social skill are rarely mean-spirited. Social skill, rather, is friendliness with a purpose: moving people in the direction you desire, whether that's agreement on a new marketing strategy or enthusiasm about a new product.

Socially skilled people tend to have a wide circle of acquaintances, and they have a knack for finding common ground with people of all kinds—a knack for building rapport. That doesn't mean they socialize continually; it means they work according to the assumption that nothing important gets done alone. Such people have a network in place when the time for action comes.

Social skill is the culmination of the other dimensions of emotional intelligence. People tend to be very effective at managing relationships when they can understand and control their own emotions and can empathize with the feelings of others. Even motivation contributes to social skill. Remember that people who are driven to achieve tend to be optimistic, even in the face of setbacks or failure. When people are upbeat, their "glow" is cast upon conversations and other social encounters. They are popular, and for good reason.

Because it is the outcome of the other dimensions of emotional intelligence, social skill is recognizable on the job in many ways that will by now sound familiar. Socially skilled people, for instance, are adept at managing teams—that's their empathy at work. Likewise, they are expert persuaders— a manifestation of self-awareness, self-regulation, and empathy combined. Given those skills, good persuaders know when to make an emotional plea, for instance, and when an appeal to reason will work better. And motivation, when publicly visible, makes such people excellent collaborators; their passion for the work spreads to others, and they are driven to find solutions.

But sometimes social skill shows itself in ways the other emotional intelligence components do not. For instance, socially skilled people may at times appear not to be working while at work. They seem to be idly schmoozing—chatting in the hallways with colleagues or joking around with people who are not even connected to their "real" jobs. Socially skilled people, however, don't think it makes sense to arbitrarily limit the scope of their relationships. They build bonds widely because they know that in these fluid times, they may need help someday from people they are just getting to know today.

For example, consider the case of an executive in the strategy department of a global computer manufacturer. By 1993, he was convinced that the company's future lay with the Internet. Over the course of the next year, he found kindred spirits and used his social skill to stitch together a virtual community that cut across levels, divisions, and nations. He then used this de facto team to put up a corporate Web site, among the first by a major company. And on his own initiative, with no budget or formal status, he signed up the company to participate in an annual Internet industry convention. Calling on his allies and persuading various divisions to donate funds, he recruited more than fifty people from a dozen different units to represent the company at the convention.

Management took notice: Within a year of the conference, the executive's team formed the basis for the company's first Internet division, and he was formally put in charge of it. To get there, the executive had ignored conventional boundaries, forging and maintaining connections with people in every corner of the organization.

Is social skill considered a key leadership capability in most companies? The answer is yes, especially when compared with the other components of emotional intelligence. People seem to know intuitively that leaders need to manage relationships effectively; no leader is an island. After all, the leader's task is to get work done through other people, and social skill makes that possible. A leader who cannot express her empathy may as well not have it at all. And a leader's motivation will be useless if he cannot communicate his passion to the organization. Social skill allows leaders to put their emotional intelligence to work.

It would be foolish to assert that good old-fashioned IQ and technical ability are not important ingredients in strong leadership. But the recipe would not be complete without emotional intelligence. It was once thought that the components of emotional intelligence were "nice to have" in business leaders. But now we know that, for the sake of performance, these are ingredients that leaders "need to have."

It is fortunate, then, that emotional intelligence can be learned. The process is not easy. It takes time and, most of all, commitment. But the benefits that come from having a well-developed emotional intelligence, both for the individual and for the organization, make it worth the effort.

14

~

Don't Bother Putting
Leadership into People

Joseph A. Raelin

Most leadership training that is being conducted in corporate off-sites is ill advised. I make this bold statement because the intent of most of this training is to put leadership into people so that they can transform themselves and then their organizations upon their return. In this article, I shall address why the latter process is unlikely to succeed and what alternatives exist that can more effectively put leadership directly into the organization, where it belongs.

THE "LIST APPROACH" TO LEADERSHIP

The sheer amount of investment put into leadership training is enormous. Although no one has done a definitive study, an annual price tag of approximately $50 billion is often used. How is this money spent?

Most investment in leadership training subscribes to a "list" approach. What I mean is that the provider of the training typically has either an explicit or tacit list in mind of what attributes it takes to be a good leader. Trainees who attend the sessions are expected to learn and practice this list of leadership attributes. The presumption is that once they become experts in this list, they will have graduated into leadership. It should be noted that the list can be quite "scientific"—that is, empirically derived—and behaviorally

Reprinted with permission from *Academy of Management Executive* 18: 3 (August 2004), pp. 131–135. Copyright 2004 Academy of Management.

complex, not only in its origin but in its measurement. The measures might also be assembled from a variety of sources, for example, using 360-degree feedback.

The problem with the list approach is that most trainees find that, as a leadership development method, it doesn't work that well upon their return to their professional homes. The main reason for the lack of success is that though they have learned the list of leadership, no one else in their shop has. What was covered in class, though well presented by instructors and well understood by trainees, may not necessarily jibe with organizational realities. Hence, the new knowledge and practices may have to be strategically tucked away by our junior executives as they discover that no one has learned except for themselves.

This very condition was acknowledged by Steve Kerr when he was once asked about the basis for changing GE's leadership development program. "It's Organization Development 101," he quipped. "You should never send a changed person back to an unchanged environment."[1]

THE POSITION APPROACH TO LEADERSHIP

A parallel drawback of the list approach is that a sizable portion of leadership development activity is devoted to preparing people for leadership, defined as upper managerial "positions."[2] I submit that this very presupposition is flawed to begin with as long as we insist that leadership is built into positions or people in positions and not into an organizational unit or organization as a whole. The presumption that appears to be taken for granted is that only certain people are eligible for leadership; the remainder have to take their place as reliable followers.

We can draw the conclusion that much of leadership development prepares some people to assume leadership over others who are the followers. The very nature of this relationship between leaders and followers may be outdated. Consider that there appears to be consensus on how our twenty-first-century organizations are now being structured. We are witness to the breaking down of bureaucracy, as more widely distributed, interconnected, and virtual forms emerge built on webs of information.

Such forms require us to unlock the knowledge of our organizational members, empowering them to act on their own behalf and on behalf of their enterprises. Robert Kelley described the qualities that make for an effective follower. He claimed that such people should have the vision to see both the forest and the trees, the social capacity to work well with others, the strength of character to flourish without heroic status, the moral and psychological balance to pursue personal and corporate goals at no cost to either, and above all the desire to participate in a team effort for the accomplishment of some greater common purpose.[3]

How many of you would like to see these same characteristics in your leaders? If we have reached a point in our organizational evolution where we no longer need leaders "out in front," then in the same vein, we no longer need our followers "back in line." What are the implications of using the concept of follower within our knowledge enterprises since it connotes "doing what you are told" because you are less valuable than the leader? Might our leadership development efforts be better directed toward the role of leadership as a mutual social phenomenon rather than as a position of authority?

MANAGERS AND LEADERS

Two other significant implications of using the list and position approaches in leadership development appear to disconnect from the realities of our twenty-first-century organizational environment. The first is the degrading of the role of manager in the construction of contrasting lists between "managers" and "leaders." The origin of this dualism probably dates to a classic 1977 article in the *Harvard Business Review* by Abraham Zaleznik,[4] in which he depicted the manager as a rational, bureaucratic, dutiful, practical, and unimaginative dullard but the leader as a visionary, restless, experimental, even "twice-born" dynamo. By twice-born, he suggested that leaders emerge because of not having had a secure childhood, so they now have a second shot to shine. John Kotter[5] followed Zaleznik with his enumeration of distinctions between leaders and managers, though his classification was more benign. Kotter felt that organizations needed both leaders and managers, but each had a different role to perform. The manager is in charge of coping with complexity, while the leader handles change. Hence, managers focus on planning and budgeting, follow with organizing and staffing, and finish with controlling and problem solving. It is interesting to note that these functions fall into traditional control tasks long associated with bureaucratization.

Leaders, meanwhile, have a different set of functions, namely, setting a direction, aligning people to the direction, and motivating and inspiring them to fulfill the direction. In developing leadership, what are the implications of saying that managers are one thing and leaders another? It is true that managers are usually bureaucratically appointed and thus have position power throughout the middle of the organization. But they don't have to be "hired hands" (the root word for management is *manus* from the Latin for "hand") who are condemned to a life of unimaginatively carrying out corporate goals or endorsing the status quo. Managers are hardly excluded from leadership. They need to work with their peers, bosses, subordinates, and others, and in this constant interaction, there is opportunity for leadership to emerge from anyone. What might be most impressive about the manager is not taking the reins but supporting others to take them as the situation warrants.

THE LEADER AS MOTIVATOR

Another critical item on any list of leadership attributes is the practice of motivating. One of a leader's critical roles is to find the right combination of inducements to get subordinates to do things. In fact, what makes a leadership presumably transformative is when this motivation is designed to get subordinates to do things altruistically on behalf of the wider organization.

Although a noble goal, it is quite doubtful that motivation can be taught in one setting to be applied in another. Even if through proper diagnostics one could determine the right combination of inducements, there is an even more fundamental question of whether it is possible to motivate another human being to begin with. As Bill Drath and Chuck Palus noted, "People are already in motion."[6] Much of motivation theory and practice seems to be suggesting that people are somehow static, awaiting a signal from the leader to propel them into activity.

I am not suggesting that motivation does not exist; rather, it may have to rest within the individual who can choose how and whether to motivate himself or herself. In this regard, a leader may be able to work with others to shape the contours of motivation already in operation. And perhaps the purpose of leadership is to help individuals find ways to channel this already-existing motivation toward personal meaning and contribution to the greater good of their unit and organization.

THE CONTRIBUTION OF WORK-BASED LEARNING

Given the aforementioned contradictions of transferring learning detached from its practice that arise from using the list or position approach to leadership development, consider an alternative method known as *work-based learning*. Largely based on the principles of action learning, it is a gateway to collective leadership. In brief, work-based learning:

1. Views learning as acquired in the midst of action and dedicated to the task at hand.
2. Sees knowledge creation and utilization as collective activities wherein learning becomes everyone's job.
3. Demonstrates a learning-to-learn orientation that frees learners to question underlying assumptions of practice.[7]

Expressly merging theory with practice, work-based learning recognizes that the workplace offers as many opportunities for learning as the classroom. Such learning, however, needs to be centered around reflection on work practices. Hence, it offers people faced with the relentless pace of pervasive change an opportunity to overcome time pressures by reflecting upon and learning from the artistry of their actions.

Work-based learning subscribes to the contextualized view that learning arises not from the transfer of representations from one mind to the next but from the social relations embedded within a community of practice.[8] The context for learning is not taken for granted but is critically considered as learners adapt to new problems by reflecting together on their assumptions.[9] Theory emerges, therefore, as much from hands-on practice as it does from a priori conceptualizations. Further, work-based learning calls for replacing the acquisition of skill with the development of metacompetence. Metacompetence is competence that transcends itself. Rather than focus on job-specific skills, participants learn situation-specific principles that can attend to the variability in work demands. Work-based learning uses many diverse technologies, but primary is the deployment of action projects, learning teams, and other interpersonal experiences, such as mentorships, which permit and encourage learning dialogues. Learning dialogues that arise from direct peer observation are often most insightful. One of the most extraordinary features of the International Master's Program in Practicing Management[10] is the managerial exchange program in which participants pair up across companies and spend a week at each other's workplace, observing each other and exchanging reflections. The exchange opens managers' eyes to their own problems but as mirrored in a different setting. At PAREXEL International, a global biopharmaceutical services company, managerial participants in the company's work-based Developing Future Leaders program work in teams on projects that in the first year of operation were sponsored by the CEO and COO. However, in the midst of action, team participants are asked to slow down and reflect in learning teams to digest the action and to provide feedback to one another and to their team as a whole.

LEADERSHIP DEVELOPMENT THROUGH WORK-BASED LEARNING

Through work-based learning and its dialogic approaches, participants over time appear to surface a different form of leadership that is less characterized by the "great man" model and more by a collective form that I refer to as *leaderful*.[11] This term is new but is required because the idea of involving everyone in leadership and seeing leadership as a collective property is quite distinct from the archetype of leadership based on its root definition as the "person out in front." It also falls in some respects into the domain of "shared leadership," which has roots in empowerment, self-directed work teams, and self-leadership.[12] However, unlike some traditions in shared leadership, leaderful practice is collective rather than sequential or serial.[13]

THE TENETS OF LEADERFUL PRACTICE

Leaderful practice is based on four critical tenets referred to as "the four C's." The leadership of teams and organizations can be collective, concurrent, collaborative, and compassionate. In brief, collective leadership means that everyone in the group can serve as a leader; the team is not dependent on one individual to take over. Concurrent leadership means that not only can many members serve as leaders; they can do so at the same time. No one, not even the supervisor, has to stand down when someone is making a contribution as a leader. Collaborative leadership means that everyone is in control of and can speak for the entire team. All members pitch in to accomplish the work of the team. Together they engage in a mutual dialogue to determine what needs to be done and how to do it. Finally, in compassionate leadership, members commit to preserving the dignity of every single member of the team; that is, they consider each individual whenever any decision is made or action taken.

The link between work-based learning and leaderful practice can be established across all four tenets, but collective leadership is most particularly dependent on learning as a pervasive quality that characterizes the entire organization. If everyone participates in leadership, then no one needs to stand by in a dependent capacity. Everyone is primed for learning. In such an organization, members surface their insights, become comfortable questioning their suppositions, willingly seek feedback, experiment optimistically with new behaviors, reflect mutually on their operating assumptions, demonstrably support one another, and exhibit a humility that recognizes the limits of their knowledge.

AN APPRECIATION FOR PRACTICE

Practitioners also develop an appreciation for practice in two of its meanings. First, like artists, who use practice to bring a sense of balance, proportion, design, and beauty to their creations, practitioners may use practice as an ongoing process of experimentation, skill building, attention, and reflection.[14] The Boston Consortium for Higher Education (a network of top administrators among Boston's world-renowned institutions of higher learning) sponsors the Susan Vogt Leadership Fellows Program. Fellows participate in a year-long activity to develop their own and each other's leadership potential, among the practices of which are collaborating on an experimental project to benefit and potentially transform the consortium's member universities as well as the consortium itself.

A second meaning of practice derives from viewing field settings as apt loci of learning. In the field, learning can be targeted to actual problems faced by the enterprise in question. It can also be applied just in time and in the right dose to be helpful. Eventually, the distinction between a project as a place for learning and as a place for work becomes blurred. The Learning and Development Group at the Educational Testing Service (ETS) experimented with this very process when they changed the Learning for Business Results leadership development program in the past year.

Originally, each participant developed a project at that person's own work site. In the most recent version, according to Chief Learning Officer T. J. Elliott, the entire team of participants chose a single corporatewide project and worked on it together. As is the case at ETS, while working on their projects in work-based learning, participants typically assemble into learning teams, where they begin to question one another about their project experiences. In due course, they also extend their inquiry to each other's professional and personal experiences. They come to know learning as a collective process that extends beyond the individual.

In the learning team, the questioner learns as much as the speaker; indeed, the entire group learns to learn together as all members become mutually responsible for the decisions and actions of the team. They come to realize that people at all levels in the organization no longer need to protect themselves, especially if the position leader can open himself or herself up to the challenge of others.

ATTRIBUTES OF LEARNING LEADERS

Learning leaders can be characterized by a number of attributes:

- They commit to their own and others' continuous learning-in-action, freely exchanging knowledge.
- They develop a personal self-consciousness that values reflexive self-awareness, develops insight, and engenders a commitment to examine their own defensive reactions that may inhibit learning.[15]
- They develop the capacity to make contextually relevant judgments.
- They develop a peripheral awareness of others.
- They extend time to their colleagues, to listen to them and to suspend their own beliefs during precious moments of empathy.
- They develop a systemic perspective that understands organizations as an integrated set of relationships, not as bastions of isolated expertise.

ARAMARK's action-learning-based Executive Leadership Institute in its well-cataloged eleven-year history has graduated 358 managers who not only endeavor to exemplify these attributes but who, according to Lynn McKee, executive vice president of human resources, have contributed to the company's transformation into a collaborative culture that values partnerships, teamwork, and business line integration.

THE ROLE OF REFLECTIVE PRACTICE

Henry Mintzberg, referring to action learning as second-generation management development, asserts that action learning often emphasizes action at the expense of learning. To Mintzberg, learning is not doing as much as reflecting on doing.[16] There needs to be some conversion experience to link the practice in action learning with theory and insight so that any tacit knowledge can be captured and surfaced as learning. The most prominent of such conversion experiences is reflection, especially reflection that is concurrent with the experience and collectively brought out in the company of others—what is often called *reflective practice*. Unfortunately, it is often overlooked, so much so that the firm Leadership in International Management (LIM) trademarked their practice as "action-reflection learning."

Reflective practice has a number of other distinctive features that permit its consideration within the branch of learning referred to as *praxis*. First, it is not merely a cognitive or mental process, but it is also a behavioral process. It can involve others as opposed to being an individual experience. It is typically concerned with critical inquiry, probing into the deep recesses of experience. Last, it often requires some facilitation to help learners reframe their knowledge base.

In order to be proficient, managers need to bridge the gap between theory and practice and to learn from their own workplace environment. As they engage in public reflective practices, they create genuineness among one another. They don't need to fragment their work and their personal selves. It is expected that this degree of openness over time will secure a high rate of commitment to one's organization. As one piece of evidence, consider that at SUPERVALU's Work-Based Learning program for middle managers, program director Monica Abrams reports that after the first three years of the program, all but two of the eighty-two program participants stayed with the company.

Leadership development—let's call it "leaderful" development—can be designed to release the leadership potential in everyone. People don't need to wait for their marching orders from those who have been trained to lead them. Members of the organization should be thoughtful contributors, not physical appendages. The net effect of leaderful development has enormous bottom-line implications, not to mention its endorsement of the steadfast values of authenticity, trust, humility, and compassion.

ENDNOTES

1. Rifkin, G. 1996. Leadership: Can it be learned? *Fortune ASAP,* 8 April: 100–112.

2. Ready, D. A., and Conger, J. A. 2003. Why leadership-development efforts fail. *Sloan Management Review,* Spring: 83–88.

3. Kelley, R. E. 1988. In praise of followers. *Harvard Business Review,* 66 (6): 142–148.

4. Zaleznik, A. 1977. Managers and leaders: Are they different? *Harvard Business Review,* 55 (3): 67–78.

5. Kotter, J. P. 1990. What leaders really do. *Harvard Business Review,* 68 (3): 103–111.

6. Drath, W. H., and Palus, C. J. 1994. *Making common sense.* Greensboro, NC: Center for Creative Leadership. Also see Drath, W. H. 2001. *The deep blue sea: Rethinking the source of leadership.* San Francisco: Jossey-Bass.

7. Raelin, J. A. 2000. *Work-based learning: The new frontier of management development.* Upper Saddle River, NJ: Prentice-Hall.

8. Lave, J., and Wenger, E. 1991. *Situated learning: Legitimate peripheral participation.* Cambridge: Cambridge University Press.

9. Gherardi, S. 2001. From organizational learning to practice based knowing. *Human Relations,* 54 (1): 131–139.

10. See Mintzberg, H. 2004. Third-generation management development. *T&D,* 58 (3): 28–38.

11. Raelin, J. A. 2003. *Creating leaderful organizations: How to bring out leadership in everyone.* San Francisco: Berrett-Kohler.

12. Pearce, C. L., and Conger, J. A. 2002. *Shared leadership: Reframing the hows and whys of leadership.* Thousand Oaks, CA: Sage.

13. See Pearce, C. L., and Sims, H. P., Jr. 2002. Vertical versus shared leadership as predictors of the effectiveness of change management teams: An examination of aversive, directive, transactional, transformational, and empowering leader behaviors. *Group Dynamics: Theory, Research, and Practice,* 6 (2): 172–197.

14. Jones, M. 2000. Work as practice and vocation. *Leverage Points,* 25 (March).

15. See Argyris, C. 1982. *Reasoning, learning and action.* San Francisco: Jossey-Bass; and Senge, P. M. 1990. *The fifth discipline.* New York: Doubleday.

16. See Mintzberg, op. cit.; and Mintzberg, H. 2004. *Managers not MBAs.* San Francisco: Berrett-Koehler.

15

~

Mentor Networks
and Career Success:
Lessons for Turbulent Times

Suzanne C. de Janasz
Sherry E. Sullivan
Vicki Whiting

Simply put, mentors matter. Experts agree that individuals with mentors earn higher salaries, have higher job satisfaction, get more promotions, and have greater organizational commitment. In addition to these career-related benefits, protégés receive support that enhances their sense of personal identity, role clarity, and interpersonal competence. It has been well documented that individuals, especially women and minorities, miss an important career developmental experience if they do not have a mentor. Similarly, mentors reap benefits from the mentoring process including career rejuvenation; rekindling of creativity, energy, and satisfaction; new knowledge and technical expertise contributed by protégés; organizational rewards, status, and recognition for talent development; social and emotional learning; and feedback and support from protégés. Mentors enter into these relationships for reasons ranging from the selfish (increased organizational visibility and political allies as loyal protégés mature) to the altruistic (wishing to leave a legacy and contribute to the community). Even organizations benefit from

---

Adapted and reproduced with permission of the authors from *Academy of Management Executive*, 17: 4 (2003), pp. 78–91. Copyright 2003 Academy of Management.

mentoring, as mentoring facilitates the socialization process and helps acculturate junior members of the organization.[1]

Although recent best-selling books such as Lois Zachary's 2000 *The Mentor's Guide* and Jack Carew's 1999 *The Mentor: 15 Keys to Success in Sales, Business and Life* expound the values of having a senior person guide a newcomer's development, the idea of mentoring isn't new. The first documented example of mentoring dates back to the ancient Greeks, when King Odysseus asked Mentor to guide the growth of his son, Telemachus. What is new, however, are the recent and sweeping changes that have shaken long-held beliefs about careers and organizational life, necessitating a shift in thinking about the process of mentoring. Turbulent times, as evidenced by undervalued stock options, court cases questioning corporate ethics, and rising unemployment rates, are causing professionals to rethink their career strategies. The career, once synonymous with a well-defined ladder and advancement in one or two paternalistic organizations, has become boundaryless, with individuals continually updating and remarketing their skills and changing jobs on an average of every four and one-half years.

Although much recent research has focused on how individuals survive and navigate this boundaryless career landscape, most of these writings have been more descriptive than prescriptive. The purpose of this article is to provide specific recommendations on how executives can build and utilize a network of mentors to aid in the development of the competencies needed for career success and satisfaction in these turbulent times.

When asked to identify mentors, we often think of one outstanding, caring individual who provided career guidance and support. People typically describe their mentors as someone older, more experienced, and higher in organizational or professional rank. Traditionally, a mentor recognizes a protégé's potential and offers to take the novice "under his or her wing" for instruction and protection. This relationship benefits the protégé with updated skills and knowledge and at the same time provides synergy and new ideas to the mentor. In many professions, such as academia, medicine, and the skilled crafts, the mentor-protégé relationship is part of the learning process. The apprentice works side by side with the master, getting hands-on instruction for an extended period of time.

This traditional mentoring model—a stable, long-term master-apprentice relationship—may no longer be viable. Forces such as rapidly changing technology, shifting organizational structures, and global marketplace dynamics have transformed mentoring into a process that by necessity extends beyond the services of a single mentor. As knowledge continuously changes and evolves, it becomes difficult if not impossible for individuals—or individual mentors—to possess all the requisite knowledge within them. Having multiple mentors facilitates the building of knowledge in the people who then become the primary assets and sources of competitive advantage to the firm.

One workforce change necessitating multiple mentors is the proliferation of boundaryless work practices. Ceridian Group reported that 90 percent of firms use boundaryless work arrangements including telecommuting (i.e., completing all or most of one's work from a home office), flexible scheduling, and project work.[2] Furthermore, the International Telework Association and Council reported that in 1999, nearly 20 million workers telecommuted,[3] and expected that number to increase to 137 million in 2003.[4] Organizations implementing teleworking arrangements are realizing significant gains through reduced real estate expenses, increased productivity, increased access to global markets, reduced pollution, and greater ability to attract and retain high-quality workers.

However, this technology-facilitated, boundaryless working arrangement presents a unique set of challenges to executives and managers whose experience is limited to traditional office environments. Today's managers are challenged to establish organizational and individual goals, provide performance feedback, and lead culturally and geographically diverse teams and meetings, while simultaneously maintaining a positive work climate and tracking productivity, quality, costs, and adherence to regulations with minimal if any face-to-face interaction.[5] These skills were not likely to be part of managers' formal education; thus, they would benefit from associating with mentors who have the technological and managerial expertise to succeed in a boundaryless venue.

Another reason for creating a multiple mentor network involves the dramatic shifts in organizational structures and the concurrent shift in job mobility since the early 1980s. Organizational downsizing, mergers and acquisitions, global competition, and the growth of small entrepreneurial startups have altered the "company man" ideal of stability and upward mobility. Today, people have careers characterized by flexibility, project work across multiple firms, and an emphasis on learning rather than promotions and salary increases. Managers change jobs, industries, and even careers, as they seek to maintain or improve their standard of living while developing new, more marketable skills. In such an environment, where change is the norm and continuous knowledge acquisition is critical, the traditional single mentor-protégé model is being replaced by the guidance and assistance of a diverse cadre of mentors.

However, the demand for mentors is likely to outpace the supply. Because organizational downsizing and delayering have amplified workload pressures on the dwindling supply of mid- and upper-level managers, these potential mentors may lack the ability or desire to provide the time and attention needed to build a quality mentoring relationship with junior employees. These countervailing forces—need for continuously updating skills and reduced supply of mentors—require today's managers to search for multiple mentors who can provide career and psychosocial support that varies in duration and intensity. What once was accomplished by a single mentor over many years is now available only to protégés who search out multiple mentors.

In tandem with changes in organizational and job structures are major changes in the demographic makeup of the global workplace. William Johnston, author of "Global Workforce 2000," noted that there are "massive relocations of people including immigrants, temporary workers, retirees, and visitors. The greatest relocations will involve young, well-educated workers flocking to the cities of the developed world."[6] These immigrants are expected to flock to Japan, Germany, and the United States; in addition, millions of women in industrializing nations are entering the paid workforce.[7] In this new, diverse global context, multiple perspectives provided by a diverse set of mentors will help bridge the variety of employee expectations, values, and work habits and allow executives to take advantage of the diversity that this new workforce offers.

These changing workforce demographics have altered the work of and created additional challenges for today's manager. For example, as the number of dual-career and single-parent employees continues to grow, organizations are increasingly adopting family-friendly policies and expecting their managers to implement these and other supportive company practices.[8] The changing composition of employees and the work they do creates two challenges necessitating a new type of mentor guidance: how to deal with employees' diverse employment expectations and how to balance one's own work and family roles and responsibilities. As these phenomena are fairly recent, it is likely that minimal guidance is available through human resource or other formalized functions. A mentor who has successfully addressed these challenges can provide valuable knowledge and support for today's executive.

The expected mass global migration of workers suggests increasingly diverse work populations who face challenges emanating from minority status. However, the limited supply of minorities in high-level positions requires that protégés seek the services of multiple mentors to provide the needed advice and support. To find these multiple mentors, a protégé must search beyond organizational and geographic boundaries—non-face-to-face means of communication—for mentor support.[9] In addition, each new mentor in a protégé's developmental network provides potential access to an exponentially greater number of individuals, creating even more opportunities to build a mentor relationship with individuals who share similar or compatible values and characteristics. The more diverse the workforce becomes, the greater the need for individuals to build a diverse mentor network.

In sum, mentoring has become an effective means for coping with organizational change. A collection of mentors is invaluable, providing different perspectives, knowledge, and skills while serving multiple mentoring functions. They can provide emotional support or protection from political enemies in a way no one individual can. Where firms use organizational networks to facilitate increased knowledge for a competitive advantage,[10] individuals can utilize mentor networks to facilitate access to the knowledge and experiences of others for a competitive career advantage. Moreover, individuals with multiple mentors to rely on for career assistance are less affected by a dysfunctional or unavailable mentor. Protégés with multiple mentors realize that they cannot rely on a single mentor for career development; instead, they must manage their own careers by developing and maintaining many relationships that will enable them to achieve career success and satisfaction.

INTELLIGENT CAREERS

I had female mentors, the few women who had gone before me. These women taught me what it took to be a female in a man's world. One woman, the first female pilot in the Navy, helped me understand that I just had to prove myself. She gave me practical, hard-hitting facts. I had men who showed me how to navigate through the political arena of Navy pilots. A master chief with twenty-three years of experience taught me how to gain the respect of an all-male crew. I needed his perspective and his experience to be successful in leading troops of soldiers. I had people who taught me how to act, others who taught me whom to know. Each of these mentors allowed me to be successful in a world where women had not had much of an opportunity to succeed before.

—Elizabeth Williams, lieutenant and one of the 2 percent of female pilots in the U.S. Navy in 1986.

Respected career scholars Robert DeFillippi and Michael Arthur developed the concept of the intelligent career to complement the work of strategic management scholars studying intelligent enterprises and competency-driven firms.[11] DeFillippi and Arthur suggested that personal competencies, like organizational competencies, in turbulent environments reflect different forms of knowledge that can be applied and adapted to the shifting career opportunities in today's workplace. This approach reflects the shift from the long-term loyalty of professionals to a firm, wherein competencies were built according to organizational needs, to a model of occupational excellence, wherein professionals seek to continually upgrade the skills they offer to the marketplace. Each form of knowledge, and the accumulation of knowledge, changes in response to shifting environmental, employment, and personal factors, independent of a single firm.

THE THREE CAREER COMPETENCIES

The intelligent career comprises three career competencies that are manifested in people's beliefs and identities (knowing *why*), knowledge and skills (knowing *how*), and networks or relationships (knowing *whom*).[12] Specifically, the knowing-why competency reflects a professional's values and motivation—his or her career passion. Knowing why answers the question: Who am I? It relates to an individual's identity and the fit between this identity and choices made relative to tasks, projects, and organizations.

Knowing how answers the question: What can I do? It refers to the skills and knowledge needed for job performance—a person's level of expertise. Individuals may use their various employment settings and experiences on different projects as well as the mentor network that has been developed to both apply and enlarge the skills and knowledge they possess.

Knowing whom answers the question: Whom do I know? It reflects the relationships that contribute to an individual's networking. The friends, colleagues, and professional associations in individuals' networks can help build a reputation, provide needed visibility and access to opportunities, and provide new learning resources independent of the firm. Mentors serve as a knowledge bank to support professionals in the growth and enhancement of all three career competencies.

Terri Scandura and Ethlyn Williams, noted mentoring researchers, provided a detailed conceptualization of how one type of mentor, the leader, can assist in the development of his or her subordinates' intelligent careers amid increasing interorganizational mobility. They suggested that leaders serve as mentors by providing vocational support for knowing how, psychological support for knowing whom, and role modeling for knowing why.[13] By providing protection, challenging assignments, and visibility, leaders help protégés enhance self-efficacy and promotability, and thus their knowing-how competency. Leaders provide counseling, encouragement, and emotional support to facilitate the building of networks and the enhancement of knowing-whom competencies. Through their example, leaders help protégés learn, understand, and internalize the organization's culture, thereby engaging the knowing-why competency.

Suzanne de Janasz and Sherry Sullivan applied the intelligent-career concept to examine how professors must go beyond the traditional dissertation adviser-mentor apprenticeship model and build a portfolio of mentor relationships to enhance career progression and satisfaction.[14] By mapping the knowing competencies across the professorial ranks (doctoral student, assistant, associate, full professor), they provided a framework for guiding professors in the construction of a network of developmental relationships. They suggested that professors who recognize the need for an intelligent career will actively seek out relationships to help them develop the three knowing competencies.

Developing these different career competencies makes relying on different types of mentoring relationships essential. Drawing on the ideas of the intelligent career, we examine how the career competencies of knowing why, how, and whom interact with learning demands to produce the need for different types of mentoring.

KNOWING WHY: WHO AM I?

Knowing why relates to our identity, which relates to our career-related choices. This identity begins to form at a young age, evolves through educational and work experiences, and translates into early career choices. New entrants into the workforce might ask themselves: Do I enjoy working for a large, prestigious corporation or a smaller, more close-knit firm? Am I better suited to this industry or another? Am I on the right path? They might also seek the counsel of mentors in their personal or professional networks for information and support in making difficult career decisions.

During this time, the knowing-why competency continues to be tested and developed. Was the right profession chosen? Is the work satisfying? Junior professionals may seek the advice of their peers or supervisors for help with these questions. They may seek out new mentors within their firms for more organization-specific knowledge about performance standards, how to get promoted, and learning the ropes. They also begin to build reputations about who they are and for what they will be known.

As time passes, trigger events such as a blocked promotion, job layoff, divorce, or illness may cause professionals to reevaluate their career paths. Many of the executives we interviewed recounted how they had sought the advice of one or more mentors when they reached a career or life transition. Based on their mentor's advice and their own reassessment, some professionals may veer off the fast track or take a lower-level position with less prestige. Some may strategize their eventual move up through the company's ranks, and others may leave the corporation and start their own firms.

Upon achieving career success, the need for mentoring continues. Formal networking, as well as informal conversations with other seasoned professionals, may assist in making decisions about work-family balance, midlife renewal, career changes, updating skills, and retirement options.

In sum, answering the "Who am I?" question relates to individuals' search and development of their identity and the fit between this identity and choices made relative to tasks, projects, and organizations. As individuals change career directions and need to develop new skills and abilities to support changes in their self-concept, they will need to seek out new mentors to help guide them.

KNOWING HOW: WHAT CAN I DO?

Throughout and beyond formal schooling, individuals continue to build new skills and identify those skills that require polishing through feedback from self and others. This learning process enhances individuals' self-esteem and their beliefs that they can perform a task.[15] Regardless of education, experience, or career stage, people need to learn continuously—that is, develop their knowing-how competency—particularly in turbulent times. For example, many firms lament that despite their advanced degrees, MBA graduates lack the soft skills (i.e., communications, interpersonal relations) and hands-on experience needed to succeed in business. Even as individual proficiencies are developed, demands shift, requiring a need for additional mentor help with new technologies or markets. Such mentors provide not only career guidance but also psychosocial or emotional support—an important and helpful function of mentoring. In addition to work demands, professionals must cope with simultaneous and often conflicting personal demands and obligations. Mentors may listen to and advise protégés, helping them cope with personal stress as well as work stress, such as heavy workloads, unfair treatment, inadequate feedback, problem coworkers, and unreasonable bosses.

Given the rapid changes in today's business environment, professionals need a diverse portfolio of mentors possessing sufficient breadth and depth of expertise to help them learn the ropes of their specific firm, gain knowledge of new technologies, and assist in the development of interpersonal skills (e.g., communication and conflict resolution techniques) as well as numerous other skills that may arise unexpectedly from the changing environment. Some of these mentors may be internal to the firm, and others may be members of professional organizations, volunteer groups, or even paid executive career coaches.

In sum, knowing how relates to the skills and knowledge needed for people to do their current jobs as well as any future jobs. Employees, especially temporary or project workers, who often move between boundaries, need several mentors to assist in their continuous learning and development of new expertise. These mentors may be coworkers, friends, or formal mentors established through professional organizations.

KNOWING WHOM: WHOM DO I KNOW?

I have had several mentors throughout my career at GE. I relied most on mentors at transition points, though individuals helped me navigate the corporate landscape throughout my tenure. One mentor in particular helped me make the transition from a GE subsidiary to a big corporate job with GE. This particular mentor taught me how to pitch ideas to Jack [Welch], gave me inside tips on the players, and, most important, opened doors for me. He knew folks all over the world and would ask them to give me five minutes. Without his introduction I wouldn't have been able to get an appointment.

    —Jeff Dye, CEO, GE Corporate Payment Services

According to Execunet, a career management and recruiting resource center for executives and recruiters, the old rule of thumb that it takes one month per $10,000 of salary expected to find a new job has changed, with recent findings suggesting that one's age and ease of finding a new job are inversely correlated.[16] Executive search firms capitalize on the growing difficulties in finding appropriate positions for executives and utilize their networks (in addition to workshops and coaching) to hasten executives' search. In especially tight labor markets, job hunters realize that it's not always what you know but whom you know that facilitates job acquisition.

Individuals who have knowing-whom competency may increase their mobility both within and outside the firm based on the reputation they have built through their mentor networks. Of the 3,652 executives surveyed by Drake Beam Morin, 61 percent said they had found new positions in the previous year through networking.[17] Having an extensive network of contacts also makes the individual more valuable to organizations. Management scholar Rosalie Tung wrote about the organization's need "to attract and retain people who are well connected or who excel in collaborative teamwork in order to become or remain world class."[18]

Knowing whom refers to the depth and breadth of relationships within the networks that people build to facilitate their career development. These friends, coworkers, and colleagues in professional associations may come from different organizations, occupations, or parts of the globe, but together they provide people with networks of information and emotional support to increase their mobility and improve their job skills. Building and continuously developing such networks allows individuals to stay connected and opens doors to new opportunities.

In order to develop the knowing whom, how, and why competencies in an increasingly complex and changing environment, individuals must develop relationships with multiple mentors who can assist in different aspects of their careers. In the next section, using information gleaned from our interviews with top executives as well as recent mentoring research, we provide five specific strategies for building and maintaining an intelligent career network. Such a network should provide a portfolio of "mentors of the moment" who can help protégés develop across a variety of learning experiences and over the phases of their careers.[19]

BUILDING AN INTELLIGENT MENTORING NETWORK

Recent research and current realities support the idea of constructing an intelligent mentor network. But how do professionals actually build such networks, and how can executives help professionals in their firms develop these networks? We suggest the following five steps:

1. Become the Perfect Protégé.

Linda Hill, in her well-known Harvard Business School article "Beyond the Myth of the Perfect Mentor," suggested that instead of searching for the mythical perfect mentor, an individual should become the "perfect protégé" by investing the time and energy needed to develop and maintain a network of developmental relationships.[20] Because of the give-and-take aspects of the mentoring process, protégés must be careful to invest enough time to permit the mentoring relationship to grow and mature, so that trust and respect can develop.

Protégés should be aware that mentors often risk their own credibility and reputation to aid in protégé development. When a protégé stumbles, the failure often reflects poorly on the mentor. Protégés should be careful not to underestimate the risks that their mentors assume on their behalf and should publicly acknowledge the mentor's assistance. Moreover, protégés should seek out opportunities to provide their mentors with technical information, new knowledge, or emotional support, as "the goal of building networks is to contribute to others." Mentoring is a reciprocal relationship; mentors assist protégés, and in turn protégés should assist their mentors. Helping others increases the likelihood of receiving assistance in the future as well as increasing the trust and credibility of the relationship. Protégés should provide positive feedback and thanks when their mentors help them. If mentors don't know that they have been helpful, they may be less willing to share valuable insights or opportunities in the future.

Because mentors are identified based upon their wisdom and reputations for developing others, expect quality mentors to be in high demand. Realize that mentors have work demands and personal lives as well as other protégés in their networks. Protégés must discuss their needs and ascertain the mentor's willingness to provide corresponding time and effort; they also need to be proactive in maintaining contact with their mentors. For example, mentoring researchers Lillian Eby and Tammy Allen found that 55 percent of 242 protégés studied reported that their mentors had occasionally neglected them.[21] Executives we interviewed suggested that they relied not just on one mentor but had several trusted mentors to whom they could turn.

Mentoring is all about learning—for both the protégé and the mentor. Protégés should develop the knowing why, how, and whom competencies and learn from different types of mentors; in return, those mentors will learn and grow. In addition, protégés should seek development from formal mentors as well as through coaches, sponsors, friends, and peers. By honestly sharing successes as well as mistakes, protégés enable learning—both theirs and their mentors'.

2. Engage in 360-Degree Networking.

In a study of fifteen high-ranking women executives in the male-dominated entertainment industry, Ellen Ensher, Susan Murphy, and Sherry Sullivan found that while only a few of the women had traditional mentors, many had developed a 360-degree approach to networking.[22] The women shared information and strove to maintain good relationships with those above, below, and at the same status level as themselves. Their social lives were built around, and integrated with, work contacts and friendships. Hiking outings or monthly women-only industry parties provided social satisfaction as well as a means to connect and share resources with many different types of developers.

Aspiring managers can adapt the 360-degree technique of these successful women by seeking out developers and mentors who are at different career stages and levels. Some junior executives turn to senior executives, such as Cameron Burr, who sought the advice of his father and People Express Airlines founder Don Burr, explaining, "You want someone who's been around the block a few times, who has a more seasoned perspective on life issues." Others, like Ellen Aschendorf, CEO of Egg Electric Inc., approach peers who are facing similar challenges. She sought advice from a CEO who shared several similarities: Both are women, are in the same industry, have children, and are about the same age. In addition to competency matching with mentors, aiming for similarity in values, personality, or other attributes can further enhance the value of the mentor relationship.

3. Commit to Assessing, Building, and Adjusting the Mentor Network.

A survey of 649 professional women found that approximately 50 percent of them had three or more mentors.[23] However, it is not enough just to increase the size of the mentoring network; it is important to conduct a careful analysis of what competencies you wish to build (knowing why, how, whom) and find the best resources for development. Although multiple mentors might be willing to participate in a mentoring network, there can be a point of diminishing returns. A healthy mentoring relationship is based on mutual trust and mutual obligations. Too many individuals in a network can impede the building of trust and hinder support, information, and assistance.

The analysis process begins by assessing the current mentor network and identifying which mentors currently provide support for which competences. Individuals should be available to help identify a career path and determine how to succeed to the next level within the organization. If not available, other trusted individuals who know the protégés can develop their knowing-why competency. Individuals who can help develop critical job skills and corporate knowledge provide a lifeline for developing knowing-how competence. Mentors can open their networks and assist in the development of knowing-whom competencies. With network assessment, gaps and needed mentor competencies can be identified.

As experiences and knowledge are gained and professional goals shift, a mentor network must also change. With passing time and changing needs, the frequency and intensity of interactions may alter, and members may enter and leave the network based on shifting goals and demands. Whether the employee is starting out in a new position or considering a shift in current career status, the network must be reviewed for possible needs of additional assistance. Even after you have mastered the job, think ahead to your next career move in determining whether your current network is adequate. As networks evolve, they should be continuously monitored and updated.

4. Develop Diverse, Synergistic Connections.

In the same way that work teams realize benefits such as increased creativity, innovation, and effectiveness from the synergistic combination of multiple, diverse perspectives, individuals should be able to reach their greatest potential through interaction with multiple, diverse mentors. The unique combination of the guidance, information, and support of this diverse team of developers can exceed the sum of its parts, enabling protégés to expand their competencies.

Organizational or geographic boundaries should not preclude developing a diverse set of mentors. Improved technology (e.g., Internet, inexpensive airfares) and the growth and globalization of professional organizations have made it easier for professionals to develop effective working relationships with individuals from different backgrounds and in different firms and countries. For example, a manager might select an internal mentor to learn about the ins and outs of an organization's culture, policies, and practices; she or he may also seek advice from those outside the firm, industry, or country to glean specific information about external job opportunities, international market trends, best practices, and obtaining new skills.

Moreover, formal and informal mentoring opportunities offer unique benefits; protégés might consider drawing from both. Many organizations have formal mentoring programs that assist in matching individuals based on their career plans and goals in addition to other firm-sponsored opportunities (e.g., conferences, women and minority network groups) that can expand the mentor network. Recognizing that gains can arise from the mutual-selection aspect of informal mentoring, some organizational mentoring programs allow individuals to take a role in choosing their mentors. For example, GE selects the top 20 percent of their performers and permits these protégés to personally choose their own mentors from a list of top executives. Jan Johnson, former vice president of marketing of Zions Bank, commented on the value of such programs:

> I realize now that my career could be a lot different if I had had mentors to introduce me to the right people and to provide visibility within organizations. I chose to work in startup companies while some of my friends went to work in large corporations with formal mentor programs. I saw how their mentors could open doors for them. There is a lot to be said for having a mentor to stand up for you, introduce you, and shine their successes back on you.

In addition to seeking both internal and external, informal and formal mentors, the synergy of diversity—facilitated by seeking out mentors and developers of different races, educational backgrounds, and industries, and of the opposite gender—should be considered. A diverse set of mentors provides different worldviews that will open new and refreshing ways to view old problems and will also provide potentially exciting and novel career opportunities.

In sum, by consciously targeting a diverse team of mentors, professionals building an intelligent network can capitalize on the strengths of distinct mentor characteristics as well as the synergy that often comes from a diversity of opinions, information, and knowledge.

5. Realize That Change Is Inevitable and That All Good Things Must Come to an End.

We know that mentoring relationships vary in intensity and change over time. Some relationships never mature beyond the minimum mentoring based upon on-the-job training. Other relationships are characterized by marginal mentoring; these mentors provide limited developmental assistance and are just "good enough." Still others develop into powerful colearning relationships where the parties begin to view themselves as family. Mentor relationships that are characterized by different processes and outcomes, vary in how long they last, and change over time are illustrated by Kirk Wessel, corporate consultant with Organizational Consultants to Management, Inc.:

> A mentor network is dynamic. It has to be. As a manager at Pepsi Corporation and Associated Food Stores, I would turn to a mentor in my functional area for job-related support. When I moved on from a job, I normally left my mentor relationship along with the job. In the Navy, however, as an ensign, I had a "Sea Daddy" [the Navy term for mentors]. "Sea Daddies" stick with you; it is a permanent relationship. In fact, I'm still in contact with my Navy mentor.

Ideally, mentor relationships provide rich learning experiences. Over the course of a healthy mentoring relationship, shared experiences, insights, and sacred knowledge are exchanged. At some point, however, relationships change. According to Burt Chase, a member of Gore Industries' board of directors, there came a time in his mentoring relationship with the company's founder, Bill Gore, when distance, growth, and experience made him deem it time to adopt a new sponsor. His relationship with Bill stayed strong, yet the relationship changed from a mentor-type relationship to a friendship. Burt Chase commented:

Gore Industries has a mentor-type program that we call *sponsorship*. Your sponsor is a supportive individual from whom you seek out advice. I was very fortunate as a new employee at Gore Industries to have Bill Gore as my first sponsor. Bill was a visionary leader who revolutionized the concept of corporate culture. I learned a great deal from Bill. Over time, I moved on to other sponsors. It is interesting how I identified my sponsors. I really looked for ordinary people doing extraordinary things.

All mentor relationships will change over time, and at some point they will end. Although some mentoring relationships grow across decades, research indicates that most mentoring relationships last an average of five years.[24] Some relationships, like that of Burt Chase and Bill Gore, will grow in mutual respect, indicating the end of a mentor-protégé relationship and the start of a friendship. Other mentor relationships may become distant or dysfunctional. When the relationship ceases to be beneficial, ties with those mentors need to be cut.

Regardless of how the relationship ends, individuals should write a note expressing appreciation for the sponsor's influence on their careers. This communication is not only thoughtful but also may keep the door open for future conversations. An intelligent network is one that is fed and pruned as necessary.

LESSONS LEARNED

Just as the leaders of democratic nations rely on a group of advisers to make decisions about governmental issues, individuals also need a portfolio of trustworthy mentors to provide insights and help them make decisions about complex and changing issues. This article has emphasized the desirability of professionals' developing a cadre of multiple mentors to support their career development. These mentors can assist professionals in knowing the why, how, and whom in developing intelligent networks for future opportunities. Dick Graham, CEO of Augusta Medical Center, explained why building a network of multiple mentors is so important:

The higher you rise in an organization [by whatever means], the more the skill set changes. At some point you climb beyond some imaginary clouds that keep you from recalling and exercising the skills that got you to that level in the first place. Many of these skills are no less necessary at the top than during the climb. So high perch dwellers need to find young mentors still making the climb and learn or relearn from them. You can always find bright young executives who are far better than you were on your best day and be humbled in knowing that about half of your perch came to you by sheer luck . . . and humility is also a mentorable attribute.

As can be seen from the comments of high-level executives, we are never too old or too experienced to have mentors in our lives. We all have something to learn. In the same way that organizations seek partnerships in an effort to capitalize on collaborative strengths, so can individuals at any level of an organization or any stage in their careers form facilitative mentor relationships. For an individual, this learning comes most directly from mentor relationships. To that end, we have outlined five specific strategies for identifying, managing, and nurturing these mentor relationships. We think that these strategies should aid in developing effective relationships and intelligent networks that will promote success and satisfaction in these complex and changing times.

ENDNOTES

1. Kram, K. E. 1985. *Mentoring at work: Developmental relationships in organizational life.* Glenview, IL: Scott, Foresman.

2. Boundaryless workforces vary by workers' age, position, company size. 1999. Ceridian Employer Services, 27 January. Canadian Telework Association Web site.

3. Telework facts. International Telework Association and Council. www.lecommute.org.

4. Anderson, C., Payne, S., and Smith, C. 1998. Successful enterprise telecommuting: It is not just the technology. Gartner Group publication R-RMA-101. www.gartnergroup.com.

5. Sandlund, C. 2000. Remote control: As the virtual workforce grows, so does the challenge for managers. Here's how to keep it together. *Business Week,* 27 March: F14.

6. Johnston, W. B. 1991. Global Workforce 2000: The new world labor market. *Harvard Business Review,* 69: 115–126.

7. Ibid.

8. Friedman, S. D., and Greenhaus, J. H. 2000. *Work and family—Allies or enemies?* New York: Oxford University Press.

9. For information on non-face-to-face or electronic mentoring, see Whiting, V., and de Janasz, S. C. 2004. Mentoring in the 21st century: Using the internet to build skills and networks. *Journal of Management Education,* 28(3): 275–293.

10. Tung, R. L. 2002. Building effective networks. *Journal of Management Inquiry,* 11(2): 94–101.

11. Quinn, J. B. 1992. The intelligent enterprise: A new paradigm. *Academy of Management Executive,* 6(4): 48–63.

12. Ibid. See also Arthur, M. B., et al. 1995. Intelligent enterprise, intelligent careers. *Academy of Management Executive,* 9(4): 7–22.

13.Scandura, T. A., and Williams, E. A. 2002. Leadership in the context of psychological contract breach: The role of mentoring: 167–195. In L. L. Neider and C. A. Schriesheim (Eds.), *Leadership.* Greenwich, CT: Information New Publishing.

14. de Janasz, S. C., and Sullivan, S. E. 2004. Multiple mentoring in academe: Developing the professorial network. *Journal of Vocational Behavior,* 64(2): 263–283.

15. Gouillart, F. J., and Kelly, J. N. 1995. *Transforming the organization.* New York: Mc-Graw-Hill.

16. www.execunet.com.

17. Maher, K. 2001. Career coaches. *Wall Street Journal,* 26 June: B8.

18. Tung, op. cit.

19. Baugh, S. G., and Scandura, T. A. 1999. The effect of multiple mentors on protégé attitudes toward the work setting. *Journal of Social Behavior and Personality,* 14(4): 503–522.

20. Hill, L. 1991. Beyond the myth of the perfect mentor: Building a network of developmental relationships. Harvard Business School Publication 9-491-096.

21. Eby, L. T., and Allen, T. D. 2002. Further investigation of protégés' negative mentoring experiences: Patterns and Outcomes. *Group and Organizatonal Management,* 27(4): 456.

22. Ensher, E., Murphy, S., and Sullivan, S. E. 2002. Reel women: Lessons from female TV executives on managing work and real life. *Academy of Management Executive,* 16(2): 106–121.

23. Vincent, A., and Seymour, J. 1994. Mentoring among female executives. *Women in Management Review,* 9(7): 15–20.

24. Burke, R. J., and McKeen, C. A. 1997. Benefits of mentoring relationships among managerial and professional women: A cautionary tale. *Journal of Vocational Behavior,* 51(1): 43–57.

16

~

Why Leadership-Development Efforts Fail

Douglas A. Ready
Jay A. Conger

Many corporate programs to develop next-generation leaders fall victim to three pathologies that render the investments of time and money worthless. But there are ways of fighting these diseases.

In the past couple of years, leadership has become the hottest topic in business. Companies see this hard-to-pin-down ability as essential to organizational success, and they want their executives to learn how to exercise it. As a result, leadership development has become a big business: Investment in leadership education and development approached $50 billion in 2000.[1] Publishing houses are shaking the trees in hopes of finding the author of the next blockbuster leadership book; consulting firms that once focused exclusively on strategy have aggressively launched global leadership practices; and business schools have positioned themselves as prospective partners with companies in the lucrative leadership-education market.[2]

In this atmosphere, it is difficult to find a CEO of a large company who doesn't have a carefully honed speech about the importance of developing next-generation leaders at every organizational level. And yet for most companies, the combination of eloquent statements and massive investments has

Reprinted from *Why Leadership-Development Efforts Fail* by Douglas A. Ready and Jay A. Conger, *MIT Sloan Management Review*, Spring 2003, pp. 83–88, by permission of publisher.

not produced a sufficient pipeline of leaders. Many report that they have been forced to look outside the company for a new CEO or top executive team member, even though people brought in from the outside derail at significantly higher rates than internal hires. The very high rates of CEO turnover due to poor performance in recent years points to the problem: If companies were adept at developing leadership talent internally, it should be most apparent in the performance of senior leaders.[3]

Our research and advisory work involving dozens of companies over two decades leads us to believe that three pathologies are the root cause of the failure of so many leadership-development efforts. (See "About the Research.") By pathology, we mean the causes and effects of systemic problems in the way organizations attempt to develop leadership capability. As with an actual disease, companies exhibit clear patterns that cause repeated failures or breakdowns in their capacity to create internal leadership talent. Until these pathologies are examined and understood, leadership-development initiatives will continue to produce flawed results despite the best of intentions and continual investments of time and money. Fortunately, there are ways of fighting these diseases so that companies can create healthy processes for preparing the leaders they'll need in the future.

PATHOLOGY #1:
THE "OWNERSHIP IS POWER" MIND-SET

In many organizations, older ways of managing are colliding with new realities about what makes companies and their employees tick. Leadership development suffers from this pathology when executives approach it with control, ownership, and power-oriented mind-sets rather than with an understanding of the need for shared accountability.

Consider how this pathology affects a typical global company. It will often have powerful regional heads for its dispersed operations, senior managers who oversee the company's multiple lines of business, and equally powerful executives from the functional areas embedded within the business lines, geographical organizations, and corporate center. Given such complexity, it is easy to find multiple power centers for leadership-development activities, each with a different owner but lacking any overall sense of coherence.

This was the situation not long ago at a Fortune 50 manufacturing company. The company's strong global-product business units created powerful divisional and business heads, while its technological heritage and reputation for strong financial controls gave rise to highly influential functional heads. This history presented enormous structural and cultural challenges to the newly hired head of leadership development (a highly regarded academic brought in from a top-ranked business school), whose mission was to build a global pool of next-generation leaders who would be available to move freely across divisions, businesses, locations, and functions.

The company's approach to leadership development was a reflection of its culture and the "ownership is power" pathology. The CEO was enthusiastic about leadership development but in a superficial way—he soon latched onto a management guru who told him exactly what he wanted to hear: that he would build a legacy as "the leadership CEO." The company's division and business presidents carefully controlled their involvement in leadership-development initiatives, engaging only when it was in their units' self-interest. The senior vice president for human resources (the leadership director's boss) was more of a traditional personnel professional, well versed in labor relations but not an expert in leadership development. As a result, he felt competitive pressure from the leadership director whenever there were successes in building leadership capability. Such achievements were perceived to be the leadership director's victories, and the HR executive began withholding critical information from him, such as the names of identified high-potential managers and key job openings that could serve as developmental opportunities for the company's next-generation leaders.

Thus the manufacturer's ownership-is-power mind-set produced an out-of-touch CEO, intermittently involved line managers, internal warfare within the HR function, and a pool of prospective leaders who didn't know what was expected of them, didn't understand what leadership skills to develop, and couldn't link the objectives of the company's leadership program to their businesses' priorities. As one might guess, the prognosis for a sustainable leadership-development effort at the company was poor. It wasn't long before the CEO, management guru, and senior vice president for HR were fired, and the director of leadership development returned to his academic post.

Given the confusion in this case, it's natural to ask who should own the responsibility for leadership development in large, complex global businesses. The fact is, this is the wrong question. Ownership of resources, especially human resources, is old-world thinking and does not reflect the reality of organizational life today.

At first glance, it might seem logical for the CEO to assume ownership for the development of talent—to ensure that leadership development has credibility as a companywide priority. This approach has been best exemplified by General Electric during Jack Welch's tenure. Welch was well known for his comment to his business heads about the company's top 500 executives: "I own the people. You just rent them." But it is not realistic or desirable for CEOs to be solely responsible for the development of new leaders. Not only do they have little expertise in developing talent, but they are usually exposed only to those with the highest potential and have extremely limited knowledge of up-and-coming junior-level leaders. Moreover, the demands on the typical CEO make it difficult for the top person to devote enough time to this issue.

Line managers, on the other hand, know their people well and have seen them perform under daily pressures—surely they would know best who has the ingredients to make it to the top. But one can't necessarily predict who will lead successfully at the enterprise level on the basis of how someone has managed a project, a function, or even a business. Leaving responsibility for leadership development to line managers is insufficient as well.[4]

The human resources function has become more prominent over the past decade, and HR specialists with expertise in talent development have typically designed the company's processes for identifying high-potential managers and for succession planning.[5] Once again, however, assigning ownership for leadership development to HR raises complications. In highly decentralized companies, it is common to have HR specialists in each business unit running leadership-development initiatives suited to that unit's specific needs, which are not always coordinated with the company's overall strategy. For example, in a well-known retailing company, the corporate HR staff designed and owned one set of initiatives for director-level managers, and the CEO's staff designed and owned a completely different set for vice presidents. The two groups came up with different definitions of leadership effectiveness, different approaches to teaching leadership, and different standards and expectations for grooming leaders.

The case of the Fortune 50 manufacturing company points to one final argument: that individuals should be responsible for their own leadership development. The role of the organization should be to provide opportunities for development through challenging assignments; individuals have to assume responsibility for taking advantage of those opportunities, seeking feedback on their performance, and making realistic assessments about their prospects.[6] With this approach, individuals are masters of their own destiny and, the argument goes, less vulnerable to power politics and competing self-interests.[7]

Although that logic has a certain appeal, the fact is that career self-management in large organizations would quickly deteriorate into chaos in the absence of disciplined processes for tracking developmental opportunities and the insight required to assess whether an individual is likely to succeed in a new challenge. This do-it-yourself approach would surely lead to more career derailments than successes without the support systems normally provided by line managers and human resources staff to individuals taking on stretch assignments.

When one adds the pathologies of power—guarding turf, withholding information, nonparticipation—to the many other problems associated with assigning ownership to a particular group, it becomes clear that accountability for leadership development must be the interconnected responsibility of the CEO and top teams, senior line managers, HR specialists, and the high-potential individuals themselves.

PATHOLOGY #2:
THE PRODUCTIZATION OF LEADERSHIP DEVELOPMENT

In numerous companies, leadership-development efforts are not aligned with strategic goals.[8] As with other complex organizational challenges, companies are frequently in search of quick fixes, and they orient their leadership initiatives around commercial products that have limited relevance to their actual needs.[9] In other words, executives become too focused on the products themselves rather than on the problems that need to be solved.[10] (Full disclosure: Given our own work, we have to be careful not to fall victim to the Pogo principle: "We have met the enemy, and he is us.")

For example, a human resources manager from a Fortune 100 company recently explained enthusiastically during a break in an executive education class how she had just brought a "primal leadership" course into her company. She wanted suggestions on how to convince her company's line managers of the course's value—after she had already launched the program! Another company offers a new leadership-training program approximately every two years based on a current best-selling book. The programs to date have included training experiences designed on the basis of well-known books by respected researchers, such as Stephen Covey's *The Seven Habits of*

Highly Effective People, Peter Senge's *The Fifth Discipline,* James Collins and Jerry Porras's *Built to Last,* and Daniel Goleman's *Emotional Intelligence.*[11]

The problem does not reside with the authors or their books, which contain many great ideas. The problem is the misuse of these works in the form of rush-to-action training packages. As one executive in the company explained, "This multitude of offerings has created a certain cynicism about leadership development within the organization. We build a program and then toss it over the wall to the operating units. Then we go back and build another one without linking the ideas to the context of our business. There is no consistency in our message." A division president at a Fortune 50 company made a similar comment a few years ago during a leadership-development audit: "We spend $120 million a year on this stuff, and if it all went away tomorrow, it wouldn't matter one bit. Leadership development in this company is nothing more than a series of disconnected programs sold by consultants to training managers who don't understand our business."

This is the pathology of productization at work. The phenomenon is not new, but it has become more problematic and could lead to the following scenario:[12]

Witnessing an endless stream of disconnected leadership-development models and initiatives, top management begins to view leadership development as code for products that are divorced from business issues and sold by consultants to line managers looking for quick answers and HR managers looking to help the line at almost any cost. The top team disengages, and the credibility of the company's leadership program suffers. As top-level support is reduced, it becomes far less likely that the company will build an organizational culture that promotes the thoughtfully planned development of its leaders. During tough economic times, top executives decide to curtail investments in leadership development, ushering in the return of a more Darwinian model of leadership: "The cream will rise to the top." Employees then become cynical about the company's dedication to leadership development. High-potentials hesitate before investing their energy in developmental initiatives; some of the best walk away from the organization, and others do not reach their potential for lack of strong developmental experiences. In this scenario, there are no winners.

There is nothing wrong with trying to keep up with the latest ideas in leadership and management. The rush to productize these ideas, however, creates the tendency for managers to think that leadership development can take place in one-day, paint-by-the-numbers, "edutainment" sessions. When such thinking is exposed as manifestly false, companies may be tempted to give up altogether and force individuals to sink or swim in the leadership pool, and that's rarely been an effective way of teaching people anything.

PATHOLOGY #3: MAKE-BELIEVE METRICS

Businesses search for accountability for most of their actions, and accountability is driven by metrics. There are scorecards today for every business process imaginable. So it is not surprising that leadership-development initiatives are being scrutinized, as they should be. The metrics that most companies are using to assess the effectiveness of their leadership-development efforts, however, are leading them astray.

Several years ago, a large industrial company with a strong history of technological excellence and financial discipline reviewed its leadership-development initiatives. At the upper levels of its business units and functions, the company was populated by engineers and financial experts, and its culture was characterized by no-nonsense, fact-based analysis. The HR specialists charged with leadership development, seeking top-management approval for their work, provided the top team with metrics that fit the culture.

At a quarterly review meeting with division presidents and the CEO, the HR executives demonstrated the effectiveness of their programs by focusing on quantifiable activities. They showed figures that indicated higher utilization rates of the company's leadership center, the number of people sent through the programs at below-target unit costs, and an increase in the use of the company's e-learning technologies to train managers in leadership skills. These metrics met the CEO's approval, and he never stopped the presentation to ask, "Are we better able to fill key jobs when they arise?" or "To what extent are our leadership programs building managers' commitment to our strategic direction?" Instead, he and the division presidents thanked the HR staff for their good work and commented on the improvements they were making in quantifying the impact of the company's leadership initiatives.

Their satisfaction was misplaced. The full utilization of a company's training center does not matter if employees perceive that they are wasting their time attending programs that do not build competitive capability or create the next generation of talent. Increases in technology-enabled teaching methods and reductions in unit cost per program don't matter if they fail to equip the company to fill key positions more effectively. And the attempt to prove that a new action-learning leadership program has turned a big profit for the company misses the point. Far better to be able to demonstrate that the company's leaders can now think more strategically, work more co-operatively in teams, and coordinate cross-company efforts more effectively because they understand the objectives of their counterparts in other businesses and locations.

The philosophy that dominates so many company cultures today is that initiatives that cannot be measured have no value. In most instances, that is a reasonable assumption. But it does not apply to leadership development—not, at least, in the quantifiable terms that dictate assessments of capital expenditures. To avoid relying on make-believe metrics, executives have to make sure they are asking the right questions of their leadership programs.

TREATING THE PATHOLOGIES AT IBM

Although the three pathologies run deep in many organizations, they need not be fatal—recovery is possible. Several companies, including IBM, are making great strides in leadership development. As that company's experience shows, there are three keys to the successful creation of a pipeline of next-generation leaders.

Share Ownership and Demand Accountability

The companies that still live by the ownership-is-power mind-set believe that sharing ownership for leadership development would mean that no one is responsible or accountable for outcomes. IBM rejects this view and has instituted an approach that is comprehensive and results oriented.

The CEO and top team set the tone for the whole company. Chairman and CEO Sam Palmisano puts it this way: "One key to our success over the past decade has been that we established leadership development as a top corporate priority. Every manager and every executive at IBM is accountable for identifying and developing leaders. We are completely committed to this principle as one of the cornerstones of our core values." IBM's top team (some three hundred strong) establishes clear expectations by ensuring that individuals with leadership potential are identified and discussed at top management's quarterly meetings. At the meetings, the senior executives participate in what IBM calls the "five-minute drill." During the drill, each executive is expected to be ready to forward the name of at least one individual in his or her business unit or function who shows leadership promise. Palmisano demonstrates his commitment to this process by chairing the five-minute drill sessions. It is understood that someone from the chairman's office will follow up with those executives who offered up names if the "high-potentials" have not been provided with stretch assignments in relatively short order.

In this and other ways, IBM's line managers are held accountable for leadership development: They know they will not be considered for senior executive positions unless they have demonstrated skill in developing leaders. Like the senior executives, line managers are fully engaged in recognizing promising talent and making sure high-potentials are identified in a variety of meetings and venues. According to Bob Moffat, head of IBM's Personal Systems Group, "All line managers are expected to coach and mentor their employees as a part of IBM's bedrock belief that leaders learn best from other leaders and through their experiences."

IBM has also assembled a staff of HR development specialists who combine technical knowledge with business understanding. The department, called the Global Executive and Organization Capability (GEOC), consists of approximately fifty organizational and leadership-capability consultants and succession-planning professionals who help IBM's line executives think through the human capital implications of the company's business strategies.

Invest in Processes, Not Products

Companies that excel at building leaders don't rush to buy quick-fix products; they know that panaceas are a myth, and they invest in process excellence rather than a multitude of programs. At IBM, the leadership-development process is guided by the IBM Leadership Framework, a document created by the company's most senior executives, its line leaders, and the GEOC.

A key component of the framework is the heavily researched set of executive leadership competencies: eleven skills and behaviors demonstrated by exceptional leaders at IBM. By using these competencies as touchstones, mentors and coaches can assess whether an individual is on track as a potential leader in ever more demanding situations. If so, they make sure that developmental job stretches are made available to that person.

Another key tenet of the framework is that executives learn leadership much more effectively from experiences than from educational courses. Given that way of thinking, planned on-the-job development is the preferred approach to building leaders at IBM. The GEOC's consultants work closely with line managers to ensure that high-potential individuals move into jobs that will serve as developmental vehicles. Examples of critical leadership skills learned on the job include managing a turnaround, initiating a startup, managing cultural diversity, and executing cross-border partnerships.

Companies that know how to build leaders have another trait: They believe in the importance of making long-term investments in their employees, even during lean times. The head of IBM's GEOC, Tanya Clemons, explains it this way:

> During the tough economic conditions in the mid to late 1980s, we abandoned our commitment to leadership development and paid a dear price for that in loss of market leadership later on. We had to relearn the hard way the critical importance of grooming leaders at every level of this company and in every location around the globe in which we do business.

Measure What Matters

Once accountabilities for leadership development are clarified and investments are made in process excellence, the appropriate metrics must be put in place to help managers judge whether investments in leadership development are paying off. Rather than dwelling on "activity analysis," as was the case with the company focused on make-believe metrics, companies should link leadership-development investments to building the capabilities that will produce superior business results.

According to Randy MacDonald, IBM's senior vice president for human resources, "We measure our success by the extent to which we can link our leadership-development activities to business results. It all becomes a matter of demanding accountability." More specifically, IBM seeks answers to the following: Are we better able to satisfy our customers' needs than our competitors? Do we have the right leaders ready to take on key jobs when they arise? Can we take advantage of new opportunities when they arise faster than our competitors? Do our people understand—and are they capable of executing—our vision and strategy? IBM judges its investments in leadership development to be a success when it can answer yes to those questions.

BEYOND THE FADS

Although leadership is a hot topic, many companies risk getting burned. The danger is that the combination of outdated thinking about ownership, a product-focused quick-fixes mentality, and make-believe metrics that measure activity rather than capability will sour companies on leadership development. They will, in turn, cut investment and go back to waiting passively for leaders to emerge.

But that approach has failed in the past and will continue to do so. Companies can do better; those that take leadership development seriously and treat it as a core business process can overcome the pathologies. By securing top team commitment, line management engagement and first-rate professional staff support in a system of shared ownership and accountability, they can avoid the ownership-is-power mentality. By constructing a leadership framework and focusing on process excellence, they can steer clear of products that have little relevance to their leadership-development challenges. And by building metrics that matter, they can have a clear line of sight between investments in leadership development and the ultimate goal: preparing individuals and teams that will be ready to step in and take their organizations to greater heights.

ABOUT THE RESEARCH

The research for this article is based on findings from three research initiatives and a series of in-depth interviews with executives at IBM. The research initiatives are the Building Leaders project, which included interviews at fifteen global corporations with approximately 250 individuals about organizational approaches to leadership development; the Learning to Lead project, which included interviews with 150 managers from more than fifty companies who participated in leadership-education programs; and the Global Capabilities project, which included interviews and survey-based research with nearly 3,000 managers and executives from thirty global companies on approaches they were using to link strategic challenges to organizational and leadership-development initiatives.

ENDNOTES

1. R. M. Fulmer and M. Goldsmith, *The Leadership Investment: How the World's Best Organizations Gain Strategic Advantage Through Leadership Development* (New York: AMACOM, 2000).

2. A. A. Vicere, ed., *Executive Education: Process, Practice, and Evaluation* (Princeton, N.J.: Peterson's Guides, 1990); D. A. Ready, "How Storytelling Builds Next-Generation Leaders," *MIT Sloan Management Review* 64 (Summer 2002):63–69; M. Kizilos and D. Ready, *World-Class HRD: Innovations in Practice* (Lexington, Mass.: ICEDR, 1999); A. de Meyer and D.

Ready, *Developing Global Capability* (Lexington, Mass.: ICEDR, 1998); D. A. Ready, *Champions of Change* (Boston: Gemini Consulting/ICEDR, 1994); D. A. Ready, "Executive Education: Is It Making the Grade?" *Fortune* (Dec. 14, 1992):39–48; J. A. Conger and B. Benjamin, *Building Leaders: How Successful Companies Develop the Next Generation* (San Francisco: Jossey-Bass, 1999).

3. A recent study by Booz Allen Hamilton shows that CEO turnover at major corporations in Europe and North America increased by 53 percent between 1995 and 2001, and the number of CEOs departing due to poor company performance increased by 130 percent. See C. Lucier, E. Spiegel, and R. Schuyt, "Why CEOs Fall: The Causes and Consequences of Turnover at the Top," *Strategy + Business 28* (third quarter 2002):34–47.

4. Ready, "How Storytelling Builds."

5. D. Ulrich, J. Zenger, and N. Smallwood, *Results-Based Leadership* (Boston: Harvard Business School Press, 1999).

6. M. W. McCall, Jr., *High Flyers: Developing the Next Generation of Leaders* (Boston: Harvard Business School Press, 1997).

7. N. M. Tichy and S. Sherman, *Control Your Destiny or Someone Else Will,* rev. ed. (New York: HarperBusiness, 2001).

8. Conger and Benjamin, *Building Leaders;* J. A. Conger, *Learning to Lead: The Art of Transforming Managers into Leaders* (San Francisco: Jossey-Bass, 1992); de Meyer and Ready, *Developing Global Capability.*

9. R. A. Heifetz, *Leadership Without Easy Answers* (Cambridge: Belknap Press of Harvard University Press, 1994); Ready, "How Storytelling Builds."

10. For a discussion of the differences between product-centric and solutions-centric organizations, see J. R. Galbraith, *Designing the Global Corporation* (San Francisco: Jossey-Bass, 2000), and J. R. Galbraith, *Designing Organizations: An Executive Guide to Strategy, Structure, and Process,* rev. ed. (San Francisco: Jossey-Bass, 2001).

11. S. R. Covey, *The Seven Habits of Highly Effective People: Powerful Lessons in Personal Change* (New York: Simon & Schuster, 1989); P. M. Senge, *The Fifth Discipline: The Art and Practice of the Learning Organization* (New York: Currency/Doubleday, 1990); J. C. Collins and J. I. Porras, *Built to Last: Successful Habits of Visionary Companies* (New York: HarperBusiness, 1994); D. Goleman, *Emotional Intelligence* (New York: Bantam, 1995).

12. Richard Pascale, a former Stanford Business School professor, charted the ebbs and flows of line management attention to what was considered best practice in leadership over recent decades. He cited the near-fever-pitch interest in T-groups, quality circles, confrontational feedback, assessment centers, reengineering, and a variety of other leadership initiatives. See R. T. Pascale, *Managing on the Edge: How the Smartest Companies Use Conflict to Stay Ahead* (New York: Simon & Schuster, 1990).

17

~

Global Leadership, Education,
and Human Survival

Christopher Williams

Global leadership is the pivotal point for appropriate policies and action to ensure human survival. But how do leaders maintain their knowledge and awareness in a fast-changing world of increasingly complex problems? How do we create a "learning leadership" that will ensure the survival of humanity?

Despite the relevance of global leadership for human survival, the academic world has shown little concern with this aspect of "up-system" research. There has been an interest in how power groups are created and reproduced, stemming from the work of the Italian "elite theorists" Pareto and Mosca, early in the twentieth century (Meisal, 1965). But this remains in the realms of social theory and does not contribute much to the practical development of contemporary leadership. Management theories of leadership are practical but apply essentially to commercial interests, which are often antithetical to the interests of humanity and to our survival. Kennedy Graham (2002) concluded the following: Research into leadership issues is a young and still rather shapeless discipline. Although leaders and leadership may provide the stuff of barroom wisdom and talk-show humor, it is an elusive subject from which to glean analytical insight and prescriptive value at a level approaching normal academic standards. Although some literature exists offering unfalsifiable theories about leadership behavior and personality, there is a dearth of primary empirical information about leaders,

Reprinted from *World Futures* 59, pp. 301–313. Copyright 2003 Taylor & Francis.

the philosophical prisms through which they perceive reality, and the principles by which they conduct themselves. This is especially the case with leadership on global issues.

Leadership is also undertheorized in many areas related to the survival debate, for example, national development (Lee, 2002), social movements (Barker et al., 2001, p. 1), and the education of leaders.

The United Nations University Leadership Academy (UNULA) in Amman is one of the new organizations trying to address this situation. This discussion reflects ongoing research and course development at the UNULA and examines two key questions: Why should we be concerned about the relationships between education, leadership, and survival? How do potential and serving leaders acquire the necessary attributes to recognize and address the threats and challenges to our survival in the contemporary world? But first, what exactly is "global leadership" in relation to survival?

GLOBAL LEADERSHIP AND SURVIVAL

A mention of global leadership inevitably demands definitions of *global* and *leadership,* which often then consume a large proportion of the debate with no workable conclusions. For the purposes of this discussion, a compromise between conflicting claims assumes that *global* can embrace circumstances that reflect human universals, an extended national or regional interest, and/or the condition of the global commons (see Williams, 2001, p. 46).

Similarly, *leadership* has as many definitions as texts. These are constantly evolving (Ciulla, 1998, pp. 10–13), and few embrace a global dimension. The basic concept of leadership within the standard Oxford Dictionary definition is "guiding." This is reflected in other languages. The Chinese character for *leader* means a "pointing leading person." The Hausa word *Shugaba* implies "the one in front" (Abolarin, 1997, p. 5). But not all traditions recognize this role. For example the Maori understanding of chieftainship is more akin to "trusteeship" (Kawharu, 2001). In this discussion, global leadership is taken to describe:

> guidance through act, influence or inducement including financial arrangement, by individuals, collective leaderships, organisations or States, which has actual or possible consequences affecting a human universal, an extended national or regional interest, or a common global and planetary in-

terest. Leadership may appear in many forms and derive from many sources, but all are likely to guide through act, influence, or inducement. (Williams, 2001, p. 46)

The characteristics of a globalizing world are increasingly seen as constructing a mutual interest beyond that of nation-states. This proposes that national leaders should accept that the national interest could be superseded by a greater world interest in some circumstances, which raises the question of the criteria determining that interest. Within the quasi-legal concept *planetary interest* Kennedy Graham provides a pragmatic definition, on two levels analogous to the accepted conventions delineating the national interest: The "vital planetary interest" is the survival and viability of humanity, contingent on the maintenance of the physical integrity of Earth and the protection of its ecological systems and biosphere from major anthropogenic change—the continuation of the planet in its state of natural equilibrium. The "normative planetary interest" is the universal improvement in the human condition in terms of meeting the basic human needs of each individual and observance of the fundamental human rights of each. (Graham, 1999, p. 9) It is therefore meaningful to talk of a common global or planetary interest in relation to human survival.

The main concern of this discussion is senior people at national and international levels. But in the view of Graham, the global dimension extends beyond high-profile individuals and entails leadership exhibited by men and women anywhere in the world, that serves the "planetary interest" of human unity, intercivilization harmony, global security and sustainability, and environmental integrity. It can be exhibited not only by leaders of the most senior international positions. It may be exhibited by middle-level managers or the head of the most humble household who teaches her children the art and virtues of domestic recycling (Graham, 2002, p. 4).

Although the focus is individuals with political power, many of the lessons are equally relevant to, and can be gleaned from, all levels of society.

The central implication of "survival" is basic survival—the long-term continuance of humanity and the planet. The significant problems for research, as defined by John Hertz (2001), are "questions of how human survival can be ensured in the face of the threats of extinction with which the entire human race is now confronted" (p. 1). But other forms of continuance are also relevant. In relation to global security, Gwyn Prins (1993) emphasizes *positive* survival, "a condition above bare existence" marked by the things that make us human and distinct from other forms of life. This entails continuance of knowledge, social groups, social systems, families, and what UNESCO now calls "indeterminate heritage"—traditions, philosophy, systems of calculation, poetry.

From the perspective of global leadership, ensuring basic survival and ensuring positive survival are not categorically different, as they might at first seem. It is likely that a despot who is willing to promote regional genocide would also readily employ weapons of mass destruction and threaten humanity. There seems little doubt that Hitler would have used the atomic bomb, had it been available to him. The U.S. advocate of nuclear deterrence Joseph Nye, Jr. (1986) unashamedly maintained that the total destruction of the human race was preferable to an existence that did not preserve positive survival in the form of the American way of life (pp. 45–46). We need to understand the mind-set of powerful people who think this way.

Other new security threats similarly embody a link between basic and positive survival. Leaders who permit "small-scale" "local" trials involving genetic modification are making a decision with global implications, although they rarely admit it.

Similarly, the failure to address local outbreaks of diseases such as BSE/CJD ("mad cow disease") will have consequences for human survival well beyond a single country. Suicide killings, such as those on September 11 in New York City and Washington, D.C., evidence that the killing of self, adversaries, and innocents can be justified to achieve a particular ideological goal. If pursued to its logical end, that ideology leaves everyone dead. What is the education that has led to that view? Some leaders deter the use of contraceptives and jeopardize humanity through overpopulation or HIV/AIDS. They are also promoting policy on a local level that, if promoted globally, could threaten the survival of humanity. Although seemingly diverse, many challenges at the level of positive survival have implications for the basic survival of humanity, not least for the positive survival of educational traditions.

There is another, more pragmatic reason for considering "positive survival" in relation to leadership. The total obliteration of humanity within a foreseeable time frame would require the occurrence of events that appear improbable. Our complete demise can only happen in one of four ways:

1. the simultaneous death of all humanity

2. degradation of life support systems to a degree that brings about the death of all humanity
3. a universal disease, toxin, or other environmental impact that kills before reproductive age
4. a universal disease, toxin, or other environmental impact that prevents human reproduction

Impacts that do not fulfill one of these criteria might devastate humanity, but not eliminate us. As I have argued previously, the decline of human intelligence caused by adverse environmental change is one possibility. And paradoxically, less intelligent human beings would not merely survive. They would probably survive longer, because they would not do "intelligent" things such as building nuclear weapons or modifying their DNA. But in such a society, a visit to the dentist would not be much fun (Williams, 1997).

As the legends of creation remind us, provided one man and one woman with reproductive capability are alive, biologically the human species could continue in some form. Political leaders are aware of that, and while paying lip service to the threat of extinction, it is unlikely that they will take it seriously. Despite the survival-oriented raison d'être of the United Nations, research carried out by the UNULA in 2001 found that even the leaders of the international organizations do not overtly concern themselves with fundamental human survival. The world problems as seen by Juan Somavia, of the International Labour Organization (ILO), are "poverty," "social exclusion," and the need for "decent work." At the World Trade Organization (WTO), Mike Moore identifies, in the last century, European tribalism and the "twin terrors" Marxism and fascism as the main threats. He sees "those who are locked out" of the information revolution, and the possible failure of the multilateral system, as challenges in the future. Unsurprisingly, from the perspective of the World Health Organization (WHO), Gro Harlem Brundtland considers "the health of people" very significant. But, as one would hope of the progenitor of "sustainable development," she also expresses a link between basic survival and positive survival. "Healthy people—healthy planet," she concludes (Graham and Williams, 2002).

Like it or not, contemporary political leaders are going to win more votes through preserving the American way of life than through preserving humanity. And while our only form of world governance is international rather than global, the formal views of the international leaders are likely (and not wrongly) to reflect those of their paymasters.

WHY THE CONCERN?

The significance of the relationship between leadership and education goes beyond the abilities and conduct of leaders themselves, because these same people exert considerable influence over the education of everyone else. A contemporary South Korean writer, Yun-Joo Lee (2002), makes the point succinctly:

> Although leaders are a "minority," arguably they are more important [than the populace] to examine because they are producers as well as consumers of the services that build human capital. Leaders are a product of their education, either accepting or rejecting the values being taught to them and then choosing to replicate or not the system they experienced.

Any national education system is to some extent a reflection of the ideology of those in power.

For centuries leaders have used and abused education systems to achieve their ends, and they continue to do so. Education can extend loyalty to a leader into loyalty to the *ideas* of a leader, and that is attractive to saints and despots alike. Notoriously, education was used to promote apartheid in South Africa and the United States, social hatred in Nazi Germany, and harmful nationalism in prewar Japan. This problem is not restricted to past eras. In 1998, the Taliban closed private girls' schools and ruled that other schools could not instruct girls older than eight, and that they could only teach the Koran. In Russia, the supreme mufti Ravil Gaynutdin has expressed concern about Islamic colleges that are promulgating the teachings of Wahabism. This eighteenth-century movement calls on its followers to treat all other Muslims as enemies (Lane, 1904). Current textbooks teach that anyone who is not a Wahabi should be killed (Rich, 2000, p. 11). That ideology amounts to proposing the extermination of most of humanity.

Islamic fundamentalism is not the only source of abuse. In some southern states of the United States, creationists impede knowledge about evolution and Charles Darwin. In 1929 the Arkansas and Mississippi Education Authorities banned the teaching of evolution, and the courts have argued over this ever since. The Kansas Board of Education inserted "creationism" into the school standards on science in 1999 (MacKenzie, 2000); this decision was later reversed by the courts. And then Ohio tried to introduce the idea of "intelligent design." The significance goes beyond a curriculum nicety. Through understanding evolution, students learn that human beings have survived and evolved for millions of years in relation to a comparatively stable "natural" evolutionary environment. This understanding underpins a questioning of whether or not we will continue to survive in the context of adverse human-made environmental change that radically alters that environment.

Commercial interests are also a concern. In Niger, Shell runs a significant number of schools, and Mobil has similar influence in the Amazon region. Are these schools likely to present an unbiased view about global warming? Would a nation achieve a balanced democratic debate about genetically modified organisms if many of its population had been to schools or colleges run by Monsanto? It seems unlikely in the light of Monsanto's efforts to manipulate not only genes but also the academic world through articles in medical journals, as part of "a planned series of outreach efforts to physicians" (GeneWatch, 2000).

In times of political turmoil, universities often provide the only effective check on wayward governments, and for centuries this check has engendered politically motivated interference. Academics face personal danger, and military or political security is not the only rationalization for interference. In Turkey, an expert on cyanide received an eighteen-month jail sentence in July 2000, because his opinions about environmental and occupational safety could affect the gold-mining industry (Jones, 2000). Outspoken academics may be one of the last lines of defense for human survival. Even presenting data that appear inconvenient to the biotech industry can culminate in the premature ending of an academic career, as biologist Arthur Puzstai found when he suggested in Britain that genetically modified potatoes might affect the immune system of rats (BBC, 1999).

Leaders do not only influence the education of others through their control of education systems and academia. They also do it directly through speeches and public information, and they do not always do it honestly or wisely in relation to human survival. Thabo Mbeke's idiosyncratic claims about the absence of a link between HIV and AIDS are an obvious example of the latter, but misguided views are not the only problem. There is an intrinsic unwillingness to educate the public about global problems of any type. Naive cheerfulness is more likely to win votes. As John Douglas

(1986) said in the *New York Times,* "Presidents have failed to educate the nation, preferring instead to apply a cheerful veneer. . . . Leaders fear being tagged as scare-mongers or doomsayers. Optimists are cast as winners, pessimists as losers."

Politicians usually only ride on the threat of danger retrospectively. U.S. President George W. Bush showed little interest in global matters before September 11, 2001. The symbiosis between leadership and education is not surprising. It is even reflected in etymology: *Education* derives from the Latin *educere,* "to educe," "to lead forth." And *pedagogue* derives from the Greek *pais,* "child," and *agein,* "to lead." If this relationship were more clearly part of public awareness, it might be asked why, although the state has legitimate control of the means of both violence and education and both can be used to threaten our survival, only the former is regulated at an international level. Governments seem more ready to accept international intervention and norms about what happens in their armies than in their classrooms. Perhaps they are all too aware that the pen really is mightier than the sword.

HOW DO LEADERS LEARN?

The most relevant aspect of leadership and education is, of course, the specific education of leaders. Throughout the world, beyond private tuition, this has been evident in four forms:

- Elite-creating national systems of education
- Specialist university courses and departments
- In-house pre- and in-service training
- Mid-career tuition at specialist institutions

Again, history provides insights into how survival may be jeopardized if these systems are inadequate or abused. In many countries the whole of the national system of education has been designed to create elite cadres of politicians and civil servants. France is a common example, which has global relevance because it has been replicated in many of the Francophone countries. The "Oxbridge" system in Britain is similar but less formalized, and the idea also remains evident throughout Britain's former colonies, including the United States with its "Ivy League" system. In Japan, the Todai system, with Tokyo University at its pinnacle, continues and has similarly had international influence within the former occupied countries, such as South Korea.

These systems are increasingly seen as ineffective. Selection processes are often inefficient and nonmeritocratic. Tuition is inappropriate and does little to engender an informed global leadership. Students are still required to study academic subjects that are not relevant to their future careers, in great and unnecessary depth, and there is rarely any conceptual linking or overview of subjects. Discipline-based intelligence is overvalued, yet studies of senior leaders find that this mental capacity is secondary in its significance to skills such as creativity (Rushmore, 1984). Paradoxically, the traditional systems that lay claim to selecting and educating the future world leaders at the undergraduate level hardly ever have the study of "leadership" on their curriculum, except within management courses, or as an aspect of history. They usually do not provide the right input or ethos for those who need to acquire generalist skills, to engage in global "joined-up thinking," and to make increasingly "big" decisions in the context of risk and uncertain knowledge. And they rarely encourage or facilitate ongoing learning.

The result is personified in British prime minister Tony Blair, whose Oxford education gave him an excellent grasp of law. But on his own admission he wishes in retrospect that he had studied international relations—and that he could use a word processor efficiently. In the international sphere, director general of the WTO Mike Moore would like to have learned languages and states with great honesty, "I wish I had a degree in economics" (Graham and Williams, 2002, p. 2).

Elite-creating systems are open to abuse. Nazi Germany provided an exemplary model of leadership education, at least in terms of efficiency. In Hitler's Germany, the "new nobility" was to be created from those "of hereditary Nordic substance as has been proved by actual deeds." A decree in 1937 established the Adolf-Hitler-Schules. A quarter of these graduates were to go to the "castle of an order" *(Ordensburg)* for another four years of leadership training. A further selection was to be made to create "leaders of leaders" *(Junkers)*. The Führer was clear that "The best form of State is one which with the most natural certainty raises the best brains of the community to influence and leadership" (Kneller, 1941, pp. 62, 65).

This form of abuse is not just historical. Some of Pakistan's madrassas provide a contemporary example. Before the events of September 11, Sami-ul Haq, the head of the Darul Uloom Haqqani, one of the top Islamic seminaries, stated that he was proud to have produced some of the "top leaders of Afghanistan's repressive Taliban militia," including interior minister Khairule Khairkhwa and the head of the feared religious police, Qalam

Uddin (McCarthy, 2000, p. 16). Reports from Peshawar, Pakistan, told how young boys are taught to "Pray for the destruction of the West, pray for the West to be divided into pieces so that it can be attacked, just as the West has done to Islam" (Carlton, 2001, p. 6).

Any system of education that aims to create and shape elite cadres has the potential to promote an ideology that may threaten human well-being and survival. We should perhaps look more closely at the ideologies of limitless consumption, environmental sacrifice, and "growth" that pertain in the systems in North America, Europe, and East Asia. The abuse of education systems by self-declared despots is easy to identify and therefore eventually to redress. The threat to survival arising from the ideology of unbridled progress is latent and insidious, and so far has attracted little comment.

The second form of leadership education is through specialist courses and departments, usually at the postgraduate level. The U.S. universities have many such courses (see Freeman et al., 1996), which are, in general, commercially oriented. Beyond this "leadership" can be part of training for service within religious organizations or other professions, for example "educational leadership," which essentially means upgrading teachers. Courses such as that at Westminster University, London, offer tuition for young diplomats and other international civil servants, within which language learning is central. Increasingly, political leaders have experienced this sort of education, for example, the environmentally oriented president of Costa Rica, J. M. Figueres, attained a master's degree in public administration at the John F. Kennedy School at Harvard University.

At the postgraduate level, the Jepson School of Leadership Studies, University of Richmond (USA), is virtually unique in providing an undergraduate leadership course. This is an interesting innovation, but it begs the question whether potential leaders can self-select, and/or be selected, in their late teens. Within the third form—pre- and in-service training—selection is far less problematic.

In the commercial sector, management training is now common, but the most relevant aspect is civil service training. These institutions have their antecedents in the Chinese Imperial College *(guozijian)*, built in 1306 by the grandson of Kublai Khan. The Chinese demonstrated that national elites could be created through a meritocratic system, and that this system had benefits for governance. The tradition continues at the National School of Administration in Beijing. It was not until the end of the nineteenth century, prompted by the Northcote-Trevelyan Report in 1853, that the British system of civil service promotion and training adopted a more meritocratic form. The Civil Service College then provided a model for many similar institutions around the world. At an international level, the United Nations Staff College in Turin trains UN officials.

In-service training addresses the need for ongoing education; it can be melded into daily practice; and time-efficient delivery addresses the problem that senior people are busy people. But inevitably in-house training suffers from introspection. It is unlikely to encourage fundamental questioning of governmental practice, for example, the investment of civil servant pensions in the genetic engineering industry.

The fourth, and more recent, approach is short courses through specialist organizations. These usually target mid-career professionals, can provide a "second-chance" training for people who did not have access to the elite systems, and are often more relevant to human survival. The intent is to provide a brief period of skill enhancement and global awareness, just before individuals are promoted to senior positions. Lead International, for example, provides courses promoting sustainable development for an international clientele from diverse professional backgrounds. In the United Kingdom, Forum for the Future employs a similar strategy at a national level. Courses usually embody two aspects: a particular theme, such as water management, and core leadership skills.

The "how" of learning—the pedagogical style—in these courses is very far from that of a traditional discipline-based university. At the UNULA, the instigator of the academy, former prime minister Abdul Salam Al-Majali established the approach. He uses the phrase "Expose, don't impose." Potential leaders, he maintains, are not temperamentally suited to formal lectures but learn experientially, principally through exposure to more experienced leaders. The difficulty faced by these specialist organizations is their small scale and limited resources, which mean that selecting appropriate candidates is crucial. If fees or other costs are prohibitive, or the routes of selection are limited, they can unwittingly replicate the unmeritocratic selectivity of the old elite-creating education systems.

CREATING A LEARNING LEADERSHIP—CYBERNETICS

In addition to the difficulty of selecting the right people, these four forms of leadership education embody another problem: They rarely influence serving political leaders. To be realistic, this will probably always be the case. So how do we engender a learning leadership? Leaders might not be persuaded to take time out themselves, to upgrade their abilities, but they might be persuaded to create learning-oriented institutions around them—a learning leadership, if not a learning leader. Serving leaders would claim that they learn "on the job" from one another, from their advisers, and from the population they serve, so we must build on that. Learning on the job reflects two relational aspects of leadership theory: peer interaction and *reciprocal* relationships (Williams 2001, pp. 33, 80), and *transactional* relationships—mutual give-and-take—between leaders and followers (Bass, 1990, p. 319). But transactional relationships are not so straightforward on a global scale. Relevant peers are scattered across the world, and it is hard to envisage a truly transactional relationship between leaders and followers on a global scale.

A third relational interaction therefore becomes significant—*cybernetic* learning—which complements the other two forms. In any biological system, even on a global scale, cybernetic systems provide the feedback that is vital for any form of control to be effective. The term *cybernetic* is very apposite in relation to leadership: It stems from the Greek *kybernetes,* which means "steersman." Theories of cybernetics have been utilized to explain how commercial leaders learn "on the job," but this idea has not been extended to a global scale (Hampden-Turner, 1992, pp. 421–428).

Norbert Wiener foresaw the significance of cybernetics in the 1950s, in *The Human Use of Human Beings: Cybernetics and Society* (1954). In the view of Jeremy Rifkin (1998), "Weiner came to view cybernetics as both a unifying theory and a methodological tool for reorganising the entire world." Rifkin continued, "Virtually every activity of importance in today's society is being brought under the control of cybernetic principles" (p. 184). There are four aspects that relate to global leadership: the *behavior* of humanity, the *condition* of humanity, *planetary information,* and *global ethics.*

First, global leadership must attend to the *behavior* of the global population—utilizing indicators that reflect the choices and decisions that human populations make. In the 1960s and 1970s international aid agencies realized that the day-to-day behavior of nomadic Africans, not high-tech weather projections, was one of the most reliable indicators of impending famine. If the nomads were selling cattle and becoming less willing to make long, risky journeys, famine was likely. Scanning local newspapers for conflict-related keywords is being used as an indicator of unrest in Central Asia. Similarly, on a global scale, behavior such as migration and asylum seeking, or a decline in birthrate as in Japan and Russia, provides indicators of planetary disruption or the changing dynamics of globalization and modernity. Second, the *condition* or "health" of humanity is indicated by changes such as an increasing birth/survival rate since the 1950s, a possible decline in fertility rate due to chemical impacts, an increase in mental health problems, and pandemics such as HIV/AIDS. A global leader must become a global epidemiologist, seeking out and analyzing effects in the whole population that are hardly evident in individuals or single nations, and noticing effects in small populations that may have global implications, such as Ebola. But this should also embrace a global epidemiology of success—how certain policies and strategies improve the human condition.

The third aspect is that leadership should attend to *planetary information,* for example, in the form of changes in climate, biodiversity, radiation levels, oxygen levels, or water availability and quality. Agreements such as that at Kyoto may seem inadequate, but they represent a completely new era in which global leaders attend to planetary information (see Kyoto GIS, 2001). The term *sustainable* stems from the Greek verb *prosecho,* "to take care" and "to take notice." The case of ozone depletion also provides a reminder that "attend" should mean "take notice." When data indicating the thinning of the ozone layer were first recorded by scientists, they were ignored on the belief that they were a mistake.

The idea that the planetary and ecological systems, including human life, can be viewed as a global information system has been developing for three decades. In the 1970s, James Lovelock's Gaia hypothesis (1979) introduced the perception of the Earth as a single system. Inspired by the mapping of the human genome, recent innovations propose that all the genes in an ecosystem could be considered a single genome, and we could then compare these "ecogenomes" to discover rules for how ecosystems are put together (Leslie, 2001, pp. 32–35). Howard Bloom (2000) sees planetary life as representing an evolutionary "global brain," and Alison Jolly (1999) foresees an increasingly networked information system that will eventually make the planet function as a single "superorganism." New surveillance technology—for example, remote sensing and Geographical Information Systems (GIS)—increasingly provides the means for leaderships to observe their planet in a way that has never before been possible (Harrison and Pearce, 2001).

Websites such as Globio (2002) and the United Nations Environment Programme's UNEP/GRID provide a wealth of planetary information about environmental change, yet the potential for improving human well-being is not properly exploited. The likely impacts of the flooding in Mozambique in 2000 were predicted by satellite within minutes, but the information was slow to reach the people who needed it, so remedial action was delayed. The UK nongovernmental organization (NGO) AidtoAid, which makes satellite information available to other NGOs engaged in humanitarian assistance, addresses this problem. But proposals to create an inexpensive ring of remote sensing devices, which could help predict and assess the impacts of natural and human-made disasters, has been languishing with the British civil service for three years (Graham-Rowe, 2001, p. 4). Hopefully, the United Nations Development Programme (UNDP) Millennium Ecosystem Assessment, which links the efforts of fifteen hundred scientists to assess sixteen thousand satellite images, will greatly improve this information deficit.

Well before these global visions and technological advances, information biologist Gregory Bateson (1979) defined information very simply as "news of difference." And he continued with an obvious point that provides an important warning: "All perception of difference is limited by threshold. Differences too slowly presented are not perceivable." Thresholds raise a crucial point. Humans are not adapted to notice the "creeping disasters" such as climate change and ozone depletion. The perception of global risk must be intellectual, not sensory (Seidel, 1999), and that is a concern for education, particularly the public information put out by leaders (Williams, 2002). Intellectual perception requires new forms of collaborative leadership between scientists, technologists, educationists, and politicians.

But whatever the system, strategy, or pedagogy, there remains the standard dilemma in any discussion of leadership education: It is not adequate to develop technical proficiency without a moral dimension. Technical proficiency alone is as likely to produce a Gandhi as a Hitler. It is also clear that the survival of humanity is inextricably linked to the "positive survival" of education, and that is largely a moral question.

The fourth aspect is that those with power must also be constantly aware of evolving *global ethics,* particularly in relation to leadership. There are currently no international standards that specifically address the moral conduct of leaders, simply a proposal from the UNULA (Williams, 2001). Within this code, of relevance to this discussion, leaders should recognize a moral duty to maintain their own ongoing learning: "Leaders and their agents shall seek out and consider properly all information and evidence relevant to their duties from all possible sources, particularly in relation to hatred, harm or hazard, including information from the global population and planetary and ecological systems" (Proposed Code for Global Leadership, C3.3). Any set of ethical standards for leadership also proposes a relevant curriculum for the education of leaders. For example, if it is agreed that leaders should respect international law, it follows that they should know the basics of international law. If they should uphold the "global and planetary interest," they should know what that is and the precedents upon which the idea is based.

Some of the centuries-old Indian prohibitions on leadership from the traditions of Kautilya make the point about leadership ethics very clearly: "Keep away from another person's wife"; "Avoid daydreaming, capriciousness, falsehood, extravagance"; and "Avoid association with harmful persons" (Waslekar, 2000, p. 48). There are certain of our modern leaders who might have enhanced their personal potential for survival had they learned these lessons at some point. And leadership ethics indicates the symbiosis that must be formed if we are to achieve the broader goals of this discussion.

We need to create a conspicuous coincidence of interests between the personal survival of leaders and the survival of humanity, through democratic and more innovative forms of global leadership accountability. In that context, the current dilemmas of leadership education would probably become self solving. These four aspects of cybernetic learning embody nothing new. But at present they are rarely viewed holistically as a core aspect of the duties of leadership. We need leaders who can steer humanity through intelligent responses to global information, not through outdated beliefs or self-serving ideology. A "learning leadership" is one of the most important manifestations of applied survival research.

REFERENCES

Abolarin, A. (1997). The cultural language of leadership. *LEAD Newsletter,* 7, p. 5.

Barker, C., Johnson, A., and Lavalette, M. (2001). *Leadership and social movements.* Manchester, UK: Manchester University Press.

Bass, B. M. (1990). *Bass and Stogdill's handbook of leadership: Theory, research, and managerial applications.* New York: Free Press.

Bateson, G. (1979). *Mind and nature.* New York: Ballantine Books.

BBC. (1999). GM research row moves to Internet. At http://news.bbc.co.uk/hi/english/sci/tech/newsid_368000/368089.stm.

Bloom, H. (2000). *Global brain: The evolution of the mass mind.* London: Wiley.

Bowles, S., and Gintis, H. (1976). *Schooling in capitalist America.* London: Routledge & Kegan Paul.

Carlton, G. (2001). In the frame: Peshawar, Pakistan. *Independent Magazine* (UK), 29 September, p. 6.

Ciulla, J. B. (Ed.). (1998). *Ethics: The heart of leadership*. Westport, Conn.: Praeger.

Duke, B. (1991). *Education and leadership for the twenty-first century: Japan, America, and Britain*. New York: Praeger.

Freeman, F. H., Knott, K. B., and Schwartz, M. K. (1996). *Leadership education: A sourcebook*. Greensboro, N.C.: Center for Creative Leadership.

GeneWatch. (2000). Monsanto's "desperate" propaganda campaign research global proportions. *GeneWatch*, press release, 6 September. At www.genewatch.org/Press%Releases/pr15.htm.

Globio. (2002). At http://www.grida.no/prog/polar/globio/UNEP/GRID-Arendal GIS datasets http://www.grida.no/db/gis/prod/html/toc.htm/.

Graham, K. (1999). *The planetary interest*. London: UCL Press.

Graham, K. (2002). Studies in vision and management: Interviews with UN leaders, Unpublished paper, Amman, UN University Leadership Academy.

Graham, K., and Williams, C. (Eds.). (2002). Global Leaders Interviews Series: *No. 1 Through the eyes of people—An interview with Juan Somavia. No. 2 Freedom is a universal value—An interview with Mike Moore. No. 3 Healthy people–healthy planet—An interview with Gro Harlem Brundtland*. Amman: UN University Leadership Academy.

Graham-Rowe, D. (2001). Saving planet Earth. *New Scientist*, 23 June, 1523, p. 27.

Hampden-Turner, C. (1992). Standing at the helm. In M. Syrett and C. Hogg, *Frontiers of leadership* (pp. 375–407). Oxford: Blackwell.

Harrison, P., and Pearce, F. (2001). *AAAS atlas of population and environment*. Berkeley: University of California Press.

Hertz, J. H. (2001). Some observations on engaging in "survival research." Unpublished paper, Scarsdale, N.Y.

Jolly, A. (1999). *Lucy's legacy: Sex and intelligence in human evolution*. Cambridge: Harvard University Press.

Jones, D. (2000). Cyanide expert jailed for meeting. *Times Higher Educational Supplement* (UK), 7 July, p. 10.

Kawharu, H. (2001). *Notes on the Treaty of Waitangi*. At http://www.govt.nz/aboutnz/treaty.php3.

Kneller, G. F. (1941). *The educational philosophy of national socialism*. New Haven: Yale University Press.

Kyoto GIS. (2001). At http://maps.grida.no/kyoto/.

Lane, E. W. (1904). *The modern Egyptians*. London: Dent.

Lee. Y.-J. (2002). Perceptions of leadership and development in South Korea and Egypt. Unpublished dissertation in progress, School of Oriental and African Studies, London.

Leslie, M. (2001). Tales of the sea. *New Scientist*, 2275, pp. 32–35.

Lovelock, J. (1979). *Gaia: A new look at life on earth*. Oxford: Oxford University Press.

MacKenzie, D. (2000). Unnatural selection. *New Scientist*, 22 April, p. 35.

McCarthy, R. (2000). Pakistan's clerics balk at school reforms. *The Guardian*, 13 September.

Meisal, J. H. (Ed.). (1965). *Pareto and Mosca*. Englewood Cliffs, N.J.: Prentice-Hall.

Nye, Joseph. (1986). *Nuclear ethic*. New York: Free Press.

Prins, G. (1993). *Threats without enemies*. London: Earthscan.

Rich, V. (2000). Terrorist colleges rife, says leader. *Times Higher Education Supplement,* 21 July, p. 15.

Rifkin, J. (1998). *The biotech century*. New York: Tarcher/Putnam.

Rushmore, J. T. (1984). *Executive performance and intellectual ability in organizational levels*. Not published.

Seidel, P. (1999). *Invisible walls: Why we ignore the damage we inflict on the planet . . . and ourselves*. New York: Prometheus Books.

Waslekar, S. (2000). *Dharma Rajya: Path-breaking reforms for India's governance*. Delhi: Konark Publishers.

Wiener, N. (1954). *The human use of human beings: Cybernetics and society*. New York: Avon Books.

Wilkinson, R. (Ed.). (1969). *Governing elites: Studies in training and selection*. Oxford: Oxford University Press.

Williams, C. (1997). *Terminus brain: The environmental threat to human intelligence*. London: Earthscan.

Williams, C. (2001). *Leaders of integrity: Ethics and a code for global leadership*. Amman: UN University Leadership Academy.

Williams, C. (2002). New security risks and public educating: The relevance of recent evolutionary brain science. *Journal of Risk Research,* 4(3), pp. 245–248.

– V –

LEADERSHIP AS A
PARADOX

A dilemma is defined as a choice between equally attractive or equally aversive alternatives and requires an either/or solution; you cannot have your cake and eat it, too. A paradox, on the other hand, is defined as an apparent contradiction between alternatives, but it can result in "and" choices rather than "either/or" outcomes. Narcissism can be said to result in incredible success and inevitable failure. Leadership, by its very nature, is a paradox, and leaders reframe dilemmas so that they are seen as paradoxes and, therefore, their choices are not mutually exclusive. It is not a matter of leadership versus management, but effective leadership and good management; not followership versus leadership, but recognizing that we occupy both the follower and leader role simultaneously; not transactional versus transformational leadership, but an effective balance of transactional and transformational leadership.

The human interaction between leader and followers mirrors the complexities of many personalities. Attempting to develop a set of requirements or assuming that specific tools and techniques can be adopted by each and all to ensure good leadership is folly. The result is paradox and we have identified only a few that are associated with leadership.

Individuals who possess all of the important characteristics and qualities of effective leaders don't necessarily succeed, and if they do, their efforts often result in great harm or tragedy to others. Moreover, leaders and followers often find themselves using unethical means to achieve worthy ends, and vice versa. A person who is a successful leader in one situation or context may fail in another situation, even though he or she employs the same capacity, skill, or style, whereas other individuals (although not very many) are able to successfully lead in a variety of very different situations. This assertion takes us back to the question of whether leaders are born or made. Although there is general agreement that leadership can be learned, it is certainly true that some find it much easier than others to learn the qualities of effective leadership.

Despite decades of progress, women remain underrepresented in senior leadership positions. Are they victims of discrimination, or have women chosen not to lead, or both? Is charisma a necessary quality for leaders to move their organizations from good to great, or are those leaders characterized by the seemingly contradictory qualities of compelling modesty and ferocious resolve? In this last part of the book we attempt to introduce the reader to just a few of the paradoxes of contemporary leadership.

LEADERSHIP PERSPECTIVES

In "The Disabling Shadow of Leadership" (Chapter 18), Bill McCabe suggests that leaders who want to transform their own performance and their team's effectiveness should look at how their own shadow could be getting in the way. The paradox is that one can be an effective leader but be hampered by one's shadow.

In Chapter 19, we explore "Narcissistic Leaders: The Incredible Pros, the Inevitable Cons" with Michael Maccoby. The paradox is that narcissists are good for companies that need people with vision and courage but are bad for companies when they refuse to listen to the advice of those around them when challenged with problems that can lead to trouble. Effective leaders all have some degree of ego, but the narcissistic leader must be cautious. Maccoby suggests that the narcissistic leader must find a trusted sidekick to bring rationality to the leader's vision. We need narcissistic leaders to create visions for today's organizations, but they need to understand and accept their limits. Barbara Kellerman and Deborah L. Rhode in "Viable Options: Rethinking Women and Leadership" (Chapter 20) examine why after decades of progress, women remain underrepresented in senior leadership positions. Are they victims of discrimination, or have women chosen not to lead?

Finally, in "Level 5 Leadership: The Triumph of Humility and Fierce Resolve" (Chapter 21), Jim Collins reports on the results of research that explain what catapults a company from merely good to truly great. He has found that most powerfully transformative executives possess a paradoxical mixture of compelling modesty and professional will. They are timid and ferocious, shy and fearless. They are rare—and unstoppable.

18

∼

The Disabling
Shadow of Leadership

Bill McCabe

There was an advertisement run not so long ago for Tabasco sauce. You may have seen it. In the advertisement God was shown sitting in the heavens on a cloud shaking the sauce onto a sandwich and clearly relishing the prospect of his fiery snack. However, as he was shaking the bottle he was also quite unaware that drops of the sauce were falling onto the earth below, causing havoc and destruction.

So it is with leaders everywhere. Leaders focus on what they see as important and are typically quite unconscious of the unintended but massive impact they are having on their colleagues, teams, and clients. We call this outcome of their actions the unconscious impact of their shadow(s). But why is this impact of their shadow important?

The answer is that an autocratic command-and-control approach in business is no longer appropriate. To be successful, leaders today have to find ways to engage people's ideas, energy, and inspiration, and this means they will also have to build much stronger relationships—and what will prevent such relationships from occurring is their shadow.

Let me give you a real-life example of a leader I have worked with who became very aware of the impact his shadow was having on his effectiveness.

We may think that we have choice all the time, but I would suggest that most of us are, in fact, governed by judgment. We are always assessing what

Reprinted with permission from the *British Journal of Administrative Management* (April/May 2005), pp. 16–17.

EXHIBIT 18.1

Case Study 1

Graham Cooke is factory general manager with Unilever Ice Cream and Frozen Food in Lowestoft, England. In his early career he achieved results by being a capable, forceful, and task-oriented manager. There was nothing unusual about this, but he had developed something of a reputation in the business, and when he took up a new role to drive through a large IT change project, he discovered that his new team were extremely concerned about how he might manage them.

Graham Cooke recognized that he needed to change, and my work with him started by focusing on his shadow. I helped him to become more aware of the impact he was having on others and helped him to see that he had different choices based on the future that he wanted to create for himself.

This understanding—that a greater awareness of the impact we make leads to a clearer choice around what future we want to create—is a critical one for leaders to grasp.

---

is right or wrong, good or bad. We base decisions not on what we want to create in the future but on what we have learned through experience in the past. But if we want to change, there has to be a radical interruption in this normal way of looking and responding. This interruption starts with a deep self-inquiry into how we impact on others at the moment and whether our intended impact is the same as that experienced by our colleagues.

SOFT AND GENTLE

To give you another example of how this principle plays out in real life, let me highlight the case of the leader who is perceived by his or her team as being too soft. The leader may believe that his or her style is one that helps to empower staff, but the shadow of such a leadership style may impact the team profoundly.

In such cases people in the team will often start to go "off message"— doing their own things in their own way. There may also be a continual sense of crisis in the team caused by a leadership that isn't clear enough or engaging enough.

The point here is that it isn't only strong leaders who cast a shadow. All leaders do. We may have a particular leadership style, but our shadow will affect others, and when we are unaware, it can seriously compromise people's engagement in work and their business effectiveness.

EXHIBIT 18.2

Case Study 2

This example of the shadow in action underlines the problems that can be caused. Take the case of the managing director (MD) whose team reported regularly that sales and results were in line with projections. Then, just two months before the end of the year, the sales team reported that they were in fact running more than £500,000 behind target. The MD exploded. How could this happen? Why hadn't he been told earlier? What were all the meetings about? The answer he got was that people were afraid to tell him about the real state of affairs because of his temper.

In this real-life example the MD saw in that moment that his shadow had led his people to present him with key information in such a way that he wouldn't have reason to blow up. Unfortunately, their approach had exacerbated the situation. He would have needed the information much earlier in the year in order to do something about it—but the weakness of his relationships with his key people had let him down, and these relationships were his responsibility all along.

TACKLING YOUR SHADOW

So, if you are a leader, how do you start to tackle your shadow? Your lever is this: to build fierce self-awareness of the way you behave around people. This requires you to get information about your impact on others, and you can use coaching, 360-degree questionnaires, or structures like action-learning groups to begin to get such feedback. However, you can make this even more real, right now, by looking at people with whom you do not have a strong relationship.

Take a moment to think of your manager or your manager's boss when you are about to present important information about your team, department, or performance. What spin do you put on that information? How does your attitude and behavior differ in a meeting where your boss is present and in a meeting where she or he isn't present. Do you feel you need to look after that relationship?

And now recognize that you have that same impact on the people who report directly to you. Some of your colleagues—those with whom you have strong relationships—may feel energized and inspired by your leadership. But don't kid yourself. There will be others who feel drained, demotivated, or even intimidated by you. Where this is the case you have an extraordinary opportunity for growth.

CONCLUSION

So how aware are you of your shadow? It is absolutely up to you to decide whether you want to look at it or not. But if you are prepared to continue leading, unaware of its impact, then don't be surprised when you achieve results you don't intend.

Alternatively, take your courage in your hands, adopt ways that help you to see the shadow that you cast, and start to make different choices about the impact you want to have in the world.

19

~

Narcissistic Leaders: The Incredible Pros, the Inevitable Cons

Michael Maccoby

Many leaders dominating business today have what psychoanalysts call a narcissistic personality. That's good news for companies that need passion and daring to break new ground. But even productive narcissists can be dangerous for organizations. Here is some advice on avoiding the dangers.

There's something new and daring about the CEOs who are transforming today's industries. Just compare them with the executives who ran large companies in the 1950s through the 1980s. Those executives shunned the press and had their comments carefully crafted by corporate PR departments. But today's CEOs—superstars such as Bill Gates, Andy Grove, Steve Jobs, Jeff Bezos, and Jack Welch—hire their own publicists, write books, grant spontaneous interviews, and actively promote their personal philosophies. Their faces adorn the covers of magazines like *Business Week, Time,* and *The Economist.* What's more, the world's business personalities are increasingly seen as the makers and shapers of our public and personal agendas. They advise schools on what kids should learn and lawmakers on how to invest the public's money. We look to them for thoughts on everything from the future of e-commerce to hot places to vacation.

There are many reasons today's business leaders have higher profiles than ever before. One is that business plays a much bigger role in our lives than it used to, and its leaders are more often in the limelight. Another is that the business world is experiencing enormous changes that call for visionary and charismatic leadership. But my twenty-five years of consulting both as a psychoanalyst in private practice and as an adviser to top managers suggest a third reason, namely, a pronounced change in the personality of the strategic leaders at the top. As an anthropologist, I try to understand people in the context in which they operate, and as a psychoanalyst, I tend to see them through a distinctly Freudian lens. Given what I know, I believe that the larger-than-life leaders we are seeing today closely resemble the personality type that Sigmund Freud dubbed narcissistic. "People of this type impress others as being 'personalities,'" he wrote, describing one of the psychological types that clearly fall within the range of normality. "They are especially suited to act as a support for others, to take on the role of leaders, and to give a fresh stimulus to cultural development or damage the established state of affairs."

Throughout history, narcissists have always emerged to inspire people and to shape the future. When military, religious, and political arenas dominated society, it was figures such as Napoleon Bonaparte, Mahatma Gandhi, and Franklin Delano Roosevelt who determined the social agenda. But from time to time, when business became the engine of social change, it, too, generated its share of narcissistic leaders. That was true at the beginning of this century, when men like Andrew Carnegie, John D. Rockefeller, Thomas Edison, and Henry Ford exploited new technologies and restructured American industry. And I think it is true again today.

But Freud recognized that there is a dark side to narcissism. Narcissists, he pointed out, are emotionally isolated and highly distrustful. Perceived threats can trigger rage. Achievements can feed feelings of grandiosity. That's why Freud thought narcissists were the hardest personality types to analyze. Consider how an executive at Oracle described his narcissistic CEO Larry Ellison: "The difference between God and Larry is that God does not believe he is Larry." That observation is amusing, but it is also troubling. Not surprisingly, most people think of narcissists in a primarily negative way. After all, Freud named the type after the mythical figure Narcissus, who died because of his pathological preoccupation with himself.

Yet narcissism can be extraordinarily useful—even necessary. Freud shifted his views about narcissism over time and recognized that we are all somewhat narcissistic. More recently, psychoanalyst Heinz Kohut built on Freud's theories and developed methods of treating narcissists. Of course, only professional clinicians are trained to tell whether narcissism is normal or pathological. In this article, I discuss the differences between productive and unproductive narcissism but do not explore the extreme pathology of borderline conditions and psychosis.

Leaders such as Jack Welch and George Soros are examples of productive narcissists. They are gifted and creative strategists who see the big picture and find meaning in the risky challenge of changing the world and leaving behind a legacy. Indeed, one reason we look to productive narcissists in times of great transition is that they have the audacity to push through the massive transformations that society periodically undertakes. Productive narcissists are not only risk takers willing to get the job done but also charmers who can convert the masses with their rhetoric. The danger is that narcissism can turn unproductive when, lacking self-knowledge and restraining anchors, narcissists become unrealistic dreamers. They nurture grand schemes and harbor the illusion that only circumstances or enemies block their success. This tendency toward grandiosity and distrust is the Achilles' heel of narcissists. Because of it, even brilliant narcissists can come under suspicion for self-involvement, unpredictability, and—in extreme cases—paranoia.

It's easy to see why narcissistic leadership doesn't always mean successful leadership. Consider the case of Volvo's Pehr Gyllenhammar. He had a dream that appealed to a broad international audience—a plan to revolutionize the industrial workplace by replacing the dehumanizing assembly line caricatured in Charlie Chaplin's *Modern Times*. His wildly popular vision called for team-based craftsmanship. Model factories were built and publicized to international acclaim. But his success in pushing through these dramatic changes also sowed the seeds of his downfall. Gyllenhammar started to feel that he could ignore the concerns of his operational managers. He pursued chancy and expensive business deals, which he publicized on television and in the press. On one level, you can ascribe Gyllenhammar's falling out of touch with his workforce simply to faulty strategy. But it is also possible to attribute it to his narcissistic personality. His overestimation of himself led him to believe that others would want him to be the czar of a multinational enterprise. In turn, these fantasies led him to pursue a merger with Renault, which was tremendously unpopular with Swedish employees. Because Gyllenhammar was deaf to complaints about Renault, Swedish managers were forced to take their case public. In the end, shareholders aggressively rejected Gyllenhammar's plan, leaving him with no option but to resign.

Given the large number of narcissists at the helm of corporations today, the challenge facing organizations is to ensure that such leaders do not self-destruct or lead the company to disaster. That can take some doing because it is very hard for narcissists to work through their issues—and virtually impossible for them to do it alone. Narcissists need colleagues and even therapists if they hope to break free from their limitations. But because of their extreme independence and self-protectiveness, it is very difficult to get near them. Kohut maintained that a therapist would have to demonstrate an extraordinarily profound empathic understanding and sympathy for the narcissist's feelings in order to gain his trust. On top of that, narcissists must recognize that they can benefit from such help. For their part, employees must learn how to recognize—and work around—narcissistic bosses. To help them in this endeavor, let's first take a closer look at Freud's theory of personality types.

THREE MAIN PERSONALITY TYPES

Although Freud recognized that there are an almost infinite variety of personalities, he identified three main types: erotic, obsessive, and narcissistic. Most of us have elements of all three. We are all, for example, somewhat narcissistic. If that were not so, we would not be able to survive or assert our needs. The point is, one of the dynamic tendencies usually dominates the others, making each of us react differently to success and failure.

Freud's definitions of personality types differed over time. When talking about the erotic personality type, however, Freud generally did not mean a sexual personality but rather one for whom loving and above all being loved is most important. These types of individual are dependent on those people they fear will stop loving them. Many erotics are teachers, nurses, and social workers. At their most productive, they are developers of the young as well as enablers and helpers at work. As managers, they are caring and supportive, but they avoid conflict and make people dependent on them. They are, according to Freud, outer-directed people.

Obsessives, in contrast, are inner-directed. They are self-reliant and conscientious. They create and maintain order and make the most effective operational managers. They look constantly for ways to help people listen better, resolve conflict, and find win-win opportunities. They buy self-improvement books such as Stephen Covey's *The Seven Habits of Highly Effective People*. Obsessives are also ruled by a strict conscience: They like to focus on continuous improvement at work because it fits in with their sense

EXHIBIT 19.1 Fromm's Fourth Personality Type

Not long after Freud described his three personality types in 1931, psychoanalyst Erich Fromm proposed a fourth personality type, which has become particularly prevalent in today's service economy. Fromm called this type the "marketing personality," and it is exemplified by the lead character in Woody Allen's movie *Zelig*, a man so governed by his need to be valued that he becomes exactly like the people he happens to be around.

Marketing personalities are more detached than erotics and so are less likely to cement close ties. They are also less driven by conscience than obsessives. Instead, they are motivated by a radar-like anxiety that permeates everything they do. Because they are so eager to please and to alleviate this anxiety, marketing personalities excel at selling themselves to others.

Unproductive marketing types lack direction and the ability to commit themselves to people or projects. But when productive, marketing types are good at facilitating teams and keeping the focus on adding value as defined by customers and colleagues. Like obsessives, marketing personalities are avid consumers of self-help books. Like narcissists, they are not wedded to the past. But marketing types generally make poor leaders in times of crisis. They lack the daring needed to innovate and are too responsive to current, rather than future, customer demands.

of moral improvement. As entrepreneurs, obsessives start businesses that express their values, but they lack the vision, daring, and charisma it takes to turn a good idea into a great one. The best obsessives set high standards and communicate very effectively. They make sure that instructions are followed and costs are kept within budget. The most productive are great mentors and team players. The unproductive and the uncooperative become narrow experts and rule-bound bureaucrats.

Narcissists, the third type, are independent and not easily impressed. They are innovators, driven in business to gain power and glory. Productive narcissists are experts in their industries, but they go beyond this expertise. They also pose the critical questions. They want to learn everything about everything that affects the company and its products. Unlike erotics, they want to be admired, not loved. And unlike obsessives, they are not troubled by a punishing superego, so they are able to aggressively pursue their goals. Of all the personality types, narcissists run the greatest risk of isolating themselves at the moment of success. And because of their independence and aggressiveness, they are constantly looking out for enemies, sometimes degenerating into paranoia when they are under extreme stress. (For more on personality types, see Exhibit 19.1.)

STRENGTHS OF THE NARCISSISTIC LEADER

When it comes to leadership, personality type can be instructive. Erotic personalities generally make poor managers: They need too much approval. Obsessives make better leaders: They are your operational managers, critical and cautious. But it is narcissists who come closest to our collective image of great leaders. There are two reasons: They have compelling, even gripping, visions for companies, and they have an ability to attract followers.

Great Vision

I once asked a group of managers to define a leader. "A person with vision" was a typical response. Productive narcissists understand the vision thing particularly well, because they are by nature people who see the big picture. They are not analyzers who can break up big questions into manageable problems; they aren't number crunchers either (these are usually the obsessives). Nor do they try to extrapolate to understand the future: They attempt to create it. To paraphrase George Bernard Shaw, some people see things as they are and ask why; narcissists see things that never were and ask why not.

Consider the difference between Bob Allen, a productive obsessive, and Mike Armstrong, a productive narcissist. In 1997, Allen tried to expand AT&T to reestablish the end-to-end service of the Bell System by reselling local service from the regional Bell operating companies (RBOCs). Although this was a worthwhile endeavor for shareholders and customers, it was hardly earth shattering. By contrast, through a strategy of combining voice, telecommunications, and Internet access by high-speed broadband telecommunication over cable, Mike Armstrong has "created a new space with his name on it," as one of his colleagues puts it. Armstrong is betting that his costly strategy will beat out the RBOCs' less expensive solution of digital subscriber lines over copper wire. This example illustrates the different approaches of obsessives and narcissists. The risk Armstrong took is one that few obsessives would feel comfortable taking. His vision is galvanizing AT&T. Who but a narcissistic leader could achieve such a thing? As Napoleon—a classic narcissist—once remarked, "Revolutions are ideal times for soldiers with a lot of wit—and the courage to act."

As in the days of the French Revolution, the world is now changing in astounding ways; narcissists have opportunities they would never have in ordinary times. In short, today's narcissistic leaders have the chance to change the very rules of the game. Consider Robert B. Shapiro, CEO of Monsanto.

Shapiro described his vision of genetically modifying crops as "the single most successful introduction of technology in the history of agriculture, including the plow" (*New York Times,* August 5, 1999). This is certainly a huge claim—there are still many questions about the safety and public acceptance of genetically engineered fruits and vegetables. But industries like agriculture are desperate for radical change. If Shapiro's gamble is successful, the industry will be transformed in the image of Monsanto. That's why he can get away with painting a picture of Monsanto as a highly profitable "life sciences" company—even though Monsanto's stock fell 12 percent from 1998 to the end of the third quarter of 1999. (During the same period, the S&P was up 41 percent.) Unlike Armstrong and Shapiro, it was enough for Bob Allen to win against his competitors in a game measured primarily by the stock market. But narcissistic leaders are after something more. They want—and need—to leave behind a legacy.

Scores of Followers

Narcissists have vision—but that's not enough. People in mental hospitals also have visions. The simplest definition of a leader is someone whom other people follow. Indeed, narcissists are especially gifted in attracting followers, and more often than not, they do so through language. Narcissists believe that words can move mountains and that inspiring speeches can change people. Narcissistic leaders are often skillful orators, and this is one of the talents that makes them so charismatic. Indeed, anyone who has seen narcissists perform can attest to their personal magnetism and their ability to stir enthusiasm among audiences.

Yet this charismatic gift is more of a two-way affair than most people think. Although it is not always obvious, narcissistic leaders are quite dependent on their followers: They need affirmation, and preferably adulation. Think of Winston Churchill's wartime broadcasts or JFK's "Ask not what your country can do for you" inaugural address. The adulation that follows from such speeches bolsters the self-confidence and conviction of the speakers. But if no one responds, the narcissist usually becomes insecure, overly shrill, and insistent—just as Ross Perot did.

Even when people respond positively to a narcissist, there are dangers. That's because charisma is a double-edged sword: It fosters both closeness and isolation. As he becomes increasingly self-assured, the narcissist becomes more spontaneous. He feels free of constraints. Ideas flow. He thinks he's invincible. This energy and confidence further inspire his followers. But the very adulation that the narcissist demands can have a corrosive effect. As he expands, he listens even less to words of caution and advice. After all, he has been right before, when others had their doubts. Rather than try to persuade those who disagree with him, he feels justified in ignoring them—creating further isolation. The result is sometimes flagrant risk taking that can lead to catastrophe. In the political realm, there is no clearer example of this than Bill Clinton.

WEAKNESSES OF THE NARCISSISTIC LEADER

Despite the warm feelings their charisma can evoke, narcissists are typically not comfortable with their own emotions. They listen only for the kind of information they seek. They don't learn easily from others. They don't like to teach but prefer to indoctrinate and make speeches. They dominate meetings with subordinates. The result for the organization is greater internal competitiveness at a time when everyone is already under as much pressure as they can possibly stand. Perhaps the main problem is that the narcissist's faults tend to become even more pronounced as he becomes more successful.

Sensitive to Criticism

Because they are extraordinarily sensitive, narcissistic leaders shun emotions as a whole. Indeed, perhaps one of the greatest paradoxes in this age of teamwork and partnering is that the best corporate leader in the contemporary world is the type of person who is emotionally isolated. Narcissistic leaders typically keep others at arm's length. They can put up a wall of defense as thick as those in the Pentagon. And given their difficulty with knowing or acknowledging their own feelings, they are uncomfortable with other people expressing theirs—especially their negative feelings.

Indeed, even productive narcissists are extremely sensitive to criticism or slights, which feel to them like knives threatening their self-image and their confidence in their visions. Narcissists are almost unimaginably thin-skinned. Like the fairy-tale princess who slept on many mattresses and yet knew she was sleeping on a pea, narcissists—even powerful CEOs—bruise easily. This is one reason that narcissistic leaders do not want to know what people think of them unless this opinion is causing them a real problem. They cannot tolerate dissent. In fact, they can be extremely abrasive with employees who doubt them or with subordinates who are tough enough to fight back. Steve Jobs, for example, publicly humiliates subordinates. Thus, although narcissistic leaders often say that they want teamwork, what that means in practice is that they want a group of yes-men. As the more independent-minded players leave or are pushed out, succession becomes a particular problem.

Poor Listeners

One serious consequence of this oversensitivity to criticism is that narcissistic leaders often do not listen when they feel threatened or attacked. Consider the response of one narcissistic CEO I had worked with for three years who asked me to interview his immediate team and report back to him on what they were thinking. He invited me to his summer home to discuss what I had found. "So what do they think of me?" he asked with seeming nonchalance. "They think you are very creative and courageous," I told him, "but they also feel that you don't listen." "Excuse me, what did you say?" he shot back at once, pretending not to hear. His response was humorous, but it was also tragic. In a very real way, this CEO could not hear my criticism because it was too painful to tolerate. Some narcissists are so defensive that they go so far as to make a virtue of the fact that they don't listen. As another CEO bluntly put it, "I didn't get here by listening to people!" Indeed, on one occasion when this CEO proposed a daring strategy, none of his subordinates believed it would work. His subsequent success strengthened his conviction that he had nothing to learn about strategy from his lieutenants. But success is no excuse for narcissistic leaders not to listen.

Lack of Empathy

Best-selling business writers today have taken up the slogan of "emotional competencies"—the belief that successful leadership requires a strongly developed sense of empathy. But although they crave empathy from others, productive narcissists are not noted for being particularly empathetic themselves. Indeed, lack of empathy is a characteristic shortcoming of some of the most charismatic and successful narcissists, including Bill Gates and Andy Grove. Of course, leaders do need to communicate persuasively. But a lack of empathy did not prevent some of history's greatest narcissistic leaders from knowing how to communicate—and inspire. Neither Churchill, de Gaulle, Stalin, nor Mao Tse-tung was empathetic. And yet they inspired people because of their passion and their conviction at a time when people longed for certainty. In fact, in times of radical change, lack of empathy can actually be a strength. A narcissist finds it easier than other personality types to buy and sell companies, to close and move facilities, and to lay off employees—decisions that inevitably make many people angry and sad. But narcissistic leaders typically have few regrets. As one CEO says, "If I listened to my employees' needs and demands, they would eat me alive."

Given this lack of empathy, it's hardly surprising that narcissistic leaders don't score particularly well on evaluations of their interpersonal style. What's more, neither 360-degree evaluations of their management style nor workshops in listening will make them more empathic. Narcissists don't want to change—and as long as they are successful, they don't think they have to. They may see the need for operational managers to get touchy-feely training, but that's not for them.

There is a kind of emotional intelligence associated with narcissists, but it's more street smarts than empathy. Narcissistic leaders are acutely aware of whether or not people are with them wholeheartedly. They know whom they can use. They can be brutally exploitive. That's why, even though narcissists undoubtedly have "star quality," they are often unlikable. They easily stir up people against them, and it is only in tumultuous times, when their gifts are desperately needed, that people are willing to tolerate narcissists as leaders.

Distaste for Mentoring

Lack of empathy and extreme independence make it difficult for narcissists to mentor and be mentored. Generally speaking, narcissistic leaders set very little store by mentoring. They seldom mentor others, and when they do they typically want their protégés to be pale reflections of themselves. Even those narcissists like Jack Welch who are held up as strong mentors are usually more interested in instructing than in coaching.

Narcissists certainly don't credit mentoring or educational programs for their own development as leaders. A few narcissistic leaders such as Bill Gates may find a friend or consultant—for instance, Warren Buffet, a superproductive obsessive—whom they can trust to be their guide and confidant. But most narcissists prefer "mentors" they can control. A thirty-two-year-old marketing vice president, a narcissist with CEO potential, told me that she had rejected her boss as a mentor. As she put it, "First of all, I want to keep the relationship at a distance. I don't want to be influenced by emotions. Second, there are things I don't want him to know. I'd rather hire an outside consultant to be my coach." Although narcissistic leaders appear to be at ease with others, they find intimacy—which is a prerequisite for mentoring—to be difficult. Younger narcissists will establish peer relations with authority rather than seek a parentlike mentoring relationship. They want results and are willing to take chances arguing with authority.

An Intense Desire to Compete

Narcissistic leaders are relentless and ruthless in their pursuit of victory. Games are not games but tests of their survival skills. Of course, all successful managers want to win, but narcissists are not restrained by conscience. Organizations led by narcissists are generally characterized by intense internal competition. Their passion to win is marked by both the promise of glory and the primitive danger of extinction. It is a potent brew that energizes companies, creating a sense of urgency, but it can also be dangerous. These leaders see everything as a threat. As Andy Grove puts it, brilliantly articulating the narcissist's fear, distrust, and aggression, "Only the paranoid survive." The concern, of course, is that the narcissist finds enemies that aren't there—even among his colleagues.

AVOIDING THE TRAPS

There is very little business literature that tells narcissistic leaders how to avoid the pitfalls. There are two reasons. First, relatively few narcissistic leaders are interested in looking inward. And second, psychoanalysts don't usually get close enough to them, especially in the workplace, to write about them. (The noted psychoanalyst Harry Levinson is an exception.) As a result, advice on leadership focuses on obsessives; this is the reason that so much of it is about creating teamwork and being more receptive to subordinates. But as we've already seen, this literature is of little interest to narcissists, nor is it likely to help subordinates understand their narcissistic leaders. The absence of managerial literature on narcissistic leaders doesn't mean that it is impossible to devise strategies for dealing with narcissism. In the course of a long career counseling CEOs, I have identified three basic ways in which productive narcissists can avoid the traps of their own personality.

Find a Trusted Sidekick

Many narcissists can develop a close relationship with one person, a sidekick who acts as an anchor, keeping the narcissistic partner grounded. However, given that narcissistic leaders trust only their own insights and view of reality, the sidekick has to understand the narcissistic leader and what he is trying to achieve. The narcissist must feel that this person, or in some cases

EXHIBIT 19.2   The Rise and Fall of a Narcissist

The story of Jan Carlzon, the former CEO of the Scandinavian airline SAS, is an almost textbook example of how a narcissist's weaknesses can cut short a brilliant career. In the 1980s, Carlzon's vision of SAS as the businessperson's airline was widely acclaimed in the business press; management guru Tom Peters described him as a model leader. In 1989, when I first met Carlzon and his management team, he compared the ideal organization to the Brazilian soccer team—in principle, there would be no fixed roles, only innovative plays. I asked the members of the management team if they agreed with this vision of an empowered front line. One vice president, a former pilot, answered no. "I still believe that the best organization is the military," he said. I then asked Carlzon for his reaction to that remark. "Well," he replied, "that may be true, if your goal is to shoot your customers."

That rejoinder was both witty and dismissive; clearly, Carlzon was not engaging in a serious dialogue with his subordinates. Nor was he listening to other advisers. Carlzon ignored the issue of high costs, even when many observers pointed out that SAS could not compete without improving productivity. He threw money at expensive acquisitions of hotels and made an unnecessary investment in Continental Airlines just months before it declared bankruptcy.

Carlzon's story perfectly corroborates the often-recorded tendency of narcissists to become overly expansive and hence isolated at the very pinnacle of their success. Seduced by the flattery he received in the international press, Carlzon's self-image became so enormously inflated that his feet left the ground. And given his vulnerability to grandiosity, he was propelled by a need to expand his organization rather than develop it. In due course, as Carlzon led the company deeper and deeper into losses, he was fired. Now he is a venture capitalist helping budding companies. And SAS has lost its glitter.

---

persons, is practically an extension of himself. The sidekick must also be sensitive enough to manage the relationship. Don Quixote is a classic example of a narcissist who was out of touch with reality but who was constantly saved from disaster by his "squire," Sancho Panza. Not surprisingly, many narcissistic leaders rely heavily on their spouses, the people they are closest to. But dependence on spouses can be risky, because they may further isolate the narcissistic leader from his company by supporting his grandiosity and feeding his paranoia. I once knew a CEO in this kind of relationship with his spouse. He took to accusing loyal subordinates of plotting against him just because they ventured a few criticisms of his ideas.

It is much better for a narcissistic leader to choose a colleague as his sidekick. Good sidekicks are able to point out the operational requirements of

EXHIBIT 19.3 Working for a Narcissist

Dealing with a narcissistic boss isn't easy. You have to be prepared to look for another job if your boss becomes too narcissistic to let you disagree with him. But remember that the company is typically betting on his vision of the future—not yours. Here are a few tips on how to survive in the short term:

- Always empathize with your boss's feelings, but don't expect any empathy back. Look elsewhere for your own self-esteem. Understand that behind his display of infallibility, there hides a deep vulnerability. Praise his achievements and reinforce his best impulses, but don't be shamelessly sycophantic. An intelligent narcissist can see through flatterers and prefers independent people who truly appreciate him. Show that you will protect his image, inside and outside the company. But be careful if he asks for an honest evaluation. What he wants is information that will help him solve a problem about his image. He will resent any honesty that threatens his inflated self-image and is likely to retaliate.

- Give your boss ideas, but always let him take the credit for them. Find out what he thinks before presenting your views. If you believe he is wrong, show how a different approach would be in his best interest. Take his paranoid views seriously; don't brush them aside—they often reveal sharp intuitions. Disagree only when you can demonstrate how he will benefit from a different point of view.

- Hone your time-management skills. Narcissistic leaders often give subordinates many more orders than they can possibly execute. Ignore the requests he makes that don't make sense. Forget about them. He will. But be careful: Carve out free time for yourself only when you know there's a lull in the boss's schedule. Narcissistic leaders feel free to call you at any hour of the day or night. Make yourself available, or be prepared to get out.

---

the narcissistic leader's vision and keep him rooted in reality. The best sidekicks are usually productive obsessives. Gyllenhammar, for instance, was most effective at Volvo when he had an obsessive COO, Hakan Frisinger, to focus on improving quality and cost, as well as an obsessive HR director, Berth Jonsson, to implement his vision. Similarly, Bill Gates can think about the future from the stratosphere because Steve Ballmer, a tough obsessive president, keeps the show on the road. At Oracle, CEO Larry Ellison can afford to miss key meetings and spend time on his boat contemplating a future without PCs because he has a productive obsessive COO in Ray Lane to run the company for him. But the job of sidekick entails more than just executing the leader's ideas. The sidekick also has to get his leader to accept new ideas. To do this, he must be able to show the leader how the new ideas fit with his views and serve his interests. (For more on dealing with narcissistic bosses, see Exhibit 19.3, "Working for a Narcissist.")

Indoctrinate the Organization

The narcissistic CEO wants all his subordinates to think the way he does about the business. Productive narcissists—people who often have a dash of the obsessive personality—are good at converting people to their point of view. One of the most successful at this is GE's Jack Welch. Welch uses toughness to build a corporate culture and to implement a daring business strategy, including the buying and selling of scores of companies. Unlike other narcissistic leaders such as Gates, Grove, and Ellison, who have transformed industries with new products, Welch was able to transform his industry by focusing on execution and pushing companies to the limits of quality and efficiency, bumping up revenues and wringing out costs. In order to do so, Welch hammers out a huge corporate culture in his own image—a culture that provides impressive rewards for senior managers and shareholders.

Welch's approach to culture building is widely misunderstood. Many observers, notably Noel Tichy in *The Leadership Engine,* argue that Welch forms his company's leadership culture through teaching. But Welch's "teaching" involves a personal ideology that he indoctrinates into GE managers through speeches, memos, and confrontations. Rather than create a dialogue, Welch makes pronouncements (either be the number one or two company in your market or get out), and he institutes programs (such as Six Sigma quality) that become the GE party line. Welch's strategy has been extremely effective. GE managers must either internalize his vision, or they must leave. Clearly, this is incentive learning with a vengeance. I would even go so far as to call Welch's teaching brainwashing. But Welch does have the rare insight and know-how to achieve what all narcissistic business leaders are trying to do, namely, get the organization to identify with them, to think the way they do, and to become the living embodiment of their companies.

Get into Analysis

Narcissists are often more interested in controlling others than in knowing and disciplining themselves. That's why, with very few exceptions, even productive narcissists do not want to explore their personalities with the help of insight therapies such as psychoanalysis. Yet since Heinz Kohut, there has been a radical shift in psychoanalytic thinking about what can be done to help narcissists work through their rage, alienation, and grandiosity. Indeed, if they can be persuaded to undergo therapy, narcissistic leaders can use tools such as psychoanalysis to overcome vital character flaws.

Consider the case of one exceptional narcissistic CEO who asked me to help him understand why he so often lost his temper with subordinates. He lived far from my home city, and so the therapy was sporadic and very unorthodox. Yet he kept a journal of his dreams, which we interpreted together either by phone or when we met. Our analysis uncovered painful feelings of being unappreciated that went back to his inability to impress a cold father. He came to realize that he demanded an unreasonable amount of praise and that when he felt unappreciated by his subordinates, he became furious. Once he understood that, he was able to recognize his narcissism and even laugh about it. In the middle of our work, he even announced to his top team that I was psychoanalyzing him and asked them what they thought of that. After a pregnant pause, one executive vice president piped up, "Whatever you're doing, you should keep doing it, because you don't get so angry anymore." Instead of being trapped by narcissistic rage, this CEO was learning how to express his concerns constructively.

Leaders who can work on themselves in that way tend to be the most productive narcissists. In addition to being self-reflective, they are also likely to be open, likable, and good-humored. Productive narcissists have perspective; they are able to detach themselves and laugh at their irrational needs. Although serious about achieving their goals, they are also playful. As leaders, they are aware of being performers. A sense of humor helps them maintain enough perspective and humility to keep on learning.

THE BEST AND WORST OF TIMES

As I have pointed out, narcissists thrive in chaotic times. In more tranquil times and places, however, even the most brilliant narcissist will seem out of place. In his short story *The Curfew Tolls*, Stephen Vincent Benet speculates on what would have happened to Napoleon if he had been born some thirty years earlier. Retired in prerevolutionary France, Napoleon is depicted as a lonely artillery major boasting to a vacationing British general about how he could have beaten the English in India. The point, of course, is that a visionary born in the wrong time can seem like a pompous buffoon.

Historically, narcissists in large corporations have been confined to sales positions, where they use their persuasiveness and imagination to best effect. In settled times, the problematic side of the narcissistic personality usually conspires to keep narcissists in their place, and they can typically rise to top management positions only by starting their own companies or by leaving to lead startups. Consider Joe Nacchio, formerly in charge of both the business and consumer divisions of AT&T. Nacchio was a supersalesman and a popular leader in the mid-1990s. But his desire to create a new network for business customers was thwarted by colleagues who found him abrasive, self-promoting, and ruthlessly ambitious.

In 1998, Nacchio left AT&T to become CEO of Qwest, a company that is creating a long-distance fiber-optic cable network. Nacchio had the credibility—and charisma—to sell Qwest's initial public offering to financial markets and gain a high valuation. Within a short space of time, he turned Qwest into an attractive target for the RBOCs, which were looking to move into long-distance telephony and Internet services. Such a sale would have given Qwest's owners a handsome profit on their investment. But Nacchio wanted more. He wanted to expand—to compete with AT&T—and for that he needed local service. Rather than sell Qwest, he chose to make a bid himself for local telephone operator U.S. West, using Qwest's highly valued stock to finance the deal. The market voted on this display of expansiveness with its feet: Qwest's stock price fell 40 percent between June 1999, when he made the deal, and the end of the third quarter of 1999. (The S&P index dropped 5.7 percent during the same period.)

Like other narcissists, Nacchio likes risk—and sometimes ignores the costs. But with the dramatic discontinuities going on in the world today, more and more large corporations are getting into bed with narcissists. They are finding that there is no substitute for narcissistic leaders in an age of innovation. Companies need leaders who do not try to anticipate the future so much as create it. But narcissistic leaders—even the most productive of them—can self-destruct and lead their organizations terribly astray. For companies whose narcissistic leaders recognize their limitations, these will be the best of times. For other companies, these could turn out to be the worst.

20

~

Viable Options:
Rethinking Women and Leadership

Barbara Kellerman
Deborah L. Rhode

Some forty years ago, Betty Friedan's *The Feminine Mystique* helped launch the contemporary women's movement by naming a "problem that has no name." In answer to Freud's classic question, "What do women want?" Friedan proclaimed, "We can no longer ignore that voice within women that says: 'I want something more than my husband and my children and my home.'"

Except that now, it seems, a husband and children and a home are exactly what some women want—the very women whose education and professional attainments qualify them for positions of high leadership. From *Time* to the *New York Times Magazine*, from talk shows to the water cooler, the buzz is all about women dropping out of full-time work, even at the highest professional levels, to stay home with their children. It's this "opt-out revolution," Lisa Belkin argued in the *New York Times Magazine,* and not persistent inequities and stereotypes, that accounts for women's underrepresentation in the leadership ranks of American business and government. As the term *opt out* implies, Belkin is at odds with Friedan. Whereas Friedan and other leaders of the women's movement stressed women's desire for something more than husbands, children, and well-appointed homes, Belkin and her allies claim that many women are reasonably content, for years at a stretch, with exactly that.

Reprinted with permission from *Compass: A Journal of Leadership,* published by the Kennedy School of Government at Harvard University, Fall 2004, pp. 14–37.

Friedan described a society that limited women's choices; Belkin sees a society in which women are exercising choices to reject the workplace.

Jamie Gorelick, a former high-ranking official in the Clinton-era Justice Department and a member of the independent 9/11 investigative commission, might be the poster child for Belkin's revolution. In 2003, she left her position as vice chair of Fannie Mae and declined to be considered for its COO post, explaining to *Fortune* magazine that she had two children and didn't want that "pace in my life." The "dirty little secret," she added, "is that women demand a lot more satisfaction in their lives than men do."

Who is correct, Friedan or Belkin? Is the relative shortage of women leaders in government and private enterprise the result of discrimination, or have women *chosen* not to lead? The two answers, we suggest, are not mutually exclusive. Our findings do not lead us to suspend the struggle to expand women's opportunities for power, authority, and influence. Rather, we argue for reframing the problem of leadership to account for both gender *biases,* which can be addressed through greater *equity* in the workplace and in society more generally, and gender *differences,* which must be addressed through greater *diversity* in the workplace and society. To gain a sense of the interplay of the two forces, we consider where women are now, why we are where we are, and what needs to change.

PROGRESS AND FRUSTRATION

In the forty years that have passed since Friedan's manifesto, American society has experienced a transformation in gender-related attitudes, practices, and policies. About 16 percent of *Fortune* 500 corporate officers are now women; that percentage has doubled since the mid-1990s. The percentage of women holding top corporate positions—executive vice president to CEO—quadrupled during the same period, up from 2 percent to over 8 percent. Eight *Fortune* 500 companies have a female chief executive, compared with only two in 1995. Women hold fourteen Senate seats and sixty House seats in the 108th U. S. Congress. Women now constitute nearly 14 percent of members of Congress, up from 10 percent in 1992, and nearly one-quarter of the members are women of color. Twenty-one percent of college presidents are female, compared with almost none in the mid-1990s.

But progress has been partial and painfully slow. With respect to leadership, in particular, women still have a long way to go. Almost a sixth of the *Fortune* 500 companies still have no female officers. Fewer than 2 percent of corporate offices are held by African-American, Asian-American, or Hispanic women. The vast majority of women in top jobs in corporate America hold staff jobs rather than the line positions that typically produce CEOs. Women account for just 6 percent of the top corporate earners. In academia, women faculty members earn 14 percent less than men. Despite four decades of equal opportunity legislation, the workforce remains segregated and stratified by gender. Women are overrepresented at the bottom and underrepresented at the top, even controlling for educational qualifications. The best-trained women are still concentrated in different kinds of jobs from men—jobs with less pay, status, and power. As for politics and government, the United States ranks fifty-ninth in the world in electing women leaders. Congress gained three fewer women since the mid-1990s than it did in the single 1992 election, the fabled "year of the woman." Fewer women ran for state legislative offices in 2000 than did in 1992, and the number of women in state politics has been stagnant at about 20 percent since the mid-1990s. What accounts for such persistent and pervasive disparities? Why, forty years after Friedan wrote of the problem that has no name, have we done so well at labeling the problem but are still so far from solving it?

For one thing, gender bias has not been—and cannot be—legislated away. Women remain underrepresented in positions of leadership in part because of the mismatch between the characteristics traditionally associated with women and the characteristics traditionally associated with leadership. As Rakesh Khurana has observed, the Great Man model of leadership—the heroic savior—is still with us. And the term *man* is not used generically. Although recent theories of leadership stress interpersonal qualities commonly associated with women, such as cooperation and collaboration, most qualities associated with leaders are still masculine: dominance, authority, driving ambition, unflinching decisiveness, fierce determination, and so on.

Such expectations of leaders confront women with a double standard and a double bind. They may appear too soft, unable, or unwilling to make the tough calls required in the positions of greatest influence. Or if they mimic the male model, they are often viewed as strident and overly aggressive. An overview of more than a hundred studies confirms that women are rated lower when they adopt stereotypically masculine authoritative styles, particularly when the evaluators are men or when the woman's role is one typically occupied by men. Since other research suggests that individuals with masculine styles are more likely to emerge as leaders than those with feminine styles, women face trade-offs that men do not. Even in experimental situations where male and female performances are objectively equal, women are held to higher standards, and their competence is rated lower.

Many women internalize these stereotypes, which create a self-fulfilling prophecy. Researchers consistently find that most women see themselves as less deserving of rewards than men are for the same performance. On average, female workers are also less willing to take the risks, or to seek the challenges, that would equip them for leadership roles.

Commentators who focus on women's choice to leave the workplace typically fail to acknowledge the social forces that constrain it. Women are, and are expected to be, the primary caregivers, especially of the very young and very old. Many men are committed to equality more in principle than in practice; they are unwilling or (in their own view) unable to structure their lives to promote it. If, as Belkin and others insist, women are choosing not to run the world, it is partly because, to paraphrase Gloria Steinem, men are choosing not to run the washer-dryer.

Double standards in domestic roles are deeply rooted in cultural attitudes, managerial policies, and social priorities. Fewer than 15 percent of *Fortune* 100 companies offer the same paid parental leave to fathers as to mothers, and an even smaller percentage of men take any extended period of time away from their jobs for family reasons. As one director of professional development noted, the traditional expectation was that fathers with newborn infants would "just go to the hospital, take a look, and come right back to work." This pattern no longer holds, but workplaces that only grudgingly accommodate mothers can be even more resistant to fathers. Daddy tracks are noticeable for their absence. As one man put it, it is now "okay [for fathers] to say that they would like to spend more time with the kids, but it is not okay to do it, except once in a while."

As long as work-family issues are seen as problems primarily for women, potential solutions are likely to receive inadequate attention in decision-making structures still dominated by men. Within those structures, caretaking is considered primarily an individual rather than a social responsibility, adding to women's work in the home and limiting their opportunities in the world outside it. America is almost alone among industrialized nations in failing to guarantee paid parental leaves. And high-quality, affordable child care is unavailable for many women attempting to work their way up the leadership ladder.

Since the mid-1960s we have made more progress in getting women access to roles traditionally occupied by men than in getting men to assume domestic roles traditionally occupied by women. And we have made even less progress in altering social policy to accommodate the needs of both sexes on family-related issues. The resilience of traditional gender patterns is reflected in two especially telling sets of statistics. Three-quarters of women have a spouse or a partner with a full-time job; three-quarters of men have a spouse or a partner who spends at least part time at home. Almost a fifth of women with graduate or professional degrees are not in the paid labor force; only 5 percent of similarly credentialed men have opted out.

WHAT PRICE POWER?

Various researchers have attempted to find a biological basis for this achievement gap. But for every piece of data that supports the hypothesis that gender roles are biologically determined, there are at least as many data to challenge it. More compelling is a growing body of research that challenges conventional views that women want just what men want. Put another way, if women are underrepresented in leadership positions, the reason is not simply that men stand in their way. Recent surveys indicate that many women, especially women with young children, are not sufficiently determined to get to the top. For a variety of reasons, women are often ambivalent about seeking power and making the sacrifices necessary to obtain it.

There is countervailing evidence for this hypothesis as well. A recent survey by Catalyst, a New York research group that studies gender and workplace issues, reports that a majority of senior executives want to become their employer's chief executive. The numbers remain roughly the same whether the respondents are male or female, childless or not. Those findings, says Catalyst, seem to challenge "the assertion that there aren't more women at the top because they don't want to be there." But it is important to note that the survey sample consisted of those who already had made the choices necessary to become senior executives.

Belkin's small sample was skewed in the other direction. It consisted of an Atlanta book group of full-time homemakers with Princeton degrees, a group of San Francisco mothers with MBAs, and "countless" readers with whom the author had corresponded. All were well educated and economically

privileged women who could afford to choose to leave the paid workforce because their high-earning partners chose differently. Such selective samples
preclude definitive conclusions.

Countering both the Catalyst and the Belkin arguments are studies that
suggest that at least some differences in women's and men's positions in the
workplace reflect different choices, many of which involve small children. A
recent *Fortune* magazine article described a number of such studies and then
raised the heretical question: "Do women lack power in business because
they just don't want it enough?"

As the article acknowledged, the very question comes treacherously
close to blaming the victim. But the signs that women have mixed feelings
about conventional measures of workplace achievement are too striking to
ignore. For example, Catalyst recently reported that about a quarter of
women not yet in senior posts say they don't want those jobs. About a fifth
of the hundred-odd women who have appeared on the *Fortune* 50 over the
past five years have left their prestigious positions, generally of their own vo-
lition. And a recent survey by *Fast Company* identifies a significant minority
of high-ranking women who have not opted out entirely but have chosen a
life less consumed by work—which means, among other things, a life less
consumed by leadership.

Such studies reinforce a conclusion unnerving to many feminists: When
women aren't in positions that carry the greatest power, authority, and influence, it is not always because women can't get them; it is sometimes because
they don't want them. The question is why. At least some of the reasons take
us back to the gender roles and stereotypes with which we began.

First and foremost, forever foremost, there are the children. Women both
bear the children and remain their primary caretakers. Most women want to
have at least one child, and they are increasingly aware that involved parenting is difficult for anyone at the top.

The difficulties of reconciling family and leadership responsibilities are
starkly demonstrated by the demographics. Fully 42 percent of high-achieving
women in corporate America are childless at the age of forty. Moreover,
among those who do have children, 40 percent feel that their husbands create more work around the house than they contribute. Men, in contrast, do
not experience the same conflict between success and parenting or, to put it
more pointedly, between leadership and parenting. In one representative
survey, 79 percent of high-achieving men reported wanting children—and
75 percent had them.

Motherhood, it is apparent, entails more significant personal and professional implications than does fatherhood, which in turn affects access to leadership. More women than men drop out of the paid workforce, typically for periods ranging from several months to several years. More women than men work part time. And more women than men leave large organizations to strike out on their own for jobs with fewer and more flexible hours.

Yet family considerations are not the only reason that women appear less committed than men to climbing the leadership ladder. The gender biases noted earlier take a toll as well. Women who do seek leadership are slammed for seeming overly ambitious or aggressive. Others decline to risk the negative evaluations that such "unfeminine" styles evoke.

That's not the whole story, though. Many women are less professionally ambitious than men because they are more personally ambitious than men. They dream of making a difference in ways that are personally more meaningful than achievement in conventional corporate and professional settings. Many women also have personal commitments and interests that seem impossible to reconcile with the all-consuming demands of leadership roles.

THE PATH TO LEADERSHIP

Of course, only economically privileged women confront such questions as whether to work, how much to work, and whether to pursue leadership roles in the paid labor force or in the community. Yet the women who have those options also tend to be the ones with the greatest education and the best chance of achieving leadership positions. They were expected to be the role models, and if they did hold positions of power they could, in theory at least, create change for the benefit of others. Ruth Mandel, a pioneer in the field of women's studies, has well captured the current dilemma, an impasse partly created by women who could aim higher, but opt not to:

Nothing will change the picture of leadership and perhaps the practice of leadership unless women themselves choose to pursue leadership. In the United States, far and away, this matter of women's choice stands as the single greatest remaining challenge to achieve parity for women in leadership. . . . I am not saying that women at one time were choosing to lead and now are not. I am saying that today women can enter a path to leadership that has been cleared of many of the old impediments. They confront more opportunities and options than ever before. Nonetheless, women must choose to walk the path.

We have argued that the reasons for women's still-limited access to power, authority, and influence reflects both gender *biases* and gender *differences*. For women to gain ground at the leadership level, they must pursue two related but distinct strategies. Women must fight against gender biases by demanding equity; and they must fight for recognition of gender differences by demanding accommodation of diversity. These battles should be intertwined, fought simultaneously, and planned strategically, with tactics that are both political and legal.

The goals that women should be fighting for are substantially the same as those that inspired the contemporary women's movement. They include:

- Changes in public policy concerning equal opportunity enforcement, affirmative action, quality child and elder care, paid family leave, and meaningful part-time work
- Changes in organizational policies that increase those organizations' commitment to equity and diversity and that place a priority on accommodating workers with significant family, community, or other socially valued commitments
- Changes in the academy to support research on gender-related issues, particularly the socialization patterns, workplace practices, and public policies that could promote gender equality and a better quality of life for both sexes
- Changes in individual and group behaviors that will revitalize the women's movement and enable it to work more effectively toward shared goals

To promote those goals, the law can be an important tool, but its effectiveness should not be overstated and the need for its reform should not be underestimated. Legal prohibitions on sex-based discrimination and harassment, and legal entitlements concerning family leave and affirmative action, remain crucial forces in the struggle for equal employment opportunity. Multi-million-dollar victories in class action lawsuits like those against Merrill Lynch, Salomon Smith Barney, and Morgan Stanley, as well as the pending litigation against Wal-Mart, send a powerful message about the price of gender inequities. Women must continue to pursue such remedies while also pressing for changes that would make the law more effective in enhancing employment opportunities. As experts have frequently noted, our current legal framework is a highly inadequate response to "second-generation" sex discrimination, which is based less on demonstrable prejudice than on unconscious stereotypes and workplace structures that are gender neutral in form but not in fact. For the vast majority of victims, the difficulties of proof are insurmountable, or the financial and psychological costs of litigation are prohibitive. Women who pursue more informal internal remedies often experience an arbitration or mediation system stacked against them; employers control the system and are generally adept at minimizing the risk of adverse decisions, substantial financial liability, and unfavorable publicity. For victims who lack the resources to pursue litigation, federal and state enforcement agencies are a poor backup; their resources are insufficient to pursue more than a small fraction of complaints. And even the rare women who win in court often end up losing in life, given the informal blacklisting and unflattering personal disclosures that may result from litigation.

Many hard-won legal guarantees remain limited in scope. The federal Family and Medical Leave Act still leaves more than half the labor force unprotected. It provides job security only to those who can afford to take unpaid leave and excludes individuals who work for small employers or in part-time positions. And temporary-leave provisions do little to solve the long-term needs of those with substantial child-rearing or elder-care responsibilities.

There are no simple solutions. Gender-related laws remain too limited in scope and too expensive in application to reach most of the causes of women's underrepresentation in leadership positions. But we can certainly work to make those laws more effective and accessible. We can insist on greater resources for governmental enforcement agencies. We can provide financial contributions to women's rights organizations that litigate important cases and lobby for essential reforms. We can press for legislative mandates and workplace policies that will ensure more equitable informal dispute resolution systems. And we can support candidates for political and judicial positions who are committed to gender equality and the legal strategies that might help achieve it. Expanding parental leave entitlements and child-care programs, creating tax incentives for family-friendly workplace policies, and mandating more affirmative action in fields where women are underrepresented are obvious priorities for a society that is committed to equal opportunity in practice as well as principle.

Legal reforms cannot be obtained without political strategies. Our agenda, although ambitious, should be viewed in context. We do not see most American women as downtrodden. We realize that more than a few American women control large sums of money and that many (ourselves included) have very good jobs. And we are certainly aware that, by global standards, the overwhelming majority of American women are extremely well off. But in terms of basic gender equity, American women still have a long way to go. And neither governmental policy nor business practices ensure that women (or men for that matter) can care adequately for their families and participate actively in their communities while exercising leadership roles.

Women are not well positioned to address that problem. Despite their numerical majority, women still lack the positions of influence, in both the public and the private sectors, necessary to achieve the agenda set forth above. That, in turn, means that women need to employ the strategies most readily available to those without conventional sources of leverage. We refer to three in particular:

First, women must envision themselves as agents of change. Instead of reconciling ourselves to unequal burdens in the home and to unequal pay, status, and power in the world outside, we need to demand gender equity and the strategies necessary to achieve it.

Second, women must be ready, willing, and able to take a stand. The first step is a revival of old-fashioned consciousness-raising. We need to increase awareness of gender inequities and inspire a passion for challenging them. This will, in turn, require some willingness to assume short-term risks in the interest of long-term gains. As political theorists and activists across the globe remind us, there are no substitutes for speaking truth to power. Of course, that strategy must be selective. In order to reach positions of influence, women need to target their efforts and pick battles that they have some prospect of winning. But the challenge is to succeed within organizations without losing the capacity or commitment to change them. Silence in the face of inequality can only perpetuate it.

Third, women must take collective action. Fundamental change begins with individual commitment, but it requires group efforts. Women need to be more strategic in forging alliances and enlisting the collaboration of other individuals, small groups, and large organizations in the interest of common causes. Since the 1960s, both national and grassroots women's groups, all with their own particular missions and constituencies, have dramatically increased in size and number. But there has been insufficient unity even around key issues, as well as equally insufficient attempts to involve women from different points along the socioeconomic and demographic spectrum.

We need also to include men in our struggle. Women must insist, endlessly it seems, that the most crucial women's issues are issues not only for women. They are concerns in which both sexes have a stake. Increasing numbers of men want more balance in their lives. And their families, communities, and workplaces would benefit greatly if they achieved it. As a growing body of research makes clear, balanced lives serve bottom lines; they reduce employers' training and recruitment expenses and improve workers' health and productivity. A diverse workforce serves equally important objectives. In today's increasingly competitive global economy, no organization can secure long-term success with policies that penalize half the talent pool for leadership.

We cannot know with any certainty what, in an ideal world, women would truly want. But in this far from perfect world, we know well enough what women do not want—enough to forge a constructive agenda for reform. Forcing professionals of either sex to opt on or off leadership tracks as they are currently structured is not the answer. Choice on these terms is not a solution. It is part of the problem.

21

~

Level 5 Leadership:
The Triumph of Humility
and Fierce Resolve

Jim Collins

In 1971, a seemingly ordinary man named Darwin E. Smith was named chief executive of Kimberly-Clark, a stodgy old paper company whose stock had fallen 36 percent behind the general market during the previous twenty years. Smith, the company's mild-mannered in-house lawyer, wasn't so sure the board had made the right choice—a feeling that was reinforced when a Kimberly-Clark director pulled him aside and reminded him that he lacked some of the qualifications for the position. But CEO he was, and CEO he remained for twenty years.

What a twenty years it was. In that period, Smith created a stunning transformation at Kimberly-Clark, turning it into the leading consumer paper products company in the world. Under his stewardship, the company beat its rivals Scott Paper and Procter & Gamble. And in doing so, Kimberly-Clark generated cumulative stock returns that were 4.1 times greater than those of the general market, outperforming venerable companies such as Hewlett-Packard, 3M, Coca-Cola, and General Electric.

Smith's turnaround of Kimberly-Clark is one the best examples in the twentieth century of a leader taking a company from merely good to truly great. And yet few people—even ardent students of business history—have heard of

EXHIBIT 21.1   The Level 5 Hierarchy

The Level 5 leader sits on top of a hierarchy of capabilities and is, according to our research, a necessary requirement for transforming an organization from good to great. But what lies beneath? Four other layers, each one appropriate in its own right but none with the power of Level 5. Individuals do not need to proceed sequentially through each level of the hierarchy to reach the top, but to be a full-fledged Level 5 requires the capabilities of all the lower levels, plus the special characteristics of Level 5.

LEVEL 5 Level 5 Executive
Builds enduring greatness through a paradoxical combination of personal humility plus professional will.

LEVEL 4 Effective Leader
Catalyzes commitment to and vigorous pursuit of a clear and compelling vision; stimulates the group to high performance standards.

LEVEL 3 Competent Manager
Organizes people and resources toward the effective and efficient pursuit of predetermined objectives.

LEVEL 2 Contributing Team Member
Contributes to the achievement of group objectives; works effectively with others in a group setting.

LEVEL 1 Highly Capable Individual
Makes productive contributions through talent, knowledge, skills, and good work habits.

Darwin Smith. He probably would have liked it that way. Smith is a classic example of a *Level 5 leader*—an individual who blends extreme personal humility with intense professional will. According to our five-year research study, executives who possess this paradoxical combination of traits are catalysts for the statistically rare event of transforming a good company into a great one.

Level 5 refers to the highest level in a hierarchy of executive capabilities that we identified during our research. Leaders at the other four levels in the hierarchy can produce high degrees of success but not enough to elevate companies from mediocrity to sustained excellence. (For more details about this concept, see Exhibit 21.1) And while Level 5 leadership is not the only requirement for transforming a good company into a great one—other factors include getting the right people on the bus (and the wrong people off the bus) and creating a culture of discipline—our research shows it to be essential. Good-to-great transformations don't happen without Level 5 leaders at the helm. They just don't.

NOT WHAT YOU WOULD EXPECT

Our discovery of Level 5 leadership is counterintuitive. Indeed, it is countercultural. People generally assume that transforming companies from good to great requires larger-than-life leaders—big personalities like Iacocca, Dunlap, Welch, and Gault, who make headlines and become celebrities.

Compared with those CEOs, Darwin Smith seems to have come from Mars. Shy, unpretentious, even awkward, Smith shunned attention. When a journalist asked him to describe his management style, Smith just stared back at the scribe from the other side of his thick black-rimmed glasses. He was dressed unfashionably, like a farm boy wearing his first J. C. Penney suit. Finally, after a long and uncomfortable silence, he said, "Eccentric." Needless to say, the *Wall Street Journal* did not publish a splashy feature on Darwin Smith.

But if you were to consider Smith soft or meek, you would be terribly mistaken. His lack of pretense was coupled with a fierce, even stoic, resolve toward life. Smith grew up on an Indiana farm and put himself through night school at Indiana University by working the day shift at International Harvester. One day, he lost a finger on the job. The story goes that he went to class that evening and returned to work the very next day. Eventually, this poor but determined Indiana farm boy earned admission to Harvard Law School.

He showed the same iron will when he was at the helm of Kimberly-Clark. Indeed, two months after Smith became CEO, doctors diagnosed him with nose and throat cancer and told him he had less than a year to live. He duly informed the board of his illness but said he had no plans to die anytime soon. Smith held to his demanding work schedule while commuting weekly from Wisconsin to Houston for radiation therapy. He lived twenty-five more years, twenty of them as CEO.

Smith's ferocious resolve was crucial to the rebuilding of Kimberly-Clark, especially when he made the most dramatic decision in the company's history: sell the mills.

To explain: Shortly after he took over, Smith and his team had concluded that the company's traditional core business—coated paper—was doomed to mediocrity. Its economics were bad and the competition weak. But, they reasoned, if Kimberly-Clark was thrust into the fire of the *consumer* paper products business, better economics and world-class competition like Procter & Gamble would force it to achieve greatness or perish.

And so, like the general who burned the boats upon landing on enemy soil, leaving his troops to succeed or die, Smith announced that Kimberly-Clark would sell its mills—even the namesake mill in Kimberly, Wisconsin. All proceeds would be thrown into the consumer business, with investments in brands like Huggies diapers and Kleenex tissues. The business media called the move stupid, and Wall Street analysts downgraded the stock. But Smith never wavered. Twenty-five years later, Kimberly-Clark owned Scott Paper and beat Proctor & Gamble in six of eight product categories. In retirement, Smith reflected on his exceptional performance, saying simply, "I never stopped trying to become qualified for the job."

NOT WHAT WE EXPECTED EITHER

We'll look in depth at Level 5 leadership, but first let's set an important context for our findings: We were not looking for Level 5 or anything like it. Our original question was: Can a good company become a great one, and, if so, how? In fact, I gave the research teams explicit instructions to downplay the role of top executives in their analyses of this question so we wouldn't slip into the simplistic "credit the leader" or "blame the leader" thinking that is so common today.

But Level 5 found us. Over the course of the study, research teams kept saying, "We can't ignore the top executives even if we want to. There is something consistently unusual about them." I would push back, arguing, "The comparison companies also had leaders. So what's different here?" Back and forth the debate raged. Finally, as should always be the case, the data won. The executives at companies that went from good to great and sustained that performance for fifteen years or more were all cut from the same cloth—one remarkably different from that which produced executives at the comparison companies in our study. It didn't matter whether the company was in crisis or steady state, consumer or industrial, offering services or products. It didn't matter when the transition took place or how big the company, the successful organizations all had a Level 5 leader at the time of transition.

Furthermore, the absence of Level 5 leadership showed up consistently across the comparison companies. The point: Level 5 is an empirical finding, not an ideological one. And that's important to note, given how much the Level 5 finding contradicts not only conventional wisdom but much of management theory to date. (For more about our findings on good-to-great transformations, see Exhibit 21.2.)

EXHIBIT 21.2   Not By Level 5 Alone

Level 5 leadership is an essential factor for taking a company from good to great, but it's not the only one. Our research uncovered multiple factors that deliver companies to greatness. And it is the combined package—Level 5 plus these other drivers—that takes companies beyond unremarkable. There is a symbiotic relationship between Level 5 and the rest of our findings: Level 5 enables implementation of the other findings, and practicing the other findings may help you get to Level 5. We've already talked about who Level 5 leaders are; the rest of our findings describe what they do. Here is a brief look at some of the other key findings.

First who: We expected that good-to-great leaders would start with the vision and strategy. Instead, they attended to people first, strategy second. They got the right people on the bus, moved the wrong people off, ushered the right people to the right seats—and then they figured out where to drive it.

Stockdale paradox: This finding is named after Admiral James Stockdale, winner of the Medal of Honor, who survived seven years in a Vietcong POW camp by hanging on to two contradictory beliefs: His life couldn't be worse at the moment, and his life would someday be better than ever. Like Stockdale, people at the good-to-great companies in our research confronted the most brutal facts of their current reality—yet simultaneously maintained absolute faith that they would prevail in the end. And they held both disciplines—faith and facts—at the same time, all the time.

Buildup-breakthrough flywheel: Good-to-great transformations do not happen overnight or in the one big leap. Rather, the process resembles relentlessly pushing a giant, heavy flywheel in one direction. At first, pushing it gets the flywheel to turn once. With consistent effort, it goes two turns, then five, then ten, building increasing momentum until—bang!—the wheel hits the breakthrough point, and the momentum really kicks in. Our comparison companies never sustained the kind of breakthrough momentum that the good-to-great companies did; instead, they lurched back and forth with radical change programs, reactionary moves, and restructurings.

The hedgehog concept: In a famous essay, philosopher and scholar Isaiah Berlin described two approaches to thought and life using a simple parable: The fox knows a little about many things, but the hedgehog knows only one big thing very well. The fox is complex, the hedgehog simple. And the hedgehog wins. Our research shows that breakthroughs require a simple, hedgehog-like understanding of three intersecting circles: what a company can be the best in the world at, how its economics work best, and what best ignites the passions of its people. Breakthroughs happen when you get the hedgehog concept and become systematic and consistent with it, eliminating virtually anything that does not fit in the three circles.

Technology accelerators: The good-to-great companies had a paradoxical relation-ship with technology. On the one hand, they assiduously avoided jumping on new technology bandwagons. On the other, they were pioneers in the applica-tion of carefully selected technologies, making bold, farsighted investments in those that directly linked to their hedgehog concept. Like turbochargers, these technology accelerators create an explosion in flywheel momentum.

A culture of discipline: When you look across the good-to-great transformations, they consistently display three forms of discipline: disciplined people, disciplined thought, and disciplined action. When you have disciplined people, you don't need hierarchy. When you have disciplined thought, you don't need bureaucracy. When you have disciplined action, you don't need excessive controls. When you combine a culture of discipline with an ethic of entrepreneurship, you get the magical alchemy of great performance.

HUMILITY + WILL = LEVEL 5

Level 5 leaders are a study in duality: modest and willful, shy and fearless. To grasp this concept, consider Abraham Lincoln, who never let his ego get in the way of his ambition to create an enduring great nation. Author Henry Adams called him "a quiet, peaceful, shy figure." But those who thought Lincoln's understated manner signaled weakness in the man found them-selves terribly mistaken—to the scale of 250,000 Confederate and 360,000 Union lives, including Lincoln's own.

It might be a stretch to compare the eleven Level 5 CEOs in our research to Lincoln, but they did display the same kind of duality. Take Colman M. Mockler, CEO of Gillette from 1975 to 1991. Mockler, who faced down three takeover attempts, was a reserved, gracious man with a gentle, almost patrician manner. Despite epic battles with raiders—he took on Ronald Perelman twice and the former Coniston Partners once—he never lost his shy, courteous style. At the height of the crisis, he maintained a calm business-as-usual demeanor, dispensing first with ongoing business before turning to the takeover.

And yet, those who mistook Mockler's outward modesty as a sign of inner weakness were beaten in the end. In one proxy battle, Mockler and other senior executives called thousands of investors, one by one, to win their votes. Mockler simply would not give in. He chose to fight for the fu-ture greatness of Gillette even though he could have pocketed millions by flipping his stock.

Consider the consequences had Mockler capitulated. If a share-flipper had accepted the full 44 percent price premium offered by Perelman and then invested those shares in the general market for ten years, he still would have come out 64 percent behind a shareholder who stayed with Mockler and Gillette. If Mockler had given up the fight, it's likely that none of us would be shaving with Sensor, Lady Sensor, or the Mach III—and hundreds of millions of people would have a more painful battle with daily stubble.

Sadly, Mockler never had the chance to enjoy the full fruits of his efforts. In January 1991, Gillette received an advance copy of *Forbes.* The cover featured an artist's rendition of the publicity-shy Mockler standing on a mountaintop, holding a giant razor above his head in a triumphant pose. Walking back to his office, just minutes after seeing this public acknowledgment of his sixteen years of struggle, Mockler crumpled to the floor and died from a massive heart attack.

Even if Mockler had known he would die in office, he could not have changed his approach. His placid persona hid an inner intensity, a dedication to making anything he touched the best—not just because of what he would get but because he couldn't imagine doing it any other way. Mockler could not give up the company to those who would destroy it, any more than Lincoln would risk losing the chance to build an enduring great nation.

A COMPELLING MODESTY

The Mockler story illustrates the modesty typical of Level 5 leaders. (For a summary of Level 5 traits, see Exhibit 21.3.) Indeed, throughout our interviews with such executives, we were struck by the way they talked about themselves—or rather, didn't talk about themselves. They'd go on and on about the company and the contributions of other executives, but they would instinctively deflect discussion about their own role. When pressed to talk about themselves, they'd say things like "I hope I'm not sounding like a big shot," or "I don't think I can take much credit for what happened. We were blessed with marvelous people." One Level 5 leader even asserted, "There are a lot of people in this company who could do my job better than I do."

By contrast, consider the courtship of personal celebrity by the comparison CEOs. Scott Paper, the comparison company to Kimberly-Clark, hired Al Dunlap as CEO—a man who would tell anyone who would listen (and many who would have preferred not to) about his accomplishments. After

EXHIBIT 21.3   The Yin and Yang of Level 5

Personal Humility	Professional Will
Demonstrates a compelling modesty, shunning public adulation; never boastful.	Creates superb results, a clear catalyst in the transition from good to great.
Acts with quiet, calm determination; relies principally on inspired standards, not inspiring charisma, to motivate.	Demonstrates an unwavering resolve to do whatever must be done to produce the best long-term results, no matter how difficult.
Channels ambition into the company, not the self; sets up successors for even more greatness in the next generation.	Sets the standard of building an enduring great company; will settle for nothing less.
Looks in the mirror, not out the window, to apportion responsibility for poor results, never blaming other people, external factors, or bad luck.	Looks out the window, not in the mirror, to apportion credit for the success of the company to other people, external factors, and good luck.

twenty-nine months atop Scott Paper, Dunlap said in *Business Week,* "The Scott story will go down in the annals of American business history as one of the most successful, quickest turnarounds ever. It makes other turnarounds pale by comparison." He personally accrued $100 million for 603 days of work at Scott Paper—about $165,000 per day, largely by slashing the workforce, halving the R&D budget, and putting the company on growth steroids in preparation for sale. After selling off the company and pocketing his quick millions, Dunlap wrote an autobiography in which he boastfully dubbed himself "Rambo in pinstripes." It's hard to imagine Darwin Smith thinking, "Hey, that Rambo character reminds me of me," let alone stating it publicly.

Granted, the Scott Paper story is one of the more dramatic in our study, but it's not an isolated case. In more than two-thirds of the comparison companies, we noted the presence of a gargantuan ego that contributed to the demise or continued mediocrity of the company. We found this pattern particularly strong in the unsustained comparison companies—the companies that would show a shift in performance under a talented yet egocentric Level 4 leader, only to decline in later years.

Lee Iacocca, for example, saved Chrysler from the brink of catastrophe, performing one of the most celebrated (and deservedly so) turnarounds in

U.S. business history. The automaker's stock rose 2.9 times higher than the general market about halfway through his tenure. But then Iacocca diverted his attention to transforming himself. He appeared regularly on talk shows like the *Today Show* and *Larry King Live,* starred in more than eighty commercials, entertained the idea of running for president of the United States, and promoted his autobiography, which sold 7 million copies worldwide. Iacocca's personal stock soared, but Chrysler's stock fell 31 percent below the market in the second half of his tenure.

And once Iacocca had accumulated all the fame and perks, he found it difficult to leave center stage. He postponed his retirement so many times that Chrysler's insiders began to joke that Iacocca stood for "I Am Chairman of Chrysler Corporation Always." When he finally retired, he demanded that the board continue to provide a private jet and stock options. Later, he joined forces with noted takeover artist Kirk Kerkorian to launch a hostile bid for Chrysler. (It failed.) Iacocca did make one final brilliant decision: He picked a modest yet determined man—perhaps even a Level 5—as his successor. Bob Eaton rescued Chrysler from its second near-death crisis in a decade and set the foundation for a more enduring corporate transition.

AN UNWAVERING RESOLVE

Besides extreme humility, Level 5 leaders also display tremendous professional will. When George Cain became CEO of Abbott Laboratories, it was a drowsy family-controlled business, sitting in the bottom quartile of the pharmaceutical industry, living off its cash cow, erythromycin. Cain was a typical Level 5 leader in his lack of pretense; he didn't have the kind of inspiring personality that would galvanize the company. But he had something much more powerful: inspired standards. He could not stand mediocrity in any form and was utterly intolerant of anyone who would accept the idea that good is good enough. For the next fourteen years, he relentlessly imposed his will for greatness on Abbott Labs.

Among Cain's first tasks was to destroy one of the root causes of Abbott's middling performance: nepotism. By systematically rebuilding both the board and the executive team with the best people he could find, Cain made his statement. Family ties no longer mattered. If you couldn't become the best executive in the industry, within your span of responsibility, you would lose your paycheck.

Such near-ruthless rebuilding might be expected from an outsider brought in to turn the company around, but Cain was an eighteen-year insider—and a part of the family, the son of a previous president. Holiday gatherings were probably tense for a few years in the Cain clan—"Sorry I had to fire you. Want another slice of turkey?"—but in the end, family members were pleased with the performance of their stock. Cain had set in motion a profitable growth machine. From its transition in 1974 to 2000, Abbott created shareholder returns that beat the market 4.5:1, outperforming industry superstars Merck and Pfizer by a factor of 2.

Another good example of iron-willed Level 5 leadership comes from Charles R. "Cork" Walgreen III, who transformed dowdy Walgreen's into a company that outperformed the stock market 16:1 from its transition in 1975 to 2000. After years of dialogue and debate within his executive team about what to do with Walgreen's food-service operations, this CEO sensed the team had finally reached a watershed: The company's brightest future lay in convenient drugstores, not in food service. Dan Jorndt, who succeeded Walgreen in 1988, describes what happened next:

> Cork said at one of our planning committee meetings, "Okay, now I am going to draw the line in the sand. We are going to be out of the restaurant business completely in five years." At the time we had more than five hundred restaurants. You could have heard a pin drop. He said, "I want to let everybody know the clock is ticking." Six months later we were at our next planning committee meeting and someone mentioned just in passing that we had only five years to be out of the restaurant business. Cork was not a real vociferous fellow. He sort of tapped on the table and said, "Listen, you now have four and a half years. I said you had five years six months ago. Now you've got four and a half years." Well, that next day things really clicked into gear for winding down our restaurant business. Cork never wavered. He never doubted. He never second-guessed.

Like Darwin Smith selling the mills at Kimberly-Clark, Cork Walgreen required stoic resolve to make his decisions. Food service was not the largest part of the business, although it did add substantial profits to the bottom line. The real problem was more emotional than financial. Walgreen's had, after all, invented the malted milk shake, and food service had been a long-standing family tradition dating back to Cork's grandfather. Not only that, some food-service outlets were even named after the CEO, for example, a restaurant chain named Corky's. But no matter; if Walgreen had to fly in the face of family tradition in order to refocus on the one arena in which Walgreen's could be the best in the world—convenient drugstores—and terminate everything else that would not produce great results, then Cork would do it. Quietly, doggedly, simply.

One final, yet compelling, note on our findings about Level 5: Because Level 5 leaders have ambition not for themselves but for their companies, they routinely select superb successors. Level 5 leaders want to see their companies become even more successful in the next generation, comfortable with the idea that most people won't even know that the roots of that success trace back to them. As one Level 5 CEO said, "I want to look from my porch, see the company as one of the great companies in the world someday, and be able to say, 'I used to work there.'" By contrast, Level 4 leaders often fail to set up the company for enduring success—after all, what better testament to your own personal greatness than that the place falls apart after you leave?

In more than three-quarters of the comparison companies, we found executives who set up their successors for failure, chose weak successors, or both. Consider the case of Rubbermaid, which grew from obscurity to become one of *Fortune*'s most admired companies—and then, just as quickly, disintegrated into such sorry shape that it had to be acquired by Newell.

The architect of this remarkable story was a charismatic and brilliant leader named Stanley C. Gault, whose name became synonymous in the late 1980s with the company's success. Across the 312 articles collected by our research team about Rubbermaid, Gault comes through as a hard-driving, egocentric executive. In one article, he responds to the accusation of being a tyrant with the statement "Yes, But I'm a sincere tyrant." In another, drawn directly from his own comments on leading change, the word *I* appears forty-four times, whereas the word *we* appears sixteen times. Of course, Gault had every reason to be proud of his executive success: Rubbermaid generated forty consecutive quarters of earnings growth under his leadership—an impressive performance, to be sure, and one that deserves respect.

But Gault did not leave behind a company that would be great without him. His chosen successor lasted a year on the job, and the next in line faced a management team so shallow that he had to temporarily shoulder four jobs while scrambling to identify a new number-two executive. Gault's successors struggled not only with a management void but also with strategic voids that would eventually bring the company to its knees.

Of course, you might say—as one *Fortune* article did—that the fact that Rubbermaid fell apart after Gault left proves his greatness as a leader. Gault was a tremendous Level 4 leader, perhaps one of the best in the last fifty years. But he was not at Level 5, and that is one crucial reason why Rubbermaid went from good to great for a brief, shining moment and then just as quickly went from great to irrelevant.

THE WINDOW AND THE MIRROR

As part of our research, we interviewed Alan L. Wurtzel, the Level 5 leader responsible for turning Circuit City from a ramshackle company on the edge of bankruptcy into one of America's most successful electronics retailers. In the fifteen years after its transition date in 1982, Circuit City outperformed the market 18.5:1.

We asked Wurtzel to list the top five factors in his company's transformation, ranked by importance. His number one factor? Luck: "We were in a great industry, with the wind at our backs." But wait a minute, we retorted, Silo—your comparison company—was in the same industry, with the same wind, and bigger sails. The conversation went back and forth, with Wurtzel refusing to take much credit for the transition, preferring to attribute it largely to just being in the right place at the right time. Later, when we asked him to discuss the factors that would sustain a good-to-great transformation, he said, "The first thing that comes to mind is luck. I was lucky to find the right successor."

Luck. What an odd factor to talk about. Yet the Level 5 leaders we identified invoked it frequently. We asked an executive at steel company Nucor why it had such a remarkable track record of making good decisions. His response? "I guess we were just lucky." Joseph F. Cullman III, the Level 5 CEO of Philip Morris, flat out refused to take credit for this company's success, citing his good fortune to have great colleagues, successors, and predecessors. Even the book he wrote about his career—which he penned at the urging of his colleagues and which he never intended to distribute widely outside the company—had the unusual title *I'm a Lucky Guy*.

At first, we were puzzled by the Level 5 leaders' emphasis on good luck. After all, there is no evidence that the companies that had progressed from good to great were blessed with more good luck (or more bad luck, for that matter) than the comparison companies. But then we began to notice an interesting pattern in the executives at the comparison companies: They often blamed their situations on bad luck, bemoaning the difficulties of the environment they faced.

Compare Bethlehem Steel and Nucor, for example. Both steel companies operated with products that are hard to differentiate, and both faced a competitive challenge from cheap imported steel. Both companies paid significantly higher wages than most of their foreign competitors. And yet executives at the two companies held completely different views of the same environment.

Bethlehem Steel's CEO summed up the company's problems in 1983 by blaming the imports: "Our first, second, and third problems are imports." Meanwhile, Ken Iverson and his crew at Nucor viewed the imports as a blessing: "Aren't we lucky? Steel is heavy, and they have to ship it all the way across the ocean, giving us a huge advantage." Indeed, Iverson saw the first, second, and third problems facing the U.S. steel industry not as imports, telling a gathering of stunned steel executives in 1977 that the real problems facing the industry lay in the fact that management had failed to keep pace with technology.

The emphasis on luck turns out to be part of a broader pattern that we came to call *the window and the mirror*. Level 5 leaders, inherently humble, look out the window to apportion credit—even undue credit—to factors outside themselves. If they can't find a specific person or event to give credit to, they credit good luck. At the same time, they look in the mirror to assign responsibility, never citing bad luck or external factors when things go poorly. Conversely, the comparison executives frequently looked out the window for factors to blame but preened in the mirror to credit themselves when things went well.

The funny thing about the window-and-mirror concept is that it does not reflect reality. According to our research, the Level 5 leaders were responsible for their companies' transformations. But they would never admit that. We can't climb inside their heads and assess whether they deeply believed what they saw in the window and the mirror. But it doesn't really matter, because they acted as if they believed it, and they acted with such consistency that it produced exceptional results.

BORN OR BRED?

Not long ago, I shared the Level 5 finding with a gathering of senior executives. A woman who had recently become chief executive of her company raised her hand. "I believe what you've told us about Level 5 leadership," she said, "but I'm disturbed because I know I'm not there yet, and maybe I never will be. Part of the reason I got this job is because of my strong ego. Are you telling me that I can't make my company great if I'm not Level 5?"

"Let me return to the data," I responded. "Of 1,435 companies that appeared in the *Fortune* 500 since 1965, only 11 made it into our study. All of those eleven had Level 5 leaders in key positions, including the CEO role, at the pivotal time of transition. Now, to reiterate, we're not saying that Level 5 is the only element required for the move from good to great, but it appears to be essential."

She sat there, quiet for a moment, and you could guess what many people in the room were thinking. Finally, she raised her hand again: "Can you learn to become Level 5?" I still do not know the answer to that question. Our research, frankly, did not delve into how Level 5 leaders come to be, nor did we attempt to explain or codify the nature of their emotional lives. We speculated on the unique psychology of Level 5 leaders. Were they "guilty" of displacement—shifting their own raw ambition onto something other than themselves? Were they sublimating their egos for dark and complex reasons rooted in childhood trauma? Who knows? And perhaps more important, do the psychological roots of Level 5 leadership matter any more than do the roots of charisma or intelligence? The question remains: Can Level 5 be developed?

My preliminary hypothesis is that there are two categories of people: those who don't have the Level 5 seed within them and those who do. The first category consists of people who could never in a million years bring themselves to subjugate their own needs to the greater ambition of something larger and more lasting than themselves. For those people, work will always be first and foremost about what they get: the fame, fortune, power, adulation, and so on. Work will never be about what they build, create, and contribute. The great irony is that the animus and personal ambition that often drive people to become a Level 4 leader stand at odds with the humility required to rise to Level 5.

When you combine that irony with the fact that boards of directors frequently operate under the false belief that a larger-than-life, egocentric leader is required to make a company great, you can quickly see why Level 5 leaders rarely appear at the top of our institutions. We keep putting people in positions of power who lack the seed to become a Level 5 leader, and that is one major reason why there are so few companies that make a sustained and verifiable shift from good to great.

The second category consists of people who could evolve to Level 5; the capability resides within them, perhaps buried or ignored or simply nascent. Under the right circumstances—with self-reflection, a mentor, loving parents, a significant life experience, or other factors—the seed can begin to develop. Some of the Level 5 leaders in our study had significant life experiences that might have sparked development of the seed. Darwin Smith fully blossomed as a Level 5 after his near-death experience with cancer. Joe Cullman was profoundly affected by his World War II experiences, particularly the last-minute change of orders that took him off a doomed ship on which he surely would have died; he considered the next sixty-odd years a great gift. A strong religious belief or conversion might also nurture the seed. Colman Mockler, for example, converted to evangelical Christianity while getting his MBA at Harvard, and later, according to the book *Cutting Edge,* he became a prime mover in a group of Boston business executives that met frequently over breakfast to discuss the carryover of religious values to corporate life.

We would love to be able to give you a list of steps for getting to Level 5— other than contracting cancer, going through a religious conversion, or getting different parents—but we have no solid research data that would support a credible list. Our research exposed Level 5 as a key component inside the black box of what it takes to shift a company from good to great. Yet inside that black box is another: the inner development of a person to Level 5 leadership. We could speculate on what that inner box might hold, but it would mostly be just that, speculation.

In short, Level 5 is a very satisfying idea, a truthful idea, a powerful idea, and, to make the move from good to great, very likely an essential idea. But to provide "ten steps to Level 5 leadership" would trivialize the concept.

My best advice, based on the research, is to practice the other good-to-great disciplines that we discovered. Since we found a tight symbiotic relationship between each of the other findings and Level 5, we suspect that conscientiously trying to lead using the other disciplines can help you move in the right direction. There is no guarantee that doing so will turn executives into full-fledged Level 5 leaders, but it gives them a tangible place to begin, especially if they have the seed within.

We cannot say for sure what percentage of people have the seed within, nor how many of those can nurture it enough to become Level 5. Even those of us on the research team who identified Level 5 do not know whether we will succeed in evolving to its heights. And yet all of us who worked on the finding have been inspired by the idea of trying to move toward Level 5. Darwin Smith, Colman Mockler, Alan Wurtzel, and all the other Level 5 leaders we learned about have become role models for us. Whether or not we make it to Level 5, it is worth trying. For like all basic truths about what is best in human beings, when we catch a glimpse of that truth, we know that our own lives and all that we touch will be the better for making the effort to get there.

About the Editors and Contributors

EDITORS

William E. Rosenbach is the Evans Professor of Eisenhower Leadership Studies and professor of management at Gettysburg College. Formerly professor and head of the Department of Behavioral Sciences and Leadership at the U.S. Air Force Academy, he is the author or coauthor of numerous articles and books on leadership topics. He is especially interested in the elements of effective followership, and he is an active consultant to private and public organizations in North America, Europe, and Australia on executive leadership development. He is a founding partner of the Gettysburg Leadership Experiences, an innovative executive leadership development program in historic Gettysburg, Pennsylvania. He may be reached at william.e.rosenbach@gettysburg.edu.

Robert L. Taylor is professor of management and dean emeritus of the College of Business at the University of Louisville. Formerly professor and head of the Department of Management at the U.S. Air Force Academy and the Carl N. Jacobs Professor of Business at the University of Wisconsin at Stevens Point, he has been a student of leadership for nearly thirty years. Most recently, Dr. Taylor served as board chair of AACSB: the International Association for Management Education. His interests in teaching and scholarship have resulted in undergraduate and graduate seminars, presentations, and consultancies with a primary focus on the elements of effective leadership. Serving on the board of several companies and organizations, Dr. Taylor has enjoyed being a student and practitioner of leadership in countries throughout the world. He may be reached at rltayl01@gwise.louisville.edu.

CONTRIBUTORS

Marshall Sashkin is professor of human resource development of the Graduate School of Education and Human Development at the George Washington University. More than fifty of his research papers on leadership, participation, and organizational change have been published in academic journals, and he is the author or coauthor of more than a dozen books and monographs.

James M. Kouzes and **Barry Z. Posner** are coauthors of the award-winning and best-selling books *The Leadership Challenge* and *Credibility*. Their other books include *Encouraging the Heart* and *The Leadership Challenge Planner*. Jim is chairman emeritus of the Tom Peters Company and executive fellow in the Center for Innovation and Entrepreneurship at the Leavey School of Business at Santa Clara University. Barry is dean of the Leavey School and professor of leadership at Santa Clara.

Neal Thornberry is associate professor of management at Babson College and faculty director of the school of Executive Education at Babson College.

Linda Klebe Trevino is professor of organizational behavior and chair of the Department of Management and Organization at Pennsylvania State University. She holds a Ph.D. in management from Texas A&M University. Her research and writing on the management of ethical conduct in organizations is widely published and well known internationally. She coauthored a textbook with Katherine Neson of William M. Mercer Consulting, entitled *Managing Business Ethics: Straight Talk About How to Do It Right*. The second edition was published in 1999. She has presented her research findings to business groups including the Conference Board, the Conference Board of Canada, and the Ethics Officers Association.

Laura Pincus Hartman, J.D., is the associate director of DePaul University's Institute for Business and Professional Ethics, held the Wicklander Chair in Professional Ethics, and is an associate professor of legal studies and ethics at DePaul's Kellstadt Graduate School of Business. Hartman has done extensive research on the ethics of the employment relationship, employee rights, and employer responsibilities and has published the first business school textbook in the field, *Employment Law for Business,* as well as other textbooks. She has also published articles in, among other journals, *Hofstra Law Review, Columbia Business Law Journal, Harvard Journal of Law and Technology, American Business Law Journal, Labor Law Journal, Journal of Individual Employment Rights,* and *Journal of Legal Studies Education.*

Michael Brown is an assistant professor of management and organizational behavior at the Smeal College of Business Administration, Pennsylvania State University. His primary research interests are business ethics and leadership. His research includes the antecedents and consequences of ethical leadership and the development of a theoretical model of ethical leadership at the executive level.

Matthew Valle is chair of the Department of Business Administration at Elon University. He received his Ph.D. in business administration from the Florida State University in 1995. His research interests include organizational politics and politics perceptions, leadership in the public sector, and product and process improvement initiatives.

David Halberstam, who won a Pulitzer Prize at thirty for his reporting on the Vietnam War, is the author of more than a dozen books, including *The Best and Brightest, The Powers That Be,* and *War in a Time of Peace.* He is currently writing a book about the Korean War.

Mark J. Kroll is professor of management and the George W. and Robert S. Pirtle Distinguished Professor in Free Enterprise at the University of Texas at Tyler. He received his D.B.A. in management from Mississippi State University. His current research interests are business policy and strategy, agency problems, and corporate acquisitions.

Leslie A. Toombs is an associate professor of management at the University of Texas at Tyler. She received her doctor of business administration and master of business administration from Louisiana Tech University. Dr. Toombs has written many articles on quality and strategic management topics, which have appeared in publications such as the *Strategic Management Journal* and *Academy of Management Executive.* In addition, she has served as a consultant to business organizations in the areas of strategic management and quality management and has coauthored training manuals in these areas. She's also coauthor of a quality textbook, *Strategic Quality Management.*

Peter Wright is a professor of management and the holder of the University of Memphis Endowed Chair in Free Enterprise Management. He received his undergraduate degree from Ohio State University and his M.B.A. and Ph.D. degrees from Louisiana State University. His research focuses on agency theory and the valuation of firm strategies.

Albert R. Hunt was executive editor for the Washington, D.C., bureau of the *Wall Street Journal* and *Dow Jones.* He joined the *Journal* in 1965 as a reporter in New York City. He transferred to the Boston bureau in 1967 and to Washington in 1969. From 1972 to 1983, Hunt covered Congress and national politics and became Washington bureau chief in 1983. He was named executive Washington editor in 1993. Hunt writes a weekly editorial column and has been a panelist on the Public Broadcasting Service program *Washington Week in Review* and NBC's *Meet the Press*. He has also been a political analyst on the *CBS Morning News* and a member of CNN's *The Capital Gang* since its inception in 1988.

John W. Gardner served six presidents of the United States in various leadership capacities. He was secretary of Health, Education, and Welfare; founding chairman of Common Cause; cofounder of Independent Sector; and president of the Carnegie Corporation and the Carnegie Foundation for the Advancement of Teaching. The author of *On Leadership,* he served as Miriam and Peter Haas Centennial Professor at Stanford Business School.

Robert Goffee is a professor of organizational behavior at London Business School. He is the coauthor of five books and consults with large corporations in the area of organizational change and culture.

Gareth Jones is the director of human resources and international communications at the BBC and former professor of organizational development at Henley Management College in Oxfordshire, England. Along with Robert Goffee, he is a founding partner of Creative Management Associates, an organizational consulting firm in London.

Warren Bennis is retired from the University of Southern California and the founding chairman of USC's Leadership Institute. He has written eighteen books, including *On Becoming a Leader* (which was translated into nineteen languages), *Why Leaders Can't Lead,* and *The Unreality Industry,* coauthored with Ian Mitroff. Bennis was successor to Douglas McGregor as chairman of the organization studies department at M.I.T. He also taught at Harvard and Boston Universities. Later, he was provost and executive vice president of the State University of New York at Buffalo and president of the University of Cincinnati. He has published over nine hundred articles, and two of his books have earned the coveted McKinsey Award for the Best Book on Management. He has served in an advisory capacity to the past four U.S. presidents and consulted to many corporations and agencies and to the United Nations. Awarded eleven honorary degrees, Bennis has also received numerous awards, including the Distinguished Service Award of the American Board of Professional Psychologists and the Perry L. Rohrer Consulting Practice Award of the American Psychological Association.

Earl H. Potter III is provost of Southern Oregon University and former dean of the College of Business Administration at Eastern Michigan University. He has a doctorate in organizational psychology from the University of Washington and over twenty-five years of experience in research and consulting on issues of leadership, team effectiveness, and organizational change. As a leader he has led polar diving explorations, sailed a square-rigged ship with a crew of two hundred as executive officer, and chaired countless faculty meetings.

Daniel Goleman consults internationally and lectures frequently to business audiences and professional groups and on college campuses. He is founder of Emotional Intelligence Services, an affiliate of the Hay Group in Boston. A psychologist who for many years reported on the brain and behavioral sciences for the *New York Times*, Dr. Goleman previously was a visiting faculty member at Harvard. Dr. Goleman has received many journalistic awards for his writing, including two nominations for the Pulitzer Prize for his articles in the *Times* and a Career Achievement award for journalism from the American Psychological Association. In recognition of his efforts to communicate the behavioral sciences to the public, he was elected a Fellow of the American Association for the Advancement of Science. Dr. Goleman attended Amherst College, where he was an Alfred P. Sloan Scholar and graduated magna cum laude. His graduate education was at Harvard, where he was a Ford Fellow, and he received his M.A. and Ph.D. in clinical psychology and personality development.

Joseph A. Raelin is Asa S. Knowles Chair of Practice-Oriented Education at Northeastern University. He is also the director of the Center for Work and Learning. His research focuses on executive and professional education and development through work-learning. He may be reached at j.raelin@neu.edu.

Suzanne C. de Janasz is associate professor at the University of Mary Washington. She previously taught at James Madison University. Her research focuses on mentoring, careers, and work-family conflict.

Sherry E. Sullivan is at Bowling Green State University. She has published over forty articles and is the past chair of the Careers Division of the Academy of Management. Her research interests include career theory, women's careers, mentoring, and stress.

Vicki Whiting is associate professor at the Gore School of Business at Westminster College. Her teaching, consulting, and publishing interests are in organizational behavior and international management.

Douglas A. Ready is founder and president of the International Consortium for Executive Development Research in Lexington, Massachusetts. Mr. Ready can be reached at info@icedr.org.

Jay A. Conger is a professor of organizational behavior at London Business School. He can be reached at Jconger@london.edu.

Christopher Williams works at the United Nations University. He has held posts at the University of London Institute of Education and the University of Birmingham. He was a tutor in research methods for the Open University, and he was a professor in the music department of Cairo University. He also worked in South Africa during the apartheid era, teaching street children.

Bill McCabe is a partner with The McLane Group (www.mclanegroup.co.uk).

Michael Maccoby, author of *The Gamesman* and *The Leader,* is a consultant on issues of leadership, strategy, and organization to business, government, and unions. He is president of the Maccoby Group in Washington, D.C., where he lives.

Barbara Kellerman is research director at the Center for Public Research and lecturer in public policy at Harvard University's John F. Kennedy School of Government.

Deborah L. Rhode is Ernest W. McFarland Professor of Law and director of the Stanford Center on Ethics at Stanford University.

Jim Collins operates a management research laboratory in Boulder, Colorado. He is coauthor, with Jerry I. Porras, of *Built to Last: Successful Habits of Visionary Companies,* and his blockbuster book, *Good to Great,* was published in 2001.